The Iron Age hill-forts of Brown Caterthun (lower right) and White Caterthun (top left), about five miles north-west of Brechin in Angus-shire. White Caterthun has a massive stone rampart

The multivallate Iron Age fort of Bratton Castle, Wiltshire.

Danebury
Hants. 5·3 hec'
Page 185

After reading mechanical sciences at Cambridge, A. H. A. Hogg gained practical research and experience in civil engineering, and became a Lecturer in that subject at Newcastle and, later, Cambridge University. While at Newcastle he also qualified as a Town Planner. In 1949 he was appointed Secretary to the Royal Commission on Wales and Monmouthshire, remaining in that post until his retirement in 1973.

He has travelled mainly in France, but has also visited Spain, Czechoslovakia and Yugoslavia, studying hill-forts in all those countries; and publishing descriptions of forts in France and Spain. His own excavations, mostly in Wales, have been on a small scale, to investigate particular problems; but he has assisted on several major excavations both in Britain and France.

He was awarded the CBE in 1973 and in 1974 was awarded a D.Litt.(hon. causa) by the University of Wales. A Fellow of the Society of Antiquaries of London, and also that of Scotland, he was President of the Cambrian Archaeological Association for 1972.

Contents

Acknowledgements

I am greatly indebted to the following individuals, both for permission to utilize their original plans (the numbers of the relevant figures are given in parentheses), and for suggestions and unpublished information: Mr J. Collis (54); Mr D. Coombs (85); Mr R. W. Feachem (12, 20, 22, 44, 102); Mr J. Forde-Johnston (71); Lady Fox (51, 86); Mr P. S. Gelling; Mrs C. M. Guido (28, 79); Professor C. F. C. Hawkes (31); Mrs T. C. Hencken (29); Mr R. F. Jessup (25); Mr G. Jobey (107); Dr K. M. Kenyon (98, 105); Mr A. King; Professor S. Piggott (81, 106); Miss K. M. Richardson (26); Dr H. N. Savory (57); Mr A. Sorrell; Dr S. C. Stanford (13, 55); Dr K. Steer (80); Professor W. J. Varley (18, 89); Dr J. B. Ward-Perkins (88); Sir Mortimer Wheeler (11, 84, 97); Miss M. Whitley (48); and Dr A. E. Wilson. I am also grateful to the following institutions: the Ordnance Survey (1–3, 14–16); the Royal Commissions on Ancient and Historical Monuments: for England (55, 74, 77, 93); for Scotland (59, 67, 80, 95, 103); and for Wales and Monmouthshire (37, 4, 52, 56, 72, 75, 91, 92); and to the Victoria County History of England (35, 36, 38, 65); and also to the secretaries and editors of the following societies: the Society of Antiquaries of London (49, 50); the Society of Antiquaries of Scotland (47, 70); the Royal Archaeological Institute; the Cambrian Archaeological Association (68, 71, 82); the Devon Archaeological Society (76); the Wiltshire Archaeological and Natural History Society (69); also all those mentioned individually in the gazetteer.

The aerial photographs have been supplied by the Committee for Aerial Photography, of the University of Cambridge, by courtesy of Professor J. K. St Joseph, director. Copyright is reserved.

The finished plans are by Mr C. Baker and the reconstructions by Mr Dylan Roberts, from pencil drafts by the author.

List of Figures

List of Plates

Preface and Definitions

No archaeologist is satisfied with the term 'hill-fort', but all the alternatives which have been suggested are open to even more objections, so it will be used without further apology, sometimes even shortened to 'fort'. As will be seen later, if 'fort' is understood in the modern sense this is misleading: the enclosures may have corresponded to anything from a cattle kraal to a small town, but were seldom exclusively military. If a formal definition is demanded, a hill-fort may be described as an enclosure, apparently fortified, and so placed as to gain some defensive advantage from its position; as being of a type generally built during the native Iron Age; and as normally not less than 0·2 hectare in enclosed area. The restriction on date is to exclude structures such as neolithic causewayed camps or medieval earthwork castles, and that on area to separate out the recognizably different fortifications known as 'brochs' and 'duns' in Scotland. Brochs and duns are in fact contemporary with hill-forts but are on average very much smaller; they are arbitrarily excluded as a matter of convenience, to limit the field covered.

Hill-forts, then, are enclosures with ramparts built (mostly) by prehistoric man to protect his settlements or stock. These ramparts are now reduced to grassy banks or heaps of rubble, but are still conspicuous features of the countryside in many parts of Britain. Every year, new discoveries throw light on the nature of these 'hill-forts' and on the way of life of their builders, so that any attempt at a detailed definitive study of them falls out of date faster than it can be written. Nevertheless the great mass of information which has been collected does permit a fairly clear general idea of what these places were like in their prime, and when and why they were built.

This book is not a text book, and makes no attempt to summarize all work that has been done on British hill-forts; still less does it cover the Iron Age as a whole. So, although it is hoped that the collection of material may be of use to specialists, it is primarily intended for those who find that their enjoyment of the countryside is enhanced by reconstructing the past in imagination. Even companions who do not share this interest will usually find the view from a hill-fort rewarding. No footnotes are given, but for the sake of those who wish to pursue the subject the chief sources are listed in a bibliography.

The main body of the book falls into two parts. The first deals with the various elements of hill-fort structure, with sufficient background to enable the reader to place them in their historical and social context, while the second, the gazetteer, describes a representative selection of hill-forts distributed throughout the country. All sites, British or foreign, which are mentioned in the first section are included, so the second section provides the necessary references and other details, and forms an index.

Some readers may regret, or even resent, the use of metric measurements, but it would have been pedantic to cling to feet and inches after they have ceased to be the official system. Since the use of dimensions in a general work of this kind is merely to give a rough mental impression of size, it is sufficient to visualize a metre as a 'long yard', a hectare as $2\frac{1}{2}$ acres and a square kilometre as two-fifths of a square mile; more exact factors are $3\cdot281$ feet, $2\cdot47$ acres and $0\cdot386$ square mile. For smaller dimensions, 30 centimetres corresponds closely to 1 foot; and, for the benefit of cricketers, 20 metres is the length of a pitch, within 5 inches.

One further explanation is needed. At several hill-forts excavations are either in progress or have only just been completed. I have tried to avoid reference to these, even though the work is naturally of great importance; for not only does it seem undesirable to forestall the excavator with an ill-digested summary of his results, but their full significance cannot really be understood until they have received definitive publication.

Author's Preface to the Paladin Edition

Much important work has been published relating to hill-forts since 1975, but cannot be incorporated in the text of this edition, which is necessarily a straightforward reprint, apart from a few verbal corrections; the scales given in Fig. 17 are now slightly incorrect, owing to the change in page size. Even where further work has been done on individual sites, the descriptions and references have had to be left unaltered.

Most of the text remains valid, but some recent publications are noted below, especially those which substantially alter views expressed in 1975. The selection is very restricted, and much work of fully equal importance has been excluded owing to lack of space for discussion. Bibliographical abbreviations used are given on pages 103–4.

First in importance, for anyone seriously interested in the subject, is the second (1978) edition of Cunliffe's *Iron Age Communities in Britain* (Archaeology in Britain series, Routledge). The work is a general study of the period, but includes descriptions and illustrations of many hill-forts. In addition, a list of relevant radiocarbon dates is given. These, in conjunction with an extended study of pottery and other objects, are beginning to provide a reasonably sound chronology; but the rough approximations used here (see especially pp. 28–9) remain adequate for the general reader. Here also attention may be drawn once again to D. W. Harding (Editor), *Hill-forts* . . . (see p. 111), which owing to the date of its publication did not receive in 1975 the emphasis which its importance merits; M. Avery's opening chapter, 'A Student's Introduction,' is particularly valuable.

General Topographical Information (p. 106) is now supplemented by A. H. A. Hogg, *British Hill-forts; an Index*. (BAR British Series 62, 1979) which lists all hill-forts on the mainland known to the compiler at that date, with indexes, grid coordinates and selective bibliographical references, but no plans or descriptions. The three Ancient Monuments Commissions have continued their work: England; Gloucestershire and the Cotswolds (1976), and Northamptonshire, with few hill-forts (4 vols. 1975–82). Scotland; Argyll (Kintyre, 1, 1971, and Lorn, 2, 1975). Wales; Glamorgan (vol. 1, pt. 2, 1976) and Brecknockshire complete as to fieldwork.

The remaining changes in viewpoint arise from work on individual sites. In 1975, the term hill-fort was defined to exclude structures of Neolithic date; but at that time R. J. Mercer had not completed his work on Carn Brea (pp. 161–4). His report (*Cornish Archaeology* No. 20 (1981) 1–204) shows that although there was some Iron Age occupation on the site, at least the inner ramparts enclosing the knolls carrying the Monument and the Castle, some 4 hectares, are almost certainly Neolithic; and he draws attention to other known or probable fortified sites of that period. Some hill-forts, therefore, are of Neolithic origin, though without excavation they cannot be distinguished with certainty from Iron Age examples.

The other major change in outlook concerns the interiors of hill-forts. Graeme Guilbert ('Planned Hillfort Interiors', *Proc. Prehistoric Soc.* (41 (1975) 203–221) has demonstrated that in some cases distinct zones are allocated to different types of buildings. Moel y Gaer, Rhosesmor, Flintshire (SJ 211 690) is the best-studied example. This is a roughly circular enclosure of 2·7 hectares, generally bivallate. About a sixth of the area has been excavated, and *if this is representative* it suggests that an annular space about 25 metres wide within the rampart was restricted to four-post buildings, while in the central area bands, apparently radial, were alternately devoted to round buildings and to more 'four-posters'. This was in the second phase of occupation, probably in the 6th century B.C. Whether the extrapolation from the excavated area is legitimate or not, there is clear evidence for deliberate planning. Similarly at Danebury (p. 185; 2nd and 3rd interim reports, *Ant. J.* LVI (1976) 198–216; LXI (1981) 238–254), to quote from p. 250 of the third report: "in a period of major reorganisation, probably towards the end of the fourth century, the southern part of the fort . . . was replanned with rows of storage structures served by metalled roads . . ." It seems now to be the general consensus of opinion, that with rare exceptions these rectangular four- and six-post settings correspond to buildings for storage, probably of grain. Comments on these buildings, especially as regards the interior of Croft Ambrey (pp. 100–1), need reconsideration, and the reconstruction drawing of that fort (pl. 7) is probably misleading. The rows of small square buildings shown were probably interspersed with large areas where buildings were exclusively round; these were not found owing to the accident of partial excavation.

One misunderstanding displayed by some reviewers of the 1975 edition ought perhaps to be eliminated. The Gazetteer is essentially subsidiary to the first part of the book. Its primary function is to avoid the need to interrupt the general account by inserting references or descriptions which are not immediately relevant at that point; it is for that reason that the four foreign hill-forts are included. The secondary objective is, so far as possible, to provide any reader, wherever resident, with a sample of representative and accessible hill-forts.

Any such selection will inevitably be liable to regretful second thoughts, so the opportunity will be taken to mention two exceptionally noteworthy forts in Aberdeenshire: Mither Tap of Bennachie (NJ 683 224; described in Feachem, *Preh. Scot.,* P. 104), and Tap o' Noth (NJ 485 293; *Preh. Scot.*, p.106). Both are more than a mile from, and 1000 ft above, the nearest road (a factor which contributed to their omission in 1975), but the ascents are not at all difficult and are well repaid.

1
Names

Of the two thousand or more hill-forts in Britain, only one or two retain their original names in recognizable form; neither can now be interpreted. One is The Wrekin, anciently Uriconion; in Roman times the name was transferred to the new city, now Wroxeter, but has since returned to its original site. Old Sarum, too, has not departed far from its original Sorviodunon. A few others can be inferred with reasonable certainty. Almondbury, Yorkshire, was Camulodunon, the stronghold of Camulos the god of war, who also gave his name to Colchester. Less certainly, Ingleborough may have been Rigodunon, 'the royal stronghold'. At others, the ancient name may survive in a more or less corrupt form. It is an attractive suggestion, for example, that both Breedon-on-the-Hill and Bredon are derived from Brigodunon, which translates almost literally into 'hill-fort'; but there are not enough early forms of the names for proof.

Most names were either forgotten or irretrievably altered during the period of the Roman occupation and the subsequent breakdown of social order, which seems to have extended over the whole country. When the places are mentioned again it is usually as land—marks, not as inhabited sites. The people who renamed them felt no doubt as to their original use. The enclosure was a 'burgh', a 'dun', a 'caer', 'urbs antiqua', 'veterum castrum', almost always implying a fortified permanent settlement. These identifications, by people whose way of life was not very unlike that of the builders, weigh heavily against the doubts which some modern archaeologists have expressed as to the function of the forts. Most of the names given, however, are either merely descriptive or indicative of ownership. They are of the same type in all parts of the country.

The earliest references occur in boundary surveys appended to pre-Norman charters. Bredon Hill, for example, is first mentioned as a 'city with the ancient name of Baenintesbury', meaning 'Baening's fort', a name preserved in that of the Banbury Stone which stands on the hill. Chastleton Barrow, is 'the hill of Susibre, an ancient city'. The name is Celtic; the last element 'bre' means 'hill', but the meaning of the first is uncertain. Salmonsbury is 'a city called Sulemonnes-bury', which has nothing to do with Solomon or fish, but means the 'ploughman's fort'. Examples can be multiplied almost indefinitely. To cite a few of them: Almondsbury, Gloucestershire, is 'Aethelmund's fort', but Almondbury, Yorkshire is 'All-man's-bury', a fort publicly owned; Hembury, is Hean-burh, the 'high fort'; Membury is Maen-burh, the 'stone fort'. Comparable names are found in Scotland. Dunmore, the 'big fort', is common; Dunsapie, near Arthur's Seat, means the fort covered with tufts of grass; Dundurn does in fact resemble a fist from some aspects.

Names which could have been given when the place was in use are uncommon, but do occur. Winklebury was Winterburge, a 'stronghold used in winter'. Traprain Law was formerly Dunpelder, the 'fort of the palisades' – though excavation suggests that all the defences were of stone. Nevertheless, since this translation is explicable as a simple description it is to be preferred to the alternative 'fort of the spear shafts', which would fall into the same class as some which hint tantalizingly at forgotten folk tales, like Castell Nadolig ('Christmas Castle'); Old Winchester Hill, which stands 20 kilometres from Winchester; or Dun na Ban-Oige, the 'fort of the rich woman' – or perhaps 'of the young wife'. Maiden Castle in archaeological contexts almost always refers to the Dorset hill-fort, but the name is quite common and widespread. Derivation from 'Celtic' *Mai-dun* has been proposed, but this is fanciful. Another suggestion is that the fortresses so named were impregnable; but by the far most probable explanation is that these sites were known locally as places where one might hope to meet young women who were not.

More interesting names are those which even in their earliest forms contain some reference to a known mythical or historical character. There is a strong temptation, to which many archaeologists have succumbed at some time, to accept an apparent tradition of this kind at its face value. Some, indeed, may be genuine; but there are enough examples where even early identifications are demonstrably false to cast doubt on all the others.

The proliferation of 'Caesar's Camps' seems to have begun in the seventeenth century, but as early as 1279 the rampart on Bindon Hill was identified as Julius Caesar's dyke. Caer Helen, the older name of

Pen-y-Gaer above Llanbedr-y-Cennin, implies that the fort belonged to the wife of Magnus Maximus. These were reasonable attempts to link history with visible monuments. Similarly, storytellers have given verisimilitude to their tales by linking them to real places. The composer of the Mabinogion tale of Math and Mathonwy has associated Dinlle, 'Lleu's stronghold', with a mythical or imaginary character Lleu Llaw Gyffes, 'Lleu of the deft hand'. The whole of this story is woven round local place-names and topographical features; for example, it gives an account of the theft of pigs which is clearly based on a run of 'moch' (pig) place-names, and it explains a naturally-holed stone, which still exists, as having been pierced by Lleu's spear. So it seems likely that Lleu Llaw Gyffes is essentially an invention of the story-teller, whereas the Lleu after whom the fort was named may have been just as real as the Aethelmund who owned Almondsbury.

Examples of this kind cast doubt on the validity of apparently traditional identifications, and indeed it seems safer to reject them all, except as indicating interesting possibilities. The sort of evidence which would be needed to carry reasonable conviction is discussed below, when considering Dinas Emrys and South Cadbury.

As would be expected, names which hint at the survival of genuine folk memories occur almost exclusively in 'Celtic' areas. In Wales we have Dinorwig, of the Ordovices, and Dinllaen, of the Leinstermen; in Scotland Dunearn, Dumbarton, Dumyat and Dunkeld incorporate some recollection of Irishmen, Britons, Maeatae and Caledonians — the last two are tribes recorded by Roman historians as having fought against Severus. Even if these are genuine traditional names and not the result of early attempts at historical identification, the question remains as to whether they imply particularly important places within the territory of the people named, or whether they correspond to strongholds established outside their own regions. Further, in attempting to assess the possible age of such names, it is relevant that in all records *known* to originate earlier than about the fourth century AD the *dunon* element occurs *after* the descriptive term.

Associations with historical or semi-historical characters are at least equally open to suspicion. Dunsinane does in fact contain the foundations of an early medieval castle which could have belonged to Macbeth, though the surrounding earthworks are far older. At Old Oswestry none of the pottery is now regarded as post-Roman, so there is nothing except the name Caer Ogyrfan to imply occupation by King Arthur's father-in-law King Gogyrfan, if indeed he ever existed outside the minds of story tellers; but Dinas Emrys was not only fortified at about the time of Ambrosius Aurelianus, it also enclosed a curious pool and associated structures which agree remarkably well with the legend attached to the site (see pp. 186, 188).

Except perhaps at Dunsinane, these traditional associations will not really stand up to critical study. We do not know if any forts near Old Oswestry would display post-Roman occupation, and even the detailed agreement of the curious legend attached to Dinas Emrys with the results of excavation could be explained by assuming that the story was made up to account for features visible there.

Another Arthurian association, recorded in the first half of the sixteenth century, makes Barry Hill at Alyth in Perthshire the place of imprisonment of Guinevere after Arthur's death. No one in modern times has taken this very seriously, but a rather later 'tradition' has led to excavations of archaeological importance. It provides a good example of the difficulty of evaluating such evidence.

Leland, at the end of the sixteenth century, records as a local belief that South Cadbury Castle was the site of Camelot, where King Arthur held his court; and twentieth-century excavations, carried out with great care and skill, have shown that the hill-fort was indeed a place of major importance at the right date. At first sight, the agreement of tradition and reality seems all that could be hoped for, establishing the location of Camelot beyond doubt.

Some highly respected archaeologists have accepted the identification, and all must feel grateful that King Arthur's posthumous patronage assisted such a valuable piece of research. Nevertheless, as the excavator has pointed out, the name Camelot is the invention of a French romancer working seven centuries after Arthur's time; and its attribution to South Cadbury, whether by Leland or by his informants, seems to rest on no stronger foundation than the presence nearby of two villages called Queen Camel and West Camel. That South Cadbury was refortified, to become an important centre at about the time when Arthur is likely to have lived, is no longer open to question; but there is no proof that he ruled in this region. Neither is it certain, as yet, that the refortification of South Cadbury is exceptional. Excavations in adjacent hill-forts are for the most part lacking, so the regional background is obscure.

Other characters, with a clearer historical background than

Arthur, have been allotted hill-forts by local enthusiasts. Julius Caesar is the most versatile claimant, starting as already noted with Bindon Down in the thirteenth century — a reasonable identification given the state of knowledge at the time. Later he collected six prehistoric forts, ranging from Farnham to Rotherham, as well as two Norman earth and timber castles, one above Folkestone, the other at Wollaston; and in the seventeenth century, Cissbury was known locally as Caesar's Hill. Two other Romans have been commemorated in this way, but only with one hill-fort apiece. Vespasian's Camp still appears on the map, but that of Chlorus has reverted to its older name of Figsbury.

Now that the nature of the Roman camp is better known, these identifications can be dismissed at once, but 'Caer Caradoc' offers a more difficult problem. According to Tacitus, Caratacus did occupy what was apparently some sort of hill-fort before his last battle against the Romans, and one might expect its remains to be identifiable. Three earthworks now carry the appropriate name, near Clun, Church Stretton and Llanfihangl-Glyn-Myfry; the first identification was made by William Camden in his *Britannia* (London, 1586). These three hill-forts have one feature in common: they cannot possibly be the place in question, for according to Tacitus the Britons were numerous enough to cause anxiety to two Roman legions, and were accompanied by their families. It is known that two legions, fighting men only, encamped with military precision and economy of space, required 25 hectares, so the real Caer Caradoc must be at least as large; the biggest of the three pretenders only encloses a tenth of that area.

2
Modern Research

The body of archaeological knowledge is built up of items of varying reliability which have been collected more or less at random over a considerable period. Even where an investigation has formed part of a planned programme, this has almost always depended on the initiative of a single individual, and circumstances have seldom allowed it even to approach completion. There are compensating advantages, for archaeology in Britain has escaped the imposition of a rigid hierarchical structure, and no 'authority', however well established, is quite secure against critical appraisal of his work; but few if any branches of the subject have developed in a simple rational way.

None the less, in describing the development of modern research, it is convenient to formulate a logical approach as an ideal against which actual progress can be described. Such a theoretical programme would fall naturally into the following phases:

(a) All known structures regarded as hill-forts would be identified, and their generalized distribution plotted.
(bi) Broad regional varieties would be separated out on the evidence of major obvious characteristics such as size, spacing or number of ramparts and (bii) more complete descriptive surveys, with plans, of groups of forts would be provided.
(c) Accurate detailed surveys would be prepared, and hence the structural development worked out so far as this can be known from surface evidence. The most important objective at this stage would be to identify recognizable types.
(d) Selected typical sites would then be examined by excavation, one or two of each being treated on a large scale, a selection of the remainder being tested to see whether their apparent similarities were genuine.
(e) Finally, the apparently exceptional structures would be in-

vestigated, to discover how they fitted into the general background.

No subject has ever followed such an ideally logical path of development, and the study of hill-forts could not have done so, for interpretation of surface evidence often depends on knowledge of the results of excavation elsewhere. It must be emphasized that the use of this theoretical programme as a basis is imposing an appearance of orderly progress which is illusory.

Thanks to the founders of the Ordnance Survey, in particular General Roy, the theoretical stage (a) is in fact complete, or very nearly so. Until recently, the 6 inch to the mile OS maps represented, as accurately as the scale allowed, all known earthworks. Owing to government-enforced economies, all features on recent editions of these maps and on their 1/10000 successors have been coarsened and generalized, so that even such clearly defined details as the outlines of buildings are no longer faithfully portrayed, and earthworks have suffered with the rest, but the 1/2500 maps still provide accurate basic plans. They are available for much of Britain (though expensive) and the older editions of both these and the '6-inch' are available in libraries.

Detailed local research in the field and aerial photography continue to add occasional hill-forts to those recorded on the maps, but it is unlikely that as many as 10 per cent of the total remain unknown. British archaeologists are thus in the uniquely fortunate position of having available reasonably accurate plans of some 90 per cent or more of all the hill-forts which ever existed in this country, together with large-scale maps permitting a study of their topographical background. The potential riches of this immense mine of information have scarcely been touched, but the Ordnance Survey have placed archaeologists still further in their debt by publication of their Map of Southern Britain in the Iron Age. This, with much other information, shows the distribution of all known hill-forts, partly classified by size and partly by whether their ramparts are single or multiple. The size classes are: less than 1·2 hectares, 1·2–6 hectares, and larger. A similar map is in preparation for northern Britain.

S. C. Stanford, in his discussion of Croft Ambrey (*q.v.*), has utilized the data on the Iron Age map to distinguish several separate regions, but systematic numerical study of distributions, leading to stage (bi), has scarcely begun. Fairly detailed descriptive regional studies (bii), on the other hand, have been characteristic of British archaeology from an early stage.

One of the best, R. Colt Hoare's *Ancient Wiltshire*, even preceded the publication of the OS maps, and still provides the only collection of hill-fort plans for that county. A later individual pioneer was D. Christison, who almost single-handed covered the greater part of Scotland at the end of the last century. The first organized attempt to cover one country systematically, however, had to await the initiation, soon after 1900, of the Victoria County History (VCH) for England. With few exceptions, the volumes of this splendid work include descriptions of the earthworks in every English county, accompanied by plans to uniform rational scales, mostly 1/5000. The plans are generally based, with little revision, on the Ordnance Survey, and the descriptions do not aim at any analysis of the sequence of development; but as most of the work was done during the first decade of this century, or soon after, it would be unreasonable to expect more.

In 1908 the survey of antiquities of all kinds was given official support by the formation of the three Royal Commissions on Ancient and Historical Monuments. They are concerned to record all types of 'monument', and their work is necessarily slow, since their aim is to be definitive and the number of places which have to be inspected is very large. For a single Welsh county, a recent Inventory contained eighteen hundred entries, but its preparation necessitated the investigation of nearly seven thousand possibly ancient structures.

So far as hill-forts are concerned, the earlier Inventories were generally illustrated by plans based on the 1/2500 maps fairly extensively improved by fieldwork and redrawn — often with an elaborately ornate background which must have involved more labour than the plan itself. Recently, the plans are almost always the result of an original *ad hoc* survey.

A really careful and accurate survey (stage (c) above) can be almost as informative as an excavation — which, indeed, it should always precede — and the detailed study necessary to its preparation will often suggest interpretations which would otherwise have been overlooked. Some of the particular triumphs of surface survey have involved the recognition of unfinished hill-forts. Ladle Hill is the classic example.

This seems to be an appropriate point to comment on one very regrettable modern development. As noted above, the VCH plans were reproduced, almost without exception, to a rational scale such as 1/5000 or 1/2500. Of late this excellent practice has been increasingly abandoned, not through any fault of the surveyors but because some editors and printers have the impertinence deliberately to disregard the author's instructions, thinking some other ratio to page size will look prettier. This viciously innumerate arrogance is often more harmful than would be the deliberate insertion of grammatical errors; for the direct comparison of plans *to a consistent set of scales* can be more instructive than many pages of print.

One must be thankful that excavation (stage (d)) has not in fact had to wait its logical turn; it would have been unbearably tantalizing to have no clue as to what lies beneath the turf. Unrecorded digging for treasure or for lesser 'finds' to add to collections goes back a long way, and even research excavation has its beginnings in the nineteenth century, though its practitioners were rare. Young's work at Burghead may be mentioned.

Many essentials of modern techniques were developed just before 1900, by General Pitt-Rivers. His own generation, and the next, remained uninfluenced, but in the 1920s a number of young men rediscovered or re-invented a scientific approach. The basic principles were to plan the excavations to answer specific questions, and to record with meticulous accuracy the positions of all relics and the fullest possible details of stratification. The structural development of the defences could thus be worked out, in relation to the potentially datable objects found; and an approximately dated sequence could be established for types of pottery and other artifacts.

This approach did not necessarily involve large-scale excavation. To select one example: E. C. Curwen organized a series of investigations in the hill-forts of the Sussex Downs which in a decade produced a reliable framework for the history of the whole region during the Iron Age. The initiative of the Hampshire Field Club in organizing a series of excavations under the direction of C. F. C. Hawkes extended this knowledge over much of the southern chalklands. Even earlier first-rate work was being carried out in Wales by Willoughby Gardner, though his most important piece of research, at Dinorben, had to wait until the sixties for definitive publication.

Small-scale excavations, though, have the weakness that they provide relatively little comparative material and are not very informative as to the social and economic background. To remedy this, and to set knowledge of the southern British Iron Age on a sound basis, something more ambitious was needed. In the mid-1930s Dr (now Sir) Mortimer Wheeler, then director of the Institute of Archaeology, worked out a carefully integrated campaign.

The central feature of this was the large-scale excavation of Maiden Castle near Dorchester, the most impressive hill-fort in southern Britain. This was to be supplemented by a survey of the forts of the whole of northern France, with fairly extensive excavation of selected sites, and excavation of other south British forts near Maiden Castle.

To be effective, this sort of planned campaign, and large-scale excavation of the type undertaken at Maiden Castle, calls for the rare association of exceptional ability in organization and leadership with personal skill in the techniques of excavation and interpretation. Dr Wheeler combined all these requirements with a flair for the best type of publicity, which did much to raise archaeology in public esteem.

Only a small part of the fruits of this brilliantly planned and executed campaign could be harvested, though, for the events of 1939 intervened. On the last day scheduled for the excavations at Duclair by the Seine, a portable radio on the site gave the news of the German invasion of Poland. The Maiden Castle report, published in 1941, was, to quote Sir Mortimer's preface, 'the salvage of the report that should have been'; and although the finds had been recorded with meticulous care, when the opportunity for research returned they had been irretrievably shuffled by the disturbances of wartime. Even so, all subsequent investigation of the Iron Age in southern Britain, and of the nature and function of the hill-forts there, depends heavily on this programme of research.

As yet no other wide-ranging campaign comparable to this has been brought to completion, but there have been several postwar excavations at least equal in scale and quality to that at Maiden Castle. There have also been advances in details of technique, such as the abolition of balks in area excavation, and the use of much broader rampart sections. On some sites which have never been disturbed the meticulous plotting of literally every pebble exposed has revealed information which would have been overlooked by methods used only ten years ago; while on others, where ploughing has destroyed the later levels, the use of earth-shifting machinery involves changes in approach. The basic principles, however, remain unaltered. The development of geophysical methods of investigation has not been an unmixed advantage, for on some sites they may fail to detect buried features, thus giving a completely misleading idea of the distribution of occupation.

3

The Background

Hill-forts were being built and used in Britain for a thousand years or more, and were only one aspect, though an important one, of native life during that period. So although this is not a study of the Iron Age as a whole, some account of the chronology and cultural changes of that period is necessary as a background, as well as an indication of the nature of life then. What follows, though, is no more than a highly generalized outline.

As long ago as 1931 a coherent scheme of dated cultural changes was worked out by Professor Hawkes, and this, with some modifications and an extension by Professor Piggott to cover Scotland, held the field for nearly forty years. More recently, physical methods of dating have been developed, notably 'radiocarbon', depending on the proportions of radiocarbon which survive in organic remains, and 'thermoluminescence' which uses the property of minerals so that the age can be found by measuring variation of luminescence with temperature which is affected by the interval since the first heating. These methods have shown that almost all the dates deduced from the earlier scheme are much too late. This point is discussed in fuller detail below. In addition, some archaeologists believe that the detailed analysis of cultural characteristics depends too much on isolated elements, especially on pottery differences which now seem, in some cases at least, to correspond rather to the regions over which different groups of professional potters marketed their wares. Nevertheless, subject to the reservations over dating, this scheme provides the most useful basis for setting out, in broad outline, the development of the Iron Age.

The chronology presents the greatest problem. As already stated, radiocarbon determinations have demonstrated that many of the absolute dates suggested in the Hawkes-Piggott framework are a century or more too late: palisades for example, are there assigned to *c*. 450 BC, but recent radiocarbon figures indicate that some were in fact being built during the ninth century. Similarly, univallate hill-forts in Wales and the Marches are shown as starting rather after 250 BC, but the first rampart at Dinorben has given a radiocarbon date of 895 ± 95 BC. Indeed, the whole development of hill-forts before the Roman conquest has now to be spaced out over some nine or ten centuries, starting in the phase formally defined as the Late Bronze Age, and apparently at least as early in Scotland and Wales as in south-eastern England. According to the older scheme, a sixth-century date for a south-eastern fort was regarded as possible but daringly early, while all in the north and west were much later.

Despite these changes the Hawkes-Piggott scheme remains the only one consistently worked out to cover the whole of Britain, and the newer evidence does not, as yet, permit a complete new chronology. A framework recently proposed for the Welsh Marches is discussed below (p. 31). Further, most of the published material has used the older scheme as a background. It would be misleading arbitrarily to convert the dating assigned by an excavator to a supposedly more correct chronology, and the result could well be quite wrong. Equally, though, it would be misleading now to quote these dates as an absolute figure BC.

The method adopted, therefore, has been to quote the dates given by writers whose results are used, but to describe them as, for example, H 250, or second-century (H), when they appear to be based on the Hawkes-Piggott framework. This retains the carefully worked out relationships between sites in adjacent regions, which are often more important than absolute dates. It is impossible to give a conversion factor which will permit an accurate estimate of the 'true' BC date from 'H' figures, but *very* roughly they need to be multiplied by from $1\frac{1}{2}$ to $2\frac{1}{2}$ or even 3, the smaller values being applicable to the south-east, the larger to the north and west. It must be said, also, that the 'H' dates given here are sometimes inferred rather than directly quoted, and some of these inferences may be mistaken.

The other element of this scheme was the specification of the principal cultural characteristics of the British Iron Age; but probably its most important feature was the explicit recognition that culture and chronology must be treated separately. Thus the earliest cultural developments could have been entirely superseded and suppressed in one part of the country, while continuing to flourish elsewhere.

The principal characteristics of the British Iron Age can be recognized as the results of three main waves of continental influences, giving rise in this country to Iron Ages A, B and C. Their essentials are summarized below. They have now been subdivided, chronologically and geographically, so that a particular regional culture may be described, for example, as 'south-western second B', but for our purpose the simple basic classification is sufficient.

The first introduction of iron to this country seems to have been about H 600 or 700, but fully developed Iron Age A culture first appears about H 500, probably in the south and east, spreading slowly northwards and westwards to reach the remoter parts of Britain by H 300. It is characterized by pottery whose shape suggests derivation, usually at long remove, from metal bowls or buckets with carinated rims. Some of the better ware is given a red burnished coating of haematite as if to imitate bronze, but the nature of the coarser pots suggests that the population consisted mostly of descendants of the people who lived in Britain during the Late Bronze Age – a view confirmed by the survival of round houses as the predominant type, in contrast to the frequency of rectangular buildings on the continent. The hill-forts of this culture seem to have been exclusively defended by a single rampart, either a stone wall or a bank and ditch. Until recently, the first introduction of defended settlements to Britain was attributed to Iron Age A, and this probably remains true for their appearance in any numbers, but excavations at Ivinghoe Beacon have shown that the hill-fort there was associated exclusively with typically Late Bronze Age material; and radiocarbon dating has suggested a similarly early date on some other sites, notably Dinorben.

The second wave of foreign influences, Iron Age B, arrived in southern Britain about H 300 or 250, when 'A' had only just begun to replace the Late Bronze Age in the north and west. Their characteristic pottery takes the form of wide-mouthed rounded bowls. The ware is generally black or dark brown, often burnished, and the finer vessels are decorated with incised or simple stamped patterns, often with graceful curvilinear designs, especially in the later material. Much, if not all, of this pottery was produced commercially in particular districts, and distributed by trade. The new arrivals are credited with the introduction of the sling as a weapon, leading to the invention, perhaps in Britain, of defences consisting of two or more close-set banks and ditches. Again, the round house survives throughout much of Britain, indicating that these new arrivals also were a minority absorbed by or imposed on the mass of previous inhabitants. Nevertheless, along the whole of the Welsh Marches there seems to have been a settlement of groups entirely derived from abroad, indicated by the rows of square buildings as found at Croft Ambrey or Ffridd Faldwyn.

The third wave of continental influences, Iron Age C, arrived about H 100, introducing the use of coinage and of finer pottery, often wheel-turned. As settlers, they do not seem to have penetrated far outside south-eastern England. Settlements founded by them seem to have been protected by complex systems of linear earthworks, as at Colchester. They did occasionally take over existing hill-forts and improve and strengthen their defences. To judge from the evidence of Maiden Castle, moreover, they tidied up the settlements within the ramparts, sealing the stinking rubbish pits with layers of clean chalk or earth. The Belgae, whose invasion of Britain from north-east Gaul is recorded by Caesar, were the most noted among the bringers of this C culture.

The full-scale invasion by the Romans in AD 43 did not end the use of hill-forts immediately, but led to such a drastic discontinuity in their development that it is convenient to treat later events in a separate chapter.

As indicated earlier, the new evidence from radiocarbon dating has not yet been incorporated in a general chronological framework covering all Britain. An important beginning has been made in Scotland, but neither the structural sequences nor the artifacts there are as informative as those in the south. For the Welsh Marches, a comprehensive scheme covering nine centuries has been proposed by Mr S. C. Stanford, using the evidence of successive reconstructions in the gateways and other timberwork at Croft Ambrey and elsewhere and linking this to radiocarbon determinations.

The resulting chronology is likely to be much closer to the truth than the Hawkes-Piggott system, but cannot as yet be extended safely to other regions, such as the southern chalklands. Since the framework is based to a great extent on structural features, it is particularly useful in discussing their evolution (see p. 73), and it is of course directly applicable to the site of Croft Ambrey (pp. 99–101) which provided much of the information on which it is based. Nevertheless, the figures should still not be regarded as true dates BC, and are therefore referred to as 'S'. Thus stone guard chambers appear in the Marches about S 350.

The sparse documentary accounts which we have of Celtic life give the impression of a society dominated by priests (Druids) and warriors. No doubt this reflects their own estimate of their importance, but archaeologically they were no more than a thin layer of cream (or scum, according to one's social outlook) upon the great mass of people, who were essentially farmers. There was some trade, archaeologically attested in pottery as well as in utilitarian and fine metalwork, and to be inferred in livestock, but, except for the most skilled, craftsmen's markets were restricted to a radius of 30 or 40 kilometres from their base. So the population in any region, before the advent of the Romans and after their departure, would depend on the products of that region, not on imports. The sort of farming adopted was presumably that found by long experience to be most suited to the area. Generally in the south and east, and along the Welsh Marches, it seems to have been primarily arable, while in the extreme south-west, in Wales, and in the north, cattle predominated; but no area depended exclusively on a single product. It is also a fairly safe assumption that over most of the period the population would have increased to the limit imposed by the food supply. In general, then, as a rough upper approximation, the density of population may have been about the same as in the twelfth century AD; it is most unlikely to have been any greater. In the east and south, this implies something like ten to fifteen persons per square kilometre; the heavy claylands would not have been in use until just before the Roman period, so the medieval figure of twenty-five or so is likely to be too great. Elsewhere, the medieval value is probably of the right order, falling off to four to six per square kilometre in Wales, and to two or less in Scotland. In modern Britain population as sparse as this is only found near the remoter mountain districts. Even so, the mass of the population cannot have been reduced to bare subsistence. There was a surplus of production which could be creamed off for the benefit of the Druid priests, and to pay for the finely decorated metalwork of the warriors, or at least of their leaders. Time could be found, too, to build massive defences – and presumably to raid those of neighbours.

Even apart from the risk of death by violence, life was short. In Maiden Castle, for example, excluding the war cemetery, ages are known for skeletons from thirty-five bodies. Eleven of these died in infancy, nineteen below forty, four some time between forty and fifty, and one, the oldest, between forty-five and fifty-five. Those buried in the war cemetery, as might be expected, were on average younger, but included one man between fifty and sixty. Similar evidence is found elsewhere. Forty years, therefore, was the longest term one could reasonably hope for, even if one survived the dangers of childhood. This meagre life expectancy may be one reason for the extensive use of wood in structures which give the impression of intended permanence. A 30-centimetre oak beam would last for twenty years or more, so would only need to be renewed once in a man's working life.

So far as archaeological evidence goes, this brief span does not seem to have led to any great emphasis on existence after death. Cemeteries associated with hill-forts are extremely rare. Shrines have been identified in a few places, and may reasonably be inferred in others from temples of Roman date, which are fairly common, but little or nothing is known of the rituals with which they were served. What little is recorded concerning pre-Roman religious activities suggests that the main centres were located away from settlements.

4
Function

The really important part of a hill-fort was its interior. All too often, later use has obliterated any traces of the structures which stood there, so that most commonly nothing is known except the area enclosed and the arrangement of the protective ramparts. Nevertheless, even this limited information does allow some sort of classification: there is clearly a qualitative as well as a quantitative difference between enclosures of half a hectare and those fifty or a hundred times as large.

Excavation, and the evidence of visible hut emplacements where the ground has remained undisturbed, show that almost all hill-forts were inhabited. A few may have been intended as no more than temporary refuges, but the absence of relics or building traces does not necessarily prove this. Some cultures, for example, rely almost entirely on wooden or leather utensils, with no pottery; and certain types of building, such as timber houses founded on sleeper beams, may leave very little trace.

Whether the occupation of any fort was permanent or seasonal is a matter of inference. In southern Britain there would have been no practical objection to use throughout the year, for most of the sites are below 300 metres. The character of those excavated gives the impression that they were permanently inhabited. If the evidence from Tre'r Ceiri is correctly interpreted, this could apply even up to 500 metres. In Scotland, on the other hand, it seems incredible that places so far above sea level could have been occupied during the winter, so, making the reasonable assumption that the practice of transhumance goes back to prehistoric times, these high-level hill-forts could have been used for protection when the herds were moved up to the summer pastures.

Lacking excavation, size is probably the most important clue to a hill-fort's function, but it is important to realize that although modern terms have to be used in such a discussion they are at best no more than a rough approximation to the reality. Just as the military associations of the term 'fort' give a misleading idea of the true nature of one of these places, so the words 'city', 'town', 'castle' and even 'village' or 'farm' carry with them ideas which are often not appropriate to early settlements. In particular, practically nothing can be known or even guessed as to their administrative organization; even where some fairly early documentary material survives and should apparently be relevant, only the most brutally Procrustean treatment of the archaeological facts can make the details appear to fit. In what follows, these reservations must be kept in mind.

A second generalization, to which also there may be some exceptions, especially among the largest enclosures, is that the inhabitants of most British hill-forts subsisted on the produce of their immediate neighbourhood. Apart from some of the largest coastal forts, there is no reason to suppose that any substantial part of the population depended primarily on trade. This does not, of course, preclude the occurrence of seasonal 'fairs' for the exchange of produce, especially in cattle-raising areas.

Most hill-forts are simple enclosures, more or less strongly protected, the lines of defence being adapted to the form of the ground. In some regions, especially the south-west (pp. 44–5) and the Scottish borders (p. 45), subsidiary enclosures can be interpreted as intended for the protection of flocks and herds, but more often the appearance of multiple compartments is the result of successive alterations and reconstructions, so that the structure remained functionally one enclosure, the additional banks falling into disuse as at Maiden Castle and Hambledon Hill. Rarely, they may have continued in use as an extra defence, as perhaps at Pen Dinas, Aberystwyth.

The nature of the smallest enclosures is fairly certain. These would mostly correspond to the homes of single families, some of the larger including servants or slaves. The more weakly defended can be compared to the moated farms of the Middle Ages. Examples can be picked almost at random throughout Britain, but are under-represented in the gazetteer, which has concentrated on more impressive works. Nevertheless, Am Baghan Burblach, the northern enclosure on Harding's Down, Little Woodbury and Staple Howe are of this kind.

Considering Britain as a whole, these small weakly protected enclosures are numerically the commonest type of 'hill-fort', but many others, equally small internally and thus likely to be homes of a single family, have defences which now look disproportionately strong, often covering a greater area than that enclosed. The Barmekin of Echt, Chun Castle, the various Castle Laws, Dunsinane and Honington may be mentioned. For such places, the analogy with a medieval castle may be apt, since the task of construction seems too great to be the work of the occupants alone, and this implies that they were able to call in others to help.

There is no precise limit at which single family establishments give way to 'villages', but in some districts, such as south-west Wales, there is a break in the sequence of sizes, or a change in the distribution pattern, near 0·7 hectare, which suggests that the transition may occur at about that area; this is no more than a general trend, and does not as yet justify abandoning the 1·2 hectare criterion used by the Ordnance Survey. The larger enclosures can be regarded as 'villages' or 'towns'. Where the dividing line should be drawn is a matter of definition, and discussion would be unprofitable until far more work has been done on regional size distribution.

There are a few enclosures which stand out as quite exceptional, such as Llanymynech (56 hectares) or Bindon Hill (114 hectares). Even assuming no more than thirty persons per hectare, places of this size would need to draw on an improbably large district to maintain their inhabitants, so they must either have been far less densely occupied than the normal hill-fort or must have depended for their subsistence on something more than the farm produce of the adjacent countryside. No single explanation will fit all the examples. Bindon Hill has been accounted for as an invasion base, but an equally satisfactory alternative would be to regard it as a trading centre. This latter function would certainly seem appropriate for Hengistbury Head, also unusually large, where there is a fair amount of evidence of foreign contacts. Llanymynech, on the other hand, lies well inland, and seems most easily explicable as a centre for occasional assemblies by the local tribe, the Cornovii. Each of these very large enclosures needs to be considered separately, in its local context.

5

Distribution and Regional Types

Hill-forts are a characteristic feature of Iron Age culture, but it is immediately obvious from the maps (figs 1–3) that they are not an essential one. These maps require some explanation.

To give a really adequate cartographic representation of the distribution of hill-forts is not practicable, for it would require an atlas of several sheets, all at a very much larger scale. All that has been attempted, therefore, is to represent the size distribution, since area is probably the most important single quality. Even so, to avoid the excessive multiplication of different symbols, it has been necessary to use each to cover a wide range of areas. For consistency, the Ordnance Survey Iron Age map limits of 1·2 and 6 hectares have been adopted, but have been supplemented by two further critical values, 0·24 hectare to define the very small enclosures and 30 hectares to separate out those which are very large. These are not necessarily the best figures to choose, apart from the fact that the separate classes cover such a wide range of size; but further research is needed before more significant criteria can be selected. In the northern map the little fortified enclosures known as 'duns' have been shown, since there is no clear dividing line between a dun and a very small hill-fort; their distribution has been taken from the map which accompanies the work on the *Iron Age in Northern Britain*. Generally the objective has been to show every known fort, but in some very crowded areas, such as the Scottish borders, a few of the smallest have had to be omitted.

In considering the significance of the pattern shown by these maps, it is important to realize that it represents a palimpsest, built up over some thousand years. Nevertheless, since the dates of the various forts can seldom be decided, the distribution has to be considered as a whole. Some features stand out immediately. South of Hadrian's Wall about 1,420 hill-forts are known, and all but 110 of these lie south-west of a line from the Dee to Dungeness. Again, in the north

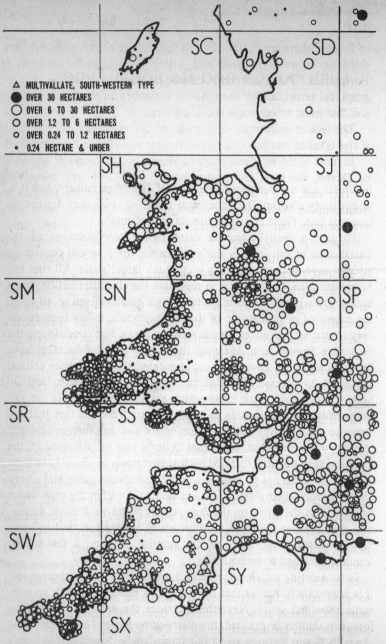

Fig. 1   Hill-forts in south-west Britain. Based upon the Ordnance Survey Map with the sanction of the Controller of Her Majesty's Stationary Office, Crown copyright reserved.

of Britain, there are 1,100 or so (if duns are rejected), and of these a third lie between the wall and a line joining north Berwick to Portpatrick. These contrasts cannot be explained simply in geographical terms, as for example by variations in the fertility of the soil, but must reflect some social differences.

The lack of uniformity in distribution becomes even more striking if size is taken into account. Several major regions can be recognized.

In most of the west and south of Wales, and in Cornwall and most of Devon, the forts are predominantly small and very numerous. Further east, in a triangle with its base extending from the Exe to Southampton Water, and its vertex just west of the Dee, large forts are common, but with a considerable admixture of smaller ones. Then up to the Dee-Dungeness line, the forts are almost all large, and appreciably less frequent. Finally, so far as the rest of Britain south of Hadrian's Wall in concerned, hill-forts become rare.

In the north there is a similar diversity. The heavy concentration in the Scottish Border region has already been mentioned. These are generally small enclosures, as indeed are most of those in the north. Then there is a fairly dense scatter round the firths of the Forth and Tay, followed by a sparse distribution of medium-sized enclosures up the east coast, while on the west coast hill-forts become rare. In the south, their infrequency is counterbalanced by the great mass of duns.

Thus there are at least seven or eight distinct regions, recognizably different though their boundaries are not sharp. These regions, moreover, are distinguishable using very broad criteria, and there is no doubt that really careful and detailed investigation would make further subdivision possible. It must be added that although regional types of fort, where identifiable, may well have corresponded to a particular tribe, this is a hypothesis which can neither be proved nor disproved; for tribal locations are seldom known before the Roman period, and their boundaries usually have an uncertainty of 30 or 40 kilometres at least. In most cases, also, the territory to be associated with a hill-fort must remain uncertain; but J. F. Dyer has put forward convincing arguments for accepting certain dykes in the eastern Chilterns as being Iron Age territorial boundaries. For the South Downs, the discussions by B. Cunliffe and R. Bradley (see p. 104) suggest the probable general areas controlled by the inhabitants of some hill-forts. Conversely, the absence of any obvious boundaries which might limit the regions appertaining to forts such as

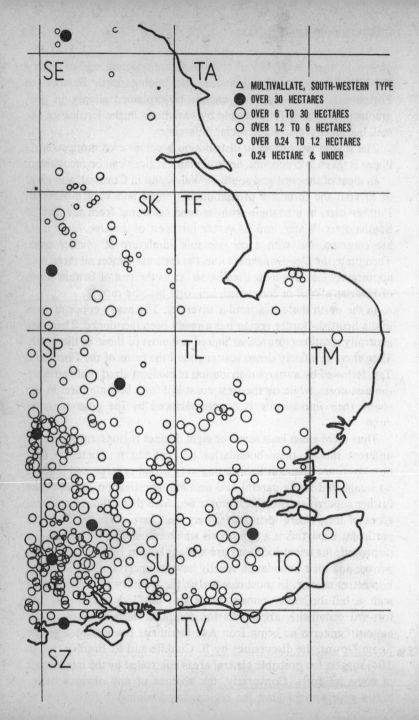

MULTIVALLATE, SOUTH-WESTERN TYPE
● OVER 30 HECTARES
○ OVER 6 TO 30 HECTARES
○ OVER 1.2 TO 6 HECTARES
○ OVER 0.24 TO 1.2 HECTARES
· 0.24 HECTARE & UNDER

Bigberry, Clare or Tasburgh gives some support to the idea that these places may have been in a sense political 'capitals'.

In the case of Bigberry, this identification is supported by the establishment of Canterbury nearby as the Roman cantonal capital – Durovernum Cantiacorum. There are similar associations of hill-forts with cantonal capitals elsewhere, as Llanmelin with Caerwent, (Venta Silurum) or St Catherine's Hill with Winchester (Venta Belgarum). But the argument is not irrefutable, for neither Llanmelin nor St Catherine's Hill is an exceptionally impressive hill-fort, and the latter seems likely to have been abandoned well before the Roman invasion.

In these eastern regions, the presence of a few isolated forts, and by implication a considerable number of undefended settlements also, must imply a fairly well organized social system, in which some centralized control prevented casual raiding by neighbours. The normally peaceful character of these regions is emphasized by the developments which took place at Stanwick in Yorkshire. There, a fairly small hill-fort of normal type, in a region where they are not common, became the nucleus of a great system of enclosures fortified by dykes, resembling the Belgic *oppida* of the south-east. All this has been convincingly interpreted as the capital of Venutius, where he collected his troops and his allies in preparation for his revolt after AD 50.

In contrast, the extreme south-west and west, and the Scottish borders, display intense concentrations of small enclosures, though a few larger ones exist there as well.

Enough of these small sites have been examined in south-west Wales to demonstrate that they are not all of the same type, nor probably of the same date, and so far as can be judged at present from surface evidence they range with no obvious break from structures to which only the most extreme purist would deny the description 'hill-fort' down to lightly protected enclosures on almost level ground. Some of these last, as at Trelissey, have proved to contain a small Roman house, which may have been the successor of a native farm. On the other hand, at Walesland Rath full excavation of what appeared on the surface to be a comparable structure has revealed a

Fig. 2   Hill-forts in south-east Britain. Based upon the Ordnance Survey Map with the sanction of the Controller of Her Majesty's Stationery Office, Crown copyright reserved.

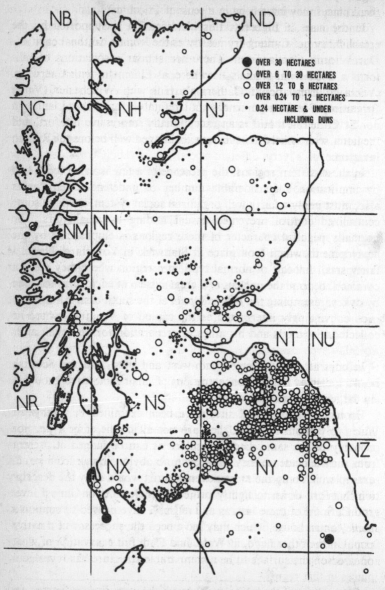

Fig. 3   Hill-forts in northern Britain. Based upon the Ordnance Survey
         Map with the sanction of the Controller of Her Majesty's
         Stationery Office, Crown copyright reserved.

two-period settlement of great complexity, with rows of rectangular buildings following the inner circuit of the rampart, and six or eight round houses in the central space. It can be explained with equal plausibility as anything from a dependent village to the 'court' of a local 'lord', with various other alternatives. The investigation has thus a double importance, both as one of the rare examples of full scientific excavation and as a warning against too facile interpretation of incomplete data.

Nevertheless, though questions of detail remain unanswered, these regions with numerous small defended enclosures must imply the existence of a very different social organization from that found further east. Perhaps a fairly close modern parallel would be the background to life on both sides of the Scottish borders in the sixteenth century. Raiding would normally be against people at a distance, but local quarrels could spark off an attack on an immediate neighbour. Keeping in mind that no analogy can be exact, we may note the range from strongly defended enclosures with several ramparts, through weaker settlements with single banks such as Walesland, to places which now appear barely defensible, and compare it to the impressive pele towers of the rich landowner, the 'bastle houses', and the peles themselves, simple enclosures without towers, which have now mostly vanished. Straining the parallel still further, we may even suspect that some of the rare larger hill-forts were the dwellings of rulers having some nominal regional authority, rather more localized than that of some English and Scottish royalty early in the Middle Ages, but equally ineffective.

In regions of intermediate type, where hill-forts are fairly large but also fairly numerous, much more detailed analysis of their distribution is needed: the apparent similarity of the pattern over a large area may conceal regional differences. In west Caernarvonshire, for example, it is possible to determine approximately the territory which might be associated with the two large forts of Garn Boduan and Carn Fadrun, and at a rough estimate this could have supported some thousand to fifteen hundred people, approximately the total population of those two hill-forts. It is therefore possible, though not of course certain, that these were the only substantial inhabited places in that region.

By contrast, if the hill-forts of west Kent, west Sussex, Surrey and the adjacent parts of Hampshire are examined similarly, it appears that they have relatively much larger areas associated with them.

They were therefore either very much more crowded than forts in similar territory further west (such as Hod Hill, where the surviving hut emplacements permit an estimate of population), or they each formed some sort of social or commercial centre for a population of which half or more normally lived at some distance. Once again using a dangerous analogy, they would be comparable to a medieval market town. Unlike the hill-forts of east Kent or East Anglia, there is no need to suppose that any part of their dependent territory lay more than 15 or 20 kilometres distant.

These settlements on the southern chalklands have received fuller attention than those elsewhere. The excavations at Quarley Hill demonstrated the relationship of that enclosure to earlier dykes, or ranch boundaries of the late Bronze Age. Professor Cunliffe and R. Bradley have emphasized the significant associations of settlements with features likely to be connected with cattle-raising and often with sacred places (inferred from the later erection of Roman temples). Many of the major hill-forts of this region can therefore be convincingly interpreted as having developed out of traditional meeting places which combined the functions of seasonal fairs or markets and those of religious centres. It is easy to devise hypotheses which will explain the evolution leading from groups of herdsmen ranging over open downland to the construction of large fortified villages, each centred on a traditional nucleus and under the control of some local leader, perhaps loosely subject to a tribal ruler.

When structural characteristics and details of design are taken into account as well as enclosed area, various regional groups can be recognized. The best known of these is characteristic of south-western Britain, the south-western wide-spaced multivallate hill-fort, to give its full description; its special characteristics were first recognized by Lady Fox. Milber Down and Clovelly Dykes are type sites. A relatively small main enclosure, seldom as much as a hectare in area and usually univallate, is surrounded by one or more additional slighter ramparts, each separated from the enclosures by wide spaces. This arrangement is convincingly interpreted as designed for the protection of cattle, the innermost small enclosure being the actual homestead. Almost all known examples occur in the south-west, and seem to be associated with B culture, dating from H 200 or later. There are several variants of the plan, the differences being mainly in the arrangement of the outer enclosures, which are not always symmetrically placed relative to the 'homestead'; but all follow the same basic principle of a small enclosure with slighter outworks widely spaced.

A few of the forts on the Scottish borders seem to have some provision for cattle. The Ringses on Doddington Moor has a compartment between inner and outer defences, with a separate entrance; but the outer rampart is stronger than in the normal 'south-western' type, and the enclosed space much smaller. At Lordenshaws the outer dyke may be a rather closer parallel. These two little forts, apart from this possible provision for cattle, may represent a 'type' which extends fairly widely into southern Scotland, characterized by strong defences enclosing a small more or less oval space, as also at Bochastle and Dunsinane, among others; but whether all these really deserve to be regarded as a single type is open to question.

At one time the 'vitrified forts' of Scotland were looked upon as a separate class, but these are now recognized as merely sharing a widespread use of timber reinforcement. Nevertheless, they do seem to include a group of characteristic and distinctive plan, though with a wide range of areas, as at Castle Law, Forgandenny, Finavon, Barry Hill near Perth and the White Caterthun. All those are more or less oblong with semicircular ends, and the type seems to have a rather localized scatter on both sides of the Firth of Tay.

Another type which seems to be exclusively Scottish, and to be post-Roman, is the nuclear fort, exemplified particularly by Dundurn, Dunadd and Ruberslaw. These have been built on craggy sites which form small irregular shelves. Each shelf is separately walled, so that the highest 'citadel' is approached through a series of defended courts, each commanded by the one above. Unfortunately no really characteristic fort of this kind has been scientifically excavated, and the possibility cannot be excluded that the apparent 'nuclear' arrangement may be the result of successive alterations and additions to what was originally a simple enclosure. That is certainly the case with some forts claimed to be of this type, but the three named at least give a strong impression of unitary design.

There are other features which seem to have a localized distribution, but which have not yet been studied fully enough for their extent to be known. One of the most important and interesting is the use of small rectangular buildings, as at Croft Ambrey; this practice seems to follow, roughly, a broad belt of territory along the Welsh Marches. Another distinctive characteristic is the use of paired guard chambers, found at Croft Ambrey but also at Dinorben (where the dwellings were round), and probably at Maiden Castle, as well as at Rainsborough, though there the chambers were round not rectangular. Massive multiple defences with elaborate entrances, as at Maiden Castle, also seem to be limited to the same general area. Nevertheless, the distributions of these three features are certainly not coincident, and multivallation is common in the Scottish borders also, though not much further north.

On the other hand, some technical devices occur in widely separated isolated patches. The *chevaux-de-frise* is discussed below (pp. 48-9). The use of large upright slabs to line entrance passages, as at Garrywhin and Duchary Rock, occurs in a fairly restricted area of north-east Scotland, but is found also at Conway Mountain and elsewhere in Wales. Multiple small entrances are also found in both these regions: they exist at Duchary Rock, and at Tre'r Ceiri. To what extent characteristics of this kind are significant is something which can only be determined when far more of our hill-forts have been the subjects of really detailed and accurate surveys. There is no doubt that when that has been done still more regional types will become recognizable.

6

Origins, Attack and Defence

Until recently, the first use of iron in Britain and the appearance of hill-forts were accepted as roughly contemporary and as having been introduced by invaders from the continent about H 500. Excavations, notably at Ivinghoe Beacon and Dinorben, but confirmed at some other sites, have now shown that some defences must have been put up within the period formally assigned to the Late Bronze Age, well before the earliest traces of ironworking here; in true dates, these sites may well go back as far as 900 or 1000 BC. Although this does not necessarily rule out the invasion hypothesis, it falsifies the dramatic picture of hordes of warriors, armed with better (and cheaper) weapons of iron, setting up fortified invasion bases on the British coasts. Once again, any sort of unitary explanation is likely to be misleading.

Walls, field banks or fences, much like those seen at many farms today, were built during the Bronze Age. To enlarge these to form a defensive rampart would require no particular inventive powers, so all that would be needed to give rise to a hill-fort would be some stimulus which would make the work seem worthwhile. Several such can be imagined, but the simplest would be merely an increase in population, especially if combined with settled farming methods, which could themselves lead to such an increase. The defences could either be the work of the original inhabitants, or could have been built by aggressors moving into new territory. Once the 'hill-fort idea' was established, also, the mere possession of defences might have carried with it some prestige.

Hill-forts, therefore, can be expected to appear as a purely local phenomenon, independently of any external influences; but that is not to say that they always did so. When technical details characteristic of forts in central Europe are found almost unchanged in Sussex, for example, the movement of ideas, and probably of actual people, can reasonably be assumed (see also pp. 61–3, 204, 274). Fortifications in central Europe provide exact parallels to the panels of dry-stone walling between timber uprights, as at Maiden Castle for example, and to an even more distinctive arrangement where the uprights, with or without stone walling, are tied together by horizontal timbers running from back to front of the rampart; Preist, in Bavaria, is the type site. This needs to be distinguished from the true *murus gallicus* described by Caesar, which is not found in Britain. Preist-type reinforcement, or arrangements very similar, occurs widely in Britain, and in some very early contexts, as at Dinorben. Bindon Hill, above Lulworth Cove, may have been an actual invasion base for people building in this style.

Technical tricks found in stone ramparts also occur abroad, but are less certainly of foreign origin. The use of multiple facing, believed to be the *murus duplex* of Caesar, is common throughout France and in Britain, as also are ramparts stepped at the back, but both techniques seem so obvious that they could have been invented independently. Double facing, presumably to reduce the risk of collapse, is found in neolithic and Bronze Age burial cairns.

Ditch profiles have not been much studied; but the use of a very broad flat-bottomed ditch in front of a massive single rampart seems characteristic of some French fortifications, mostly in the north: it is known as the Fécamp type from the site where it was first identified. It is also found at Oldbury in Kent and probably at East Hill, Hastings, among others in south-east England. It may have been developed in response to Roman methods of attack.

All these have a fairly continuous distribution, and there is no difficulty in envisaging ways in which the techniques could have been carried from place to place. One very distinctive type of additional defence, however, presents a great problem. That is the *chevaux-de-frise*, where a broad band in front of the rampart is set with a close-set pattern of small pointed stones. The known distribution in western Europe seems to be restricted to central Spain and Britain, with no intervening examples; and the British examples are sporadic, two or three in Wales, and a few in Scotland and Ireland. At one of the Welsh sites, Pen-y-Gaer near Llanbedr-y-Cennin, the belt of pointed stones is bounded on its outer edge by a slight bank and ditch, reproducing an arrangement identical with one which occurs in Spain. Possible explanations for this peculiar distribution are that of independent invention; that there is a wide spread of timber examples, all undiscovered, linking the known distributions of those in stone; or that small bodies of refugees from central Spain settled independently in various parts of Britain (but without opposition, for most of the examples are inland). None of these is satisfactory, and the problem remains unsolved.

Some element of display may often have been present in hill-fort design. For example, the panels of white stonework between the dark timber uprights at Maiden Castle must have been architecturally quite impressive until the timber rotted. Nevertheless, the primary object was to resist attack. Even if traditions which imply chariot warfare in the open were universally applicable, they would not conflict with this view, for ideally a fortress should be so strong as to make any thought of attack appear hopeless. It follows that if *both* sides wished to meet in battle, such a meeting, with or without chariots, would take place outside the ramparts. An actual assault either implies a surprise raid or an apparent numerical advantage by the attackers.

Archaeological evidence for such attacks, except at the time of the Roman invasions, is necessarily rare and seldom completely unambiguous. Those who adhere to the theory that all Iron Age warfare was in the open can explain away evidence for defenders killed in battle as a massacre of non-combatants after defeat; and any burned gateway can be written off either as due to the same circumstances or as pure accident. Nevertheless, to do this in all cases seems to be straining the evidence to fit a preconceived theory. At Sutton Walls, the skeletons showing marks of weapons and casually thrown into the ditches seem likely to be those of the young men who fell during the capture of the fortress. Similarly, at Bredon Hill the remains of bodies which had been literally cut to pieces were found scattered over the gate passage. Fragments from a handsome shield were found buried under a fallen wall at Moel Hiraddug. And while some fires were no doubt accidental, the excavator's interpretation of the burning of the first gateway at Rainsborough as the result of attack is convincing. Evidence of this kind requires that the attack ended the occupation. Even though the people of the period do not seem to have been unduly fastidious, they would surely have tidied away most of the bodies and generally have repaired the defences if the place remained inhabited.

At the time of the Roman conquest, there can be no doubt that some of the larger settlements put up a defence. It is only necessary to cite the example of Hod Hill, where additional ramparts were under construction when the place fell, and where the excavator traced the pattern of ballista bolts aimed at one of the principal dwellings. At Maiden Castle, too, even if the warriors buried in the war cemetery did not die within the town, as seems likely, the Romans considered it worthwhile to slight the gateway, making it militarily useless; clearly they regarded the ramparts as intended for defence, not merely for show.

Almost the only written account of native warfare is that given by Caesar in his *Gallic Wars*, when the influence of Roman methods had begun to be felt. The simplest method was to drive the defenders off the ramparts by a shower of missiles; the attackers, with shields above their heads, then undermined the wall and set fire to the gates. Was it perhaps in a battle of this kind that the Moel Hiraddug shield was lost?

Any form of dry-stone construction would be vulnerable to this sort of attack, though the steep slope of rubble from the collapsed wall would still be a fairly effective obstacle to the assailants. Rather surprisingly, there is no mention of the use of scaling ladders by the Gauls. Not only gateways, but in dry weather even timber revetments, could be destroyed by fire, and Caesar describes an attack on a Roman camp, using incendiary darts and red-hot slingstones of baked clay.

Perhaps the most instructive incident in Caesar's account is the siege of Uxellodunum (Puy d' Issolu, near Vayrac – *pace* the rival claimants). This is an immense plateau the size of the City of London, nearly impregnable owing to its surrounding cliffs. Yet the inhabitants depended almost entirely on water fetched from the river Dordogne far below, or from a sacred spring, nearer but still outside the defences. Unknown to the defenders, Caesar tapped its source by an adit, and this apparently supernatural blow reduced them to such despair that they surrendered.

It is evident from this account that the occupants of even a large and well organized town felt no need for a supply of water within the walls, but were prepared to bring most of their requirements from a considerable distance. The absence of any wells or cisterns in most British forts indicates that the same practice prevailed here. It also supports the view that the defences were for protection from casual raids, rather than against deliberately planned assaults in the course of systematic warfare.

In Britain, the documentary record of the Roman conquest,

confirmed by excavation, indicates that even massive fortresses such as Maiden Castle and Hod Hill fell quickly to the invaders' disciplined persistence and superior siege engines, but so far only the latter site has produced evidence of the actual methods used. There Sir Ian Richmond worked out the distribution of ballista bolts round and in one of the principal dwellings, and was able to infer the approximate position of the engine from which these came. No example has been recognized, in this country, of the method of attack by constructing a massive bank rising to the level of the ramparts; this would leave traces which should be still visible, and some may await identification.

Defence can be considered in its active and passive forms. There was one great development in the method of active defence, the introduction of the sling as a weapon, perhaps about H 200 or H 300 in this country. More precisely, of course, the same weapons are available for attack or for defence; but, as will be seen below, the sling, combined with appropriate rampart design, gave a decisive advantage to the defenders, other things being equal.

Before the introduction of sling warfare, the normal function of a rampart was to provide an elevated platform for defence, difficult for the attackers to climb, and with some frontal protection for the defenders. There was no great advantage in keeping the enemy at a distance. The ideal was to get them trapped in a ditch immediately below the rampart, so that they were vulnerable to short-range missiles, and to the spears or swords of the defenders if they did manage to get within reach. Very rarely, a *chevaux-de-frise* was provided outside the ditch, to break up a charge. Forts built before the widespread adoption of the sling as a weapon should therefore tend to have a single rampart, with a ditch where the ground permits, and with a breastwork along the outer side of the rampart walk.

The sling changed the whole principle of defence. A sling stone travels approximately in a parabola, so increased height gives greatly increased range. The ideal defensive profile therefore has a high main rampart, with two or more lesser ramparts in front, each having a steep but sloping outer face so as to give the attacker no cover, and an almost vertical back to prevent retreat. The rampart top needs no frontal breastwork, for it would hinder the use of the sling; any fence which there is will, in an ideal design, be along the back of the rampart walk as at Maiden Castle. To increase the firepower beyond what would be possible using only the top of the bank; platforms may be provided at lower levels, though no really convincing examples are known in Britain. Forts were not always built in the most up-to-date style, or exactly as this theory would suggest; indeed, sling stone hoards are found in some univallate forts. But most of the impressive monumental multivallate enclosures can be attributed to the introduction of the new weapon. It has been suggested that the use of multiple ramparts was invented in Britain as a response to this.

The most vulnerable part of the defences was the entrance. Apart from a simple gate or hurdle, the commonest elaboration was the provision of a bridge, and arrangement of the approach so that a direct rush was impossible and any attackers could be overlooked from a length of rampart. Some of the complexities which resulted are described later (chapter 9).

It is impossible to generalize about the fate of the inhabitants after an unsuccessful defence. In Caesar's wars, this varied according to circumstances from collection of tribute and hostages to execution of the leaders and mutilation of all fighting men, or to the sale of the whole tribe as slaves. Examples of destruction and massacre have been mentioned earlier, and most of these may well have been the results of native warfare. The Romans could be equally barbarous, but there are enough examples where occupation continued into the Roman period to suggest that their usual policy was to allow the inhabitants to remain, probably with their defences slighted, until they chose of their own accord to move to a more Romanized type of settlement.

7

Building the Hill-Fort

The immediate reasons for building a hill-fort, or for choosing a particular site, can usually only be guessed at. The south chalklands are exceptional in that a convincing theory has been put forward to account for the positions of the forts (p. 44), but even there the immediate stimulus which led to the construction of the actual defences remains uncertain. Claims have often been made that forts form deliberately planned strategic systems, but these hypotheses are not necessary to account for the distributions of the sites. Similarly, at the beginning of this century, several writers made a great point of the intervisibility of hill-forts; but hill tops can usually be seen from other hill tops, and it has never been demonstrated that the number of fortified sites visible one from another is greater than would occur by chance. Another theory put forward is that the exploitation of lead may have dictated the location of hill-forts in north Cardiganshire; but the region is so rich in ore that it would be difficult to find a hill which was not fairly near a vein. There are ways in which these ideas could be tested, but until that has been done they must be dismissed as unproven speculations. Even if they should prove to be true, they would not necessarily imply that the location of forts was subject to some centralized control.

There seems, in fact, to be no need to suppose that the decision to build a hill-fort, its choice of site or its form of construction, was the concern of anyone other than the group who built it, though of course they would be influenced by fashion and by the imminence of danger. Usually, too, the position chosen seems to have been that which could be effectively defended with the least work. Where this is not the case, many explanations can be imagined, ranging from a practical need to fortify a pre-existing settlement to supernatural guidance; the curious events at Dinas Emrys may have been a survival of the sort of thing which was formerly normal. Evidence, inevitably, is lacking.

For the actual details of construction there is much information available, especially from unfinished work. This has recently been studied very fully by Dr R. W. Feachem; the classic site is Ladle Hill in Hampshire, described by Professor Piggott in 1931. Despite the many examples discovered subsequently, this remains the one where the evidence is clearest. The organization of the work was perhaps rather exceptionally systematic and well planned.

The design envisaged was a roughly circular enclosure, protected by a single rampart built up of material from an external ditch. The plan was first marked out on the ground by a small bank and ditch. Material from the excavation of the main ditch was then transported to dumps within the enclosure. It may be assumed that the disadvantage of double-handling was acceptable, partly to allow the material to be sorted so that the larger chalk could be used at the base of the rampart, and partly because it was to be built up behind a timber revetment. Some parts of the rampart had been completed, when the work of fortification was given up, either because the danger was past or because the enemy arrived too soon. It seems clear that the workers were divided into gangs some of which worked faster than others, but the whole scheme must have been supervised by a single director.

Although some sort of marking out is usual, not all the unfinished enclosures show evidence of such efficient organization. Work at the easternmost fort of the group on Harding's Down in Gower stands at the other extreme. Here, the original design was for a typical 'southwestern' fort, with a fairly strong inner enclosure separated by a wide space from an outer bank. The latter was of no great strength, and seems to have been completed, but only half the inner enclosure was built; work on it must have been very haphazard.

There is no sign of a marking out ditch, so presumably the circuit was indicated by a few upright sticks. The east half of the rampart, including the entrance, seems to have been finished, with a massive stone revetment (now removed) at the rear. At the western end, also, a short length was built up to its full height. These two parts, however, are unconnected, so although a lot of work has been done the place is quite indefensible. Evidently the work was divided up among gangs, some of whom did nothing at all, and such overall control as there was could neither enforce the general decision on the inactive gangs nor arrange for the others to provide a slight rampart round the whole circuit rather than bring their own sections to full completion. To assign sections to separate gangs seems to have been the normal way in which work on ramparts was organized, for there are many examples of unfinished ditches or of ramparts only brought to their full height in places; but the work has usually been carried far enough to provide some sort of defence.

In both these examples, material for the ramparts was obtained from an exterior ditch which formed part of the defences, but hill-fort builders were not doctrinaire about this. Their objective was simply to provide a strong fortification, and on a steep hillside this could often be done more easily by building up the main rampart from quarries behind it, the material from the ditch being also thrown downhill to form a counterscarp bank. The inner quarry ditches usually provided sheltered level places for dwellings; the stratified filling which accumulated is one of the major sources of information for the excavator.

The local or national worthy laying a foundation deposit is an innocuous survival of a very ancient tradition. The earliest account of such a ceremony in Britain occurs in the story concerning Dinas Emrys. There is no way of telling whether the magical elements have been superimposed on a genuine tradition or whether the whole tale is fiction, but even in this post-Roman context the storyteller gives no hint that there was anything unusual in the idea that Druids might advise a human sacrifice in order to ensure stability for a fortress. Certainly the practice is attested much earlier at both Maiden Castle and Hod Hill. Further skeletons have also been found from bodies apparently casually deposited in the ramparts at the former site and at South Cadbury, among other places. These are usually regarded as members of the workforce who died during construction, but were more probably sacrificial deposits, for considering the care generally employed in building the ramparts it seems unlikely that the supervisor would accept such very unsuitable material unless its structural weakness were counterbalanced by the advantage of spiritual support. The number of possible examples remains very small; but proportionately to the total length of Iron Age ramparts in Britain the amount which has been completely excavated to the original surface is infinitesimal. Moreover, simpler ceremonies such as libations would leave no trace.

The setting out being completed, and any necessary ceremonies performed, work could start. The great multiple ramparts of places such as Maiden Castle or Hod Hill suggest that decades of toil are represented, and in a sense that is true; but these huge defences did not reach their present state in a single step.

Fortunately, work on the experimental earthwork at Overton Down has given an indication of the rate at which a ditch could be dug in chalk: it works out at about 1 to 1·3 cubic metres per man, per day, to loosen the material, dig it out and transport it to a bank. The tools used were picks made of deer antler, shoulderblades of oxen for shovels and baskets for transport.

Applying these figures to the projected rampart at Ladle Hill: this measured 680 metres in length, and may be assumed for this calculation to have been, in intent, 4 metres high, 7 metres wide at the base and 1 metre at the summit, giving a total volume of just under 11,000 cubic metres, requiring between 8,000 and 11,000 man-days' work. To allow for the double-handling involved on this site, this time must be increased by half: the rock did not need to be loosened before the second transference. Also, about 1,000 small trees would be needed for the timberwork. No experiments on cutting these have been published, but 500 man-days would seem reasonable for that part of the work. These add up to a total of about 12,500 to 17,000 man-days. Making the conservative assumption of 60 persons per hectare in this fort of 3·4 hectares, about 200 people would give a work-force equivalent to perhaps 150 men, for women and children would help as basket-carriers. So a total of about 85 to 115 days would be sufficient to complete a hill-fort of this kind. It must be obvious that these figures are merely an indication of possibility. They probably err rather on the high side, for one may suppose that a rather larger population would hope to benefit from the protection of the fort, and would thus assist in building it.

The rampart projected at Ladle Hill was not exceptional; huge defences such as those at Maiden Castle remain awe-inspiring. Excavation there, though, has shown that they reached their present form in several stages. There is no need to give the calculations in full, but making the same assumptions for density of population and rate of work as for Ladle Hill, the following results are obtained. The first rampart, enclosing the eastern knoll, would have taken 100 to 150 days (assuming double-handling); the extension to form the first enlarged enclosure only needed 25 to 30 days, for the population was presumably larger, much of the old rampart could be incorporated, and the glacis-type construction would not involve double-handling. Both subsequent alterations would, by contrast, have required something of the order of 150 to 250 days, perhaps needing to be spread out over two or three years. In fact, the occupants of Maiden Castle must almost certainly have been able to call upon helpers from surrounding territory; and even if they could not, these final stages were improvements to works which were already fully defensible.

The large hill-forts, then, offer no great problem. Places enclosing about 3 or 4 hectares or more, with an assumed population of sixty persons per hectare, could have been made defensible in two to four months. It is the smaller enclosures, presumed single family farms, which present difficulty. For a place a quarter the area of Ladle Hill, and thus theoretically with a quarter the population, the volume of rampart material will only be halved; so it would take at least 170 days to build, too great a proportion of the year for people who have to grow their own food. In such a case, possible explanations are a higher density of occupation, assistance from outside, or work spread over several years. The same explanation need not be applicable to every fort. As yet, excavators do not seem to have directed their attention to the difficult question of whether a single phase of rampart-building was completed in one season or spread over two or three years.

Not every small hill-fort has such massive ramparts, and many could be made defensible in a reasonable time. Take as a final example the fairly typical Camp Tops at Morebattle in Roxburghshire, where the eight dwellings of the occupants can still be traced, implying a population of about forty, equivalent to a workforce of thirty. A fairly accurate estimate can be made of the volume of material in each rampart: inner, 900 cubic metres, requiring 22 to 30 days' work; middle 570, 14 to 19 days; and outer 360, 9 to 12 days. So the inner rampart, making the site defensible, could have been finished within a month, and the whole structure in two.

The materials available to hill-fort builders were earth, stone and timber, and these were combined in almost every imaginable conjunction. Turf was seldom used. It served as filling at Carlwark and Rainsborough, but in general its rarity contrasts strongly with its very frequent employment by the Romans in semi-permanent works. Caesar notes that his enemies in northern Gaul had learned the use of turf for rampart-building from prisoners, but had no proper tools for the work and had to use their swords to cut it. Iron was used very sparingly indeed in construction in pre-Roman Britain; even at gateways it is uncommon. Mortared masonry is invariably Roman or later.

Many of the techniques were used two millennia earlier by the builders of neolithic tombs, but are not demonstrable in the intervening period, so for most of them re-introduction or re-invention must be postulated. Not enough is known as yet to decide between the two alternatives, which indeed are not mutually exclusive. On the whole, the evidence seems to favour a central European origin for some types of timberwork.

Although for convenience some attempt is made to discuss rampart design in a structurally logical way, the result does not correspond, so far as is known, to the chronological sequence in this country, and moreover imposes on the material a fictitious appearance of orderly development. The builders would have available a repertoire of methods, some of which would at any period be more fashionable than others, and radical innovations would be unlikely. Their primary objective must almost always have been to provide an effective defence as economically as possible. Occasionally a desire for display may have played some part in the design.

The simplest defence of all, when timber is available, is a strong fence or palisade. This has been found at many places, especially near the Scottish border; it is not yet certain whether its apparent frequency in that region is real, or due to the accident of discovery and preservation. The posts are usually found to have been spaced, presumably merely to economize on timber. Such an arrangement is likely to have been primarily to keep out animals or casual thieves, for it gives the defenders no advantage in height against any determined attackers.

Sometimes there are two lines of palisade, roughly parallel, 10 metres or more apart, so that the plan is comparable with a small multivallate hill-fort in the same region, such as Dunsinane. Often each circuit of palisading is double, comprising two parallel lines 2 or 3 metres apart. This arrangement could in theory have supported a fighting platform, but more probably its function was to prevent a marauding animal getting the run needed to jump the fence. Enclosures protected only by palisades can therefore hardly be classed as fortified, though many were later given more permanent defences. Effective ramparts could be built entirely of timbers laid horizontally, and have been demonstrated abroad on some water-logged sites. They would leave no surface traces on dry ground, and have not yet been identified in Britain.

In rocky country, when protection is needed, the idea of a plain wall with built faces using stone gathered on the surface seems obvious. To give the defenders access to the top, the most convenient method is to build the back in steps, sometimes supplemented by ramps as at Tre'r Ceiri (fig. 4). This profile has the added advantage that less stone is used for a given height without reducing the thickness at the base where the wall is vulnerable to attack. The steps are almost always at least 0·5 metres in height, usually more. Ordinary stairs are recorded only in the Scottish duns, and stairs of stones projecting from a nearly vertical wall face seem to be post-Roman, as in the small fort at Garn Boduan.

The third obvious way of making a rampart is to dig a ditch and pile the excavated material on the inner side, giving the glacis type of construction as found at Maiden Castle in its second phase (pl. 3). The bank there was so high and steep that scaling was almost impossible, and the front of the level summit was unprotected, presumably to avoid hindering the slingers. There was a palisade along the back, which is unusual, but whether this was to prevent them stepping incautiously onto the rearward slope during the heat of battle, or to keep children and animals off the wall walk, must remain conjectural. Some banks of this type carried a breastwork of timber or stone near the summit, but most are too eroded for the traces to survive.

Earth and timber separately are not capable of much further elaboration, but stone can be made a more effective or economical defence in several ways. It must have been realized very soon that when the facing collapsed, either owing to accident or to attack, the resulting slope left an easy way onto the rampart; this trouble was to some extent overcome by building an inner face behind the visible outer face, a system generally regarded as the arrangement mentioned by Caesar as *murus duplex*; but its use goes back far beyond

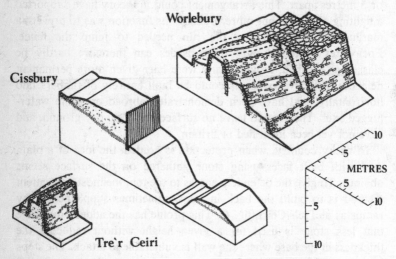

Fig. 4   Types of rampart: Tre'r Ceiri, Worlebury, Cissbury.

his time. The principle can be extended by building several internal faces. Worlebury (fig. 4) is the most elaborate example. Unfortunately it is uncertain whether the facings there were built sinuously to serve some special function, or merely because, as concealed reinforcement, their exact line did not matter. Usually the inner lines run parallel to the main wall face, and this type of construction is found as far afield as southern France.

Although they are outside the scope of this book the galleried duns and brochs of Scotland must be mentioned here. They carry the elaboration and economy of stone architecture still further, by leaving tunnels in the walls, roofed with large slabs. These may be utilized for rooms, passages or stairways, or may be merely structural.

They do not seem to occur in enclosures large enough to be termed hill-forts.

As noted above, simple banks of upcast from a ditch only become effective barriers if they are very high; otherwise an impetuous charge can carry some attackers to the summit. So a vertical or nearly vertical outer face is an advantage for defence, while a similar inner face makes a higher rampart possible for a given volume of excavation.

The simplest way of forming a vertical face using timber is to heap the earth behind a deeply founded palisade of close-set vertical posts. This was used at Cissbury (fig. 4) and at Staple Howe, where the revetment was set some way down a steep slope, and probably tied by horizontal timbers to a row of posts set further back. More commonly, the vertical posts were widely spaced and accompanied by another row at the back of the rampart; again, although not essential, transverse horizontal timbers may be inferred, and traces have occasionally been found. The type site for this sort of timbering is Preist, at Bitburg in the Rhineland. There the revetment was completed by panels of stone walling between the uprights, but this is uncommon in Britain: it has been found at Maiden Castle and South Cadbury. On other sites, such as Wandlebury (fig. 5) or Grimthorpe,

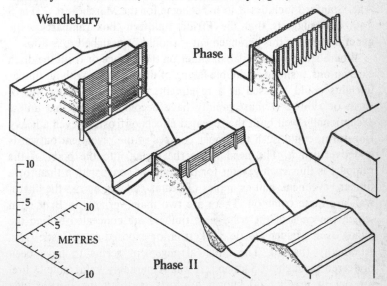

Wandlebury

Phase I

10
5
10
5
METRES
5
10

Phase II

Fig. 5   Types of rampart: Wandlebury.

a revetment of horizontal timbers must have been supported by the uprights, though this need not have been carried right down to the bottom of the bank. An open framework supporting a fighting platform above the bank is theoretically possible, but would have been very vulnerable to attack by fire. Usually, the posts in both rows were vertical. At South Cadbury, where the rows were unusually close, some in the rear row were inclined forwards, but usually there is no need to postulate diagonal timbers; such an arrangement would in fact be a disadvantage, for the wedge of earth above the inclined member would tend to push its top forwards as the material compacted.

There are great variations in the dimensions of this type of construction, ranging from 2 to nearly 5 metres between posts in one row, and similarly between rows, though for any given fort the setting out usually remains fairly uniform. Dr I. M. Stead, in discussing Grimthorpe, has suggested that the narrower ramparts correspond to fortifications thrown up hastily in an emergency. This is certainly the impression given by the structure at Ivinghoe Beacon, where the spacing of posts in each row varies from 2 to 4·5 metres and the rows are not parallel, usually 2 metres apart but sometimes converging to a metre. The fort appears to belong to the Late Bronze Age. Stanford includes it in his scheme for the Marches (p. 73) at S 740, and suggests that the Ffridd Faldwyn 'box rampart' – the general term for this arrangement – should be assigned to S 800.

Where stone was available, either on the surface or from the ditch excavations, a single or double facing of dry masonry without timber uprights could be used as a revetment, whether the filling was of earth or rubble. It must rapidly have become obvious that unless exceptionally well built the repeated effects of frost, or even a heavy rainstorm, could push the upper courses of the revetment outwards and overturn it. The need to tie the facing into the body of the rampart is thus even greater for this type of construction than for a timber revetment, and examples of beams running across the line of wall are quite common. There are two main variants in Britain, in which the ends of the transverse timbers are concealed behind the facing as at Maiden Castle, Bickerton, or exposed as at Castle Law, Abernethy (fig. 6). The latter arrangement seems to have been preferred throughout Scotland. It was remarkably vulnerable to fire, for out of nearly 260 known hill-forts north of the Forth-Clyde isthmus forty-eight show traces of having been burned, which casts

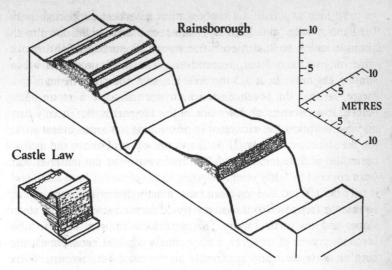

Fig. 6 Types of rampart: Castle Law (Abernethy), Rainsborough.

some doubt on the accepted view that the climate during the Iron Age was no drier than it is today. The burning was often so intense that the material of the rampart is vitrified. This was formerly regarded as an intentional attempt to consolidate the wall, but is now accepted as evidence of destruction, either accidental or deliberate.

There are many variations on these basic designs. At Dinorben, the earliest rampart was reinforced not by separate beams but by continuous layers of timber. This is of particular interest, for radiocarbon dating shows that it belongs to about the seventh century BC, and a similar arrangement was found at the Wittnauer Horn in Switzerland. By contrast, Burghead, long believed to be the nearest British parallel to true *murus gallicus* (see below), has now been shown by radiocarbon dating to belong to the sixth or eighth century AD.

Most hill-fort builders adopted some well tried and widely used type of rampart, but occasional exceptions are found. Rainsborough, for example (fig. 6), seems, so far as is known at present, to be unique. The rampart was built in three stages. The lowest was 7·3 metres wide and 0·8 metre high revetted with dry-built facing, the interior filled with crumbled soft limestone; the top was flat, laced with a layer of branches laid transversely and levelled up with turf. On this level surface was built a closely similar second stage, though only 5·5 metres wide, and (probably) filled with turf; it was set almost symmetrically, so that there were steps 0·9 metre and 0·8 metre wide at back and front, respectively. The third stage was again similar, but only about 3·5 metres wide, with filling to a depth of 0·2 metre, so that the revetments, which were about 0·5 metre high, formed low parapets on each side of the rampart walk. There seems no need to follow the excavator in postulating a wooden breastwork, for the structure is early (H 450) and missile weapons would at that period be of little importance. The rear steps were not left level, but were covered by fairly steeply sloping banks of turf or hard sand, and it may be inferred that the front (now mostly destroyed) was similar, so that the face towards the enemy would form an alternation of steep slopes and low vertical walls. This remarkable rampart was part of a bivallate system of defences, a surprisingly complex arrangement for such an early date, and apparently unconnected with the use of the sling.

Before leaving the details of rampart construction, the accepted form of classic *murus gallicus* – the 'Avaricum' type – must be described, though it is apparently unknown in Britain. Substantial beams are laid, evenly spaced, on the ground or on a prepared platform with their lengths transversely to the line of the wall, and the intervals levelled up with earth or rubble. The next layer is formed of beams similarly spaced, but set longitudinally; each is pinned to the lower beam with a long iron spike, and the intervals are again filled. This procedure is repeated, using transverse and longitudinal beams alternately, until the required height is reached. The beam ends are usually exposed in the front revetment. Caesar describes this construction in detail, and says that it is resistant both to the battering ram and to fire; but some walls of this type are found vitrified in France. The essential diagnostic feature is the presence of the long iron spikes used to pin the beams together.

In multivallate forts, the subsidiary ramparts use the same structural methods as the main banks but are generally less elaborate. Wandlebury (fig. 5) is an interesting example where the outer bank of the bivallate fort was superimposed on the ruins of an earlier single rampart. Both were timber revetted, but the details differed.

The presence of a berm between bank and ditch is almost essential where the rampart face is revetted, to prevent collapse. Whether there is any cultural significance in its width remains uncertain.

Ditches vary in form, but again there is nothing to indicate a cultural distinction between those which are V-shaped and those with flat bottoms. The difference probably depends in most cases merely on the nature of the material to be excavated. The use of a single rampart with an exceptionally broad flat-bottomed ditch (the Fécamp type, p. 48) does seem to be a distinctive and late feature.

At almost all hill-forts, banks, walls and ditches provide all the elements used in defence, but rarely these are supplemented by *chevaux-de-frise* of small pointed stones set upright. This has been discussed above (pp. 48–9).

There is one other form of supplementary defence which should be mentioned here. Mr Forde-Johnston has drawn attention to several cases where a large hill-fort is accompanied by a smaller one some distance away which commands ground concealed from observation by the occupants of the larger site. He has suggested that these are deliberate tactical arrangements, to provide advance warning of attack. From a modern point of view, it would seem that a couple of sentries would serve the same purpose, without diminishing the numbers available to defend the main enclosure. Moreover, whereas a small party in the open might reasonably hope to gain safety after the enemy were sighted, those in a relatively weak advanced fort would be almost suicidally trapped. These arguments do not necessarily discredit the theory, for the tactical principles adopted in the Iron Age were not those of today; but it is difficult to see how the hypothesis could be tested.

9

The Gateways

The most vulnerable parts of a hill-fort's defences were the gateways, for once the timber gate was destroyed by fire or battered down the way into the enclosure lay open. They are also the places where any desire for display can be most fully manifested. Hill-fort entrances thus tend to be elaborate and interesting. Further, since a gateway where the timber has rotted is worse than useless, they are more likely to retain evidence of repair and reconstruction than other parts of the defences; so particularly important information can be recovered by skilled excavation (as at Croft Ambrey), or destroyed if the work is done badly.

Functionally, the entrance arrangements fall into three parts. There is the gate itself, with the framing for its support; associated works within the enclosure, such as guard chambers; and the approaches outside the gateway.

Nothing recognizable has survived to show the actual form of any gate. They were of timber, usually entirely so; occasionally some fragments of possible iron fitments survive, but even nails are rare. The simplest were probably merely movable shutters, for some gateways show no trace of any framing to which a gate could have been hinged. Such a shutter would have been unmanageably heavy for any opening more than about 1·5 metres wide, but would have been perfectly adequate for the narrow entrances of some stone forts. Some gateways may have been closed only in emergencies. At Croft Ambrey a slot across the gateway can best be interpreted as intended to take the ends of upright posts; at this sophisticated fortress, these would have supplemented a hinged gate. Caesar notes that the entrances to Bigberry were blocked by tree trunks set close together. In stone forts gateways are often found walled up, as at Duchary Rock or Garn Boduan, and it may well be that smaller openings were normally closed in this way, but only when necessary.

Where evidence is found for a wooden frame some sort of gate can be be inferred, especially where guard houses exist, and for wide openings

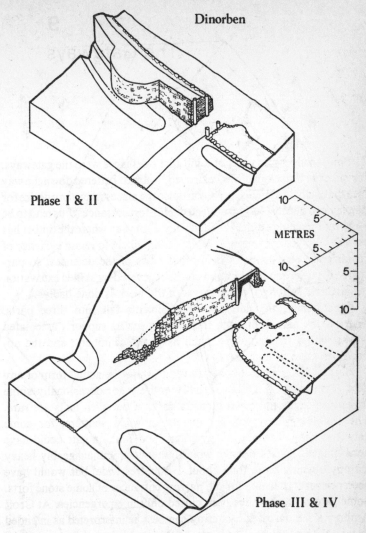

Fig. 7 Gateways: Dinorben, earlier phases.

some sort of hinged support may be postulated. The details must remain guesswork, for all timber has vanished. The iron ring for a pivot was found at Hembury, but these are extremely uncommon, as are holed stones which might have been sockets. In the absence of evidence it is fruitless to speculate as to the exact arrangement, but the builders must have been capable of devising some fairly efficient

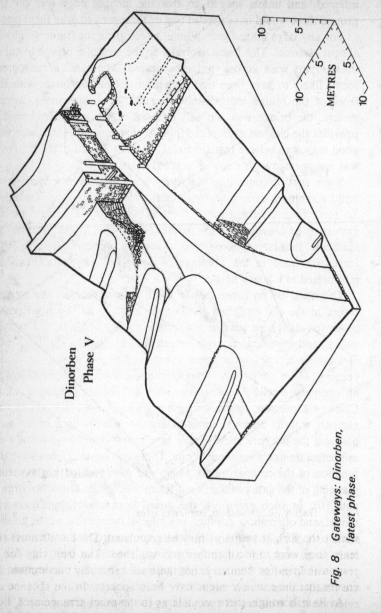

Fig. 8 Gateways: Dinorben, latest phase.

hanging for gates. Leaves up to 2·5 metres wide and high can be inferred, and unless hinged so that the moving edge was off the ground these would have needed two or three men to drag them open.

For any large hinged gate, a lintel to complete the frame would be almost essential. This leads naturally to the idea of a bridge to carry the rampart walk across the entrance gap. The usual arrangement seems likely to have been that suggested in Rainsborough, with the front of the bridge immediately over the gate. Sometimes, nevertheless, the bridge was set well in front of the gate. Bredon Hill provides the clearest example of this. At that gateway, too, there was good reason to believe that the lintel – not, in this case, the bridge – was ornamented with a row of severed heads (fig. 9).

Some sort of controlling authority is implied by the decision to build a rampart, even if no more than an *ad hoc* 'council of elders'. So some formal delegation of responsibility for the control of the gate is to be expected, to the forerunners of the 'proud porters' of medieval and later ballads and romances. Archaeologically, this leaves its trace in the presence of some building which can be interpreted as a guard house.

This need be no more than a small recess, such as the 'sentry boxes' at the east entrance of Maiden Castle in its last pre-Roman phase (pl. 4). These were semicircular in plan, of about 1·5 metres radius, and thus far too small for permanent dwellings, though one had a hearth. They must imply some sort of rota system for gate-keeping. More commonly, the guard houses are as commodious as an ordinary dwelling. Sometimes they are indistinguishable, as at Conway Mountain, where a single round hut was built on to the rampart with its doorway immediately towards the back of the gate passage; the interpretation of this as a guard chamber is merely an inference, though a reasonable one. There can be no doubt about the function of the compartments which are incorporated in the actual planning of the gate passage, as at Rainsborough or Dinorben (figs 7 and 10). In such gateways, the guard houses are almost always paired, and often show as much evidence of occupation as the houses within the fort. It seems a legitimate conjecture that sometimes, at least, they were in fact family dwellings, the tenure carrying with it responsibilities for control of the gate; and that the pairing was to ensure that the entrance need never be left unattended.

At Rainsborough, there was a large freestanding post on each side of the entrance passage, just behind the back of the ramparts; in view

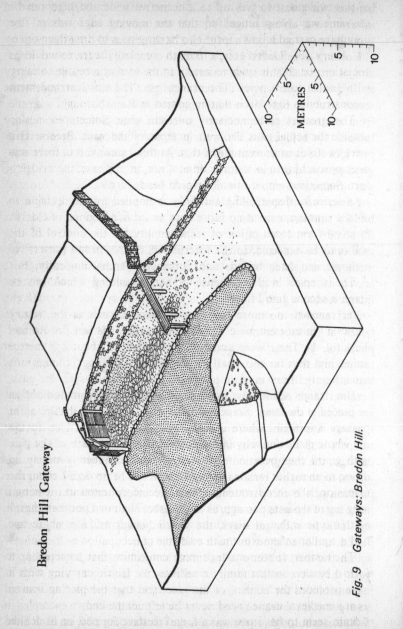

Bredon Hill Gateway

METRES

Fig. 9 Gateways: Bredon Hill.

of this evidence, two pits at St Catherine's Hill can be interpreted in the same way. No practical function can be suggested for these. They may have carried a lintel, forming a 'triumphal arch', as suggested by M. Avery for Rainsborough, though no skulls were found in association; or they may have been carved or decorated, by analogy with Indian totem poles. The carving on the lintel sketched in the reconstruction (fig. 10) is wholly conjectural.

The greatest elaboration of entrance arrangements took place outside the actual gate. From the practical standpoint, the objectives were twofold: to prevent a direct rush at the gate; and to force anyone approaching to follow a route commanded by the occupants of the fort. Sometimes, in addition, the plan seems to have been influenced by a desire for display. At Maiden Castle, for example, the complexity of the entrances in their last phase can hardly be accounted for purely by the needs of defence. On the other hand, forts with quite elaborate and sophisticated ramparts and gateways may be content with a simple straight approach to the actual gate, as at Rainsborough.

The simplest way of satisfying the two primary requirements, given a second line of defence, is to place the entrance through the outer rampart to one side of that through the inner. Chun Castle shows a typical example of this scheme applied to a small stone fort. Forcing the line of approach to turn through an angle almost inevitably results in a passage commanded from the ramparts, though only from one side.

If a straight approach was accepted as satisfactory, the gate might be placed at the inner end of a long passage. In its simplest form, this passage is formed by inturning the main ramparts, as at The Wrekin; the whole plan is merely a development of the ordinary gate passage with guard chambers. A more elaborate arrangement, often an addition to an earlier fort, is the barbican, in which a roughly triangular extension is built outwards on each side of the entrance, leaving a long narrow passage to approach the gate. The most perfect example of this type is that at Blackbury Castle; Maiden Castle, phase two, had a similar scheme, but with a double gate.

The ramparts at the entrance were sometimes given a projection to form a bastion commanding the gateway. At Blackbury they seem to have preceded the barbican, and to have been well shaped and paired as at a medieval castle gateway; but nearly all the known examples in Britain seem to have been single, and to have formed an ill defined bulge rather than a precise D-shaped projection. The best are perhaps

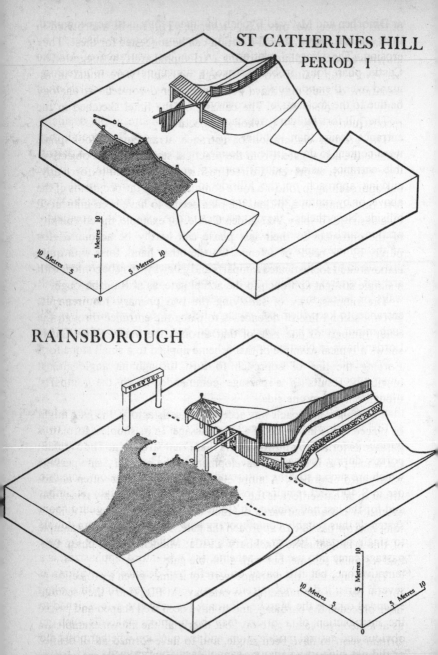

Fig. 10   Gateways: St Catherine's Hill, Rainsborough.

at Dinorben and Mynydd Bychan, but many may exist unrecognized, their rather vague original outline having become obscured by erosion. The slingers' platforms in the east entrance of Maiden Castle, phase four, probably served a similar purpose, to give command over the approaches. The extreme rarity of any parallels must be due to the accidents of discovery.

The hill-fort builders were no more doctrinaire in the details of entrance design than in other parts of their work. In general, they were content to do as little as seemed necessary to provide a defensible entrance, using natural features where appropriate, as in the curving approach up the hillside to Chalbury, overlooked from above, or by running the entrance approach along the edge of a steep hillside. Nevertheless, they sometimes undertook work of great elaboration, such as the exceptionally long inturns at Bredon Hill (fig. 29), or the complex approaches to Maiden Castle. Sites such as the last provide some of the most spectacular earthworks in Britain, but they are not typical. Neither are all outworks defensive. Lightly built walls or fences may have been needed to direct cattle towards the entrance, to keep them off adjacent fields, or to form pens. Usually such minor works have been destroyed, but good examples survive at Lordenshaws in Northumberland.

Potentially, the changes in gateway design can provide one of the most important elements in a broad chronological and cultural framework. Dr Stanford has suggested the following development in the Welsh Marches (see p. 99). Initially (S 750) the box rampart fort at Ffridd Faldwyn had a single portal. About a century later, twin portals came into fashion, to be superseded once again by single portals during the period S 350 to S 300. The twin guard rooms which are such a striking feature of hill-forts in this region came into use in S 400, and remained in fashion until S 270, initially in timber and for the last half-century in stone. The decline of the guard room system is thus roughly contemporary with the reversion from double to single portals. Finally, in S 60, the practice of bridging the gate passage came into use. This scheme, as Dr Stanford emphasizes, is a tentative one, but it is based on careful and detailed excavations at several forts; it does not introduce any very serious difficulties when extended outside the Marches. Perhaps the very late date assigned to the introduction of a bridge may be doubted; it seems such an obvious and natural modification, and the question whether posts did or did not support a gangway cannot easily be resolved.

10

The Interior

Except in temporary refuges or cattle kraals, where tents might have served, any hill-fort must have contained more or less permanent dwellings, as well as associated structures. The characteristic building in British hill-forts was round, usually of 6 to 8 metres diameter internally, though some Iron Age houses are as much as 15 metres across; the best known example of these large dwellings is that at Little Woodbury, probably built before any rampart was contemplated there. The smaller dwellings are usually referred to in a rather derogatory way as 'huts'; indeed, the term 'hut circle' is so well established that to retain it is probably better than to attempt to replace it. All the same, it gives a very misleading impression, as can be seen by comparison with modern houses. Omitting passage and bathroom, but including the kitchen, a two-bedroom bungalow of a type selling at between £8,000 and £10,000 in 1974 has a total area equivalent to a round 'hut' of just over 7 metres diameter, while even for a larger house, with three bedrooms and two reception rooms and selling at between £20,000 and £25,000, the diameter would be less than 10 metres.

An adequate account of Iron Age round houses would require, and deserve, a book to itself. The commonest internal arrangement, to which there are many exceptions, consisted of a ring of posts set upright about 1·5 to 2 metres inside the line of the wall. These served to support the roof timbers and formed a natural division between the central living space, with a hearth near the middle, and sleeping compartments against the wall. By analogy with dwellings in the north built exclusively of stone, these compartments were probably separated by hangings or boarded partitions which have left no trace. To visualize the sort of accommodation which could be provided by quite a small 'hut', 7 metres in diameter, one may assume a central living space 4 metres across. This leaves room for an entrance passage 1·3 metres wide and five sleeping compartments each 1·5 metres wide and tapering from over 4 metres long at the house wall to 2·6 metres at the inner side. It must be repeated that this is merely illustrative. There was great variety in structure and in internal arrangement. Since the object here is to indicate the general character of the settlement, no attempt has been made to illustrate these in detail.

Outside, all these round houses must have looked very much alike. Their walls were of wood, dry-stone or cob according to locality, and probably stood at most only 1·5 metres high, usually less than a metre to judge from stone examples. Above this rose a conical roof, perhaps truncated over very large houses to allow for a central court. The material was probably of thatch in most cases, but sometimes of turf. Occasionally there is evidence, from a drip mark, of wide eaves, but some relatively modern Scottish dwellings show that the occupants of simple buildings are not always concerned to avoid mere dampness, so in some, especially those of stone, the roof covering may have ended about the middle of the wall. Often a ditch was dug round the house to intercept surface water; this may have coincided with the drip from the thatch, but need not have done so. The only break in this plain conical outline would be at the entrance, sometimes no more than a simple gap, or a doorway between two uprights, but occasionally quite an elaborate projecting porch.

We have no direct knowledge of the finish of these houses, and reconstructions, whether drawn or three-dimensional, almost always show them as built of rough timbers, and shaggy with untrimmed thatch. No doubt some were of this character, but although the builders lacked lime mortar, their dry-stone masonry and their carpentry were of a standard just as high as that of the Middle Ages; and they had a sophisticated decorative art. It is reasonable to suppose, therefore, that many of their houses would display as high a technical finish as the dwelling of a prosperous farmer in later times, or a small medieval manor house. It is tempting to suggest that the woodwork was sometimes embellished with carving, but no evidence for ornamental work on building timbers of this date has ever been recorded in Britain.

During the later 1930s, the excavation of Little Woodbury first displayed convincingly all the structural remains which could be left by an Iron Age farm. With the recognition there that granaries were implied by four post holes set in a square (see below), the roundness of the houses of the British Iron Age became for many archaeologists a matter of dogma. Rectangular houses identified at Maiden Castle were explained away as misinterpretations of the evidence, and the parallel rows of post holes uncovered at Ffridd Faldwyn were regarded as inexplicable by the excavator and ignored by others; interpreted as granaries they would have implied an incredible concentration of corn-growing in that region. Recently, however, Dr Stanford's work at Croft Ambrey and elsewhere has demonstrated that square or rectangular dwellings are the only type found in some forts in the Welsh Marches, while in other parts of Britain they occur mixed, but not necessarily contemporary, with round houses. The Ffridd Faldwyn posts can now be understood as evidence for rows of small square buildings, which have been found also at Croft Ambrey. Elsewhere the rectangular buildings are sometimes larger. One rather irregular one at Maiden Castle measured 4·5 by 6 metres, and was divided into two rooms; one longer side was adjacent to a contemporary street. Other rectangular buildings could be identified there, but later structures had disturbed the area too much for the whole arrangement to be worked out.

The problem of the relationship between round and rectangular houses has not yet been solved. There is some indication that where both occur together on the same site the rectangles are the earlier. This is curious, as the round ones are generally regarded as in the Bronze Age tradition, and the others as intrusive. Pending further research, a tentative explanation could be that the rectangular houses correspond to an actual massive settlement of invaders, not merely the intrusion of foreign ideas, and that where round houses occur later there has been a renaissance of the influence of the earlier traditions, just as the official use of English reappeared after an interlude of Norman French.

Most of these dwellings survive, if at all, as levelled platforms terraced into hill slopes. Sometimes the rectangular buildings stood on recognizably elongated terraces, but at other sites the builders inconsiderately erected them on rounded platforms, so unless actual walls exist (and not always then) the predominant type of house cannot be determined from surface evidence; though it may be fairly safe to assume round houses if *all* the platforms are circular. Thus most of the evidence for the intensity of occupation and the disposition of buildings comes from regions where stone was normally used for building, and cannot be taken to apply exactly elsewhere. Fortunately, a few places such as Hod Hill, Hambledon Hill or Chalbury in southern Britain preserve the evidence in visible form, and at several on either side of the Scottish border the slots in which the timber walls stood can still be traced in the fine turf.

For round houses, the clearest evidence comes from some Caernarvonshire forts, such as Garn Boduan or Conway Mountain; both, unfortunately, are of two periods. Tre'r Ceiri (pl. 5), in the first phase, was a smaller hill-fort of the same type. The buildings are all round, and seem to have been placed in any convenient position without regard to possible trackways; the roughly aligned rows are related to the shape of the ground. This seems to apply equally to Hambledon Hill. At Hod Hill, in the surviving part, the arrangement looks random, but the aerial photograph taken before 1939 shows that there were two well defined streets curving from the north-east gateway through the mass of houses. Similarly at Maiden Castle, though the plan could not be traced, a street led from the east gate to a round building which may have been a temple (see below). Streets, where they existed, seem to have been marked out at a fairly early stage in the life of the fort, but there was no formal town-planning associated with the round houses.

In Garn Boduan and Conway Mountain there were from eight to twelve dwellings per hectare, depending on the assumptions made as to how many houses belonged to each period. This seems to be fairly typical of southern Britain, where evidence survives; the undamaged part of Hod Hill, for example, has some fifteen buildings per hectare. In Scotland, the density seems generally to be about twice this. Even in the south, though, the rule is not universal. At Moel Trigarn there are well over forty house platforms per hectare, but that is unusual.

At forts with square houses regularly arranged, such as Croft Ambrey (pl. 7) and Ffridd Faldwyn, conditions are very different. There, where the form of the ground permits, the little buildings are laid out deliberately in streets and are far more closely set, so that there may be as many as fifty or sixty per hectare. Their regularity of arrangement, and uniformity in character, have led Dr Stanford to suggest for consideration the possibility that they may correspond to barracks, forts where they occur being the centres where young warriors received their initiation and training. It is noteworthy that extensive testing of the enclosure at Croft Ambrey failed to discover any place where the small standardized dwellings gave way to some more spacious building which could be claimed as the 'chief's house'.

Conclusions as to the arrangement of the buildings and other structures in a hill-fort almost always depend on inferences, either from those features which were substantial enough to remain visible or from partial excavation. Total clearance is very uncommon. Walesland Rath therefore needs to be mentioned here, though primarily as an example of the extreme complexity which may be displayed by a superficially simple enclosure. Unfortunately, despite the exemplary care with which the excavation was conducted, it is impossible convincingly to separate out the different features so as to reconstruct the nature of the settlement in any particular phase.

Although 'hut circles', interpreted as the emplacements of houses, are generally the only features which remain visible, excavation of an intensively occupied fort, at least in the south, will usually reveal a confused medley of pits, gullies and post holes. Little Woodbury and Walesland Rath are examples which have been extensively cleared. Regular pits are now accepted as having been intended mostly for the storage of grain for consumption. When they became too sour for this they were used as rubbish dumps. Seed corn was stored in granaries above ground, now represented by four post holes set at the corners of a square, and thus not readily differentiated from a square house. For an isolated structure, the distinction can often be no more than guesswork, unless grain is actually present. Pairs of posts can be interpreted as drying racks, either for fodder or for corn which has had to be reaped unripe. Both these types of structure still survive in parts of Europe. Even when all allowance has been made for 'granaries' and 'drying racks', many post holes usually remain unaccounted for. Too little is known about the development of most forts, but the evidence from Maiden Castle suggests that in earlier periods disused storage pits half filled with decaying rubbish must have been an appreciable hazard to persons moving between the dwellings. Presumably, though, even at night, the smell would serve as a warning.

Temples dating from the Roman period are found in some hill-forts, and it is a reasonable inference that they are often the direct successors of earlier sacred sites; but these can seldom be identified with certainty. Maiden Castle offers an example which illustrates very well the problems of such an identification.

The main street from the east gate led directly to the doorway of a round 'hut', rather large but otherwise perfectly normal; but excavation indicated that the 'hut' was of the latest pre-Roman phase, Iron Age C, and that the road was not then in use. Apart from any question of religious function, there is thus an immediate problem: why was the track laid out to lead to the entrance to a building which had not then been built? Or, conversely, why was the hut located symmetrically relative to a disused road? Within the ruined outline of this 'hut' was a roughly built round structure of similar character, rather smaller, dated by numerous (171) coins to about AD 350–60. Among the debris on the floor was the base of a statuette, and in the edge of one of the holes for roof supports was another. Beneath the floor was a sparse scatter of objects which filled rather thinly the chronological interval between the Belgic and Roman 'huts'. There is nothing incontrovertibly religious about these buildings, but 12 metres north-east of them is an indisputable temple, built some ten or twenty years later than the Roman 'round hut'. Professor Piggott has pointed out that just west of this Romano-Celtic temple is a setting of four posts which can be paralleled exactly on sites abroad which are undoubtedly religious; unfortunately they can be paralleled equally exactly by posthole settings in this country which are universally accepted as the remains of granaries.

This is the evidence in summary. The writer feels no doubt whatever, as a matter of personal belief, that the whole area was a sacred centre from the establishment of the hill-fort; that there was direct continuity of sanctity right through to the end of the Roman period; and that the Roman round building was displayed to the pious but gullible visitor as the original shrine. The only difficulty in this interpretation is to understand how the attendant guides could have allowed 171 coins to slip through their fingers. Whatever one may believe as an individual, though, none of this can be maintained as having been scientifically demonstrated; the apparent 'evidence' need be no more than an assembly of coincidences. The rational approach must be that adopted by Sir Mortimer Wheeler in his excavation report, where, after setting out the facts given above, he says that all this 'justifies perhaps the passing fantasy' that there was continuity of cult at this spot.

Rarely, there are fully convincing indications of a pre-Roman Sanctuary, as at South Cadbury, where a rectangular building of unusual plan was approached between two rows of large pits each of which contained, at the bottom, an animal skull. The conclusive identification of this temple was the result not merely of careful and extensive excavation, but of the flair which enabled the excavator to choose the right place to dig. The lack of recorded pre-Roman shrines is thus no guide as to whether they were normal or exceptional. It is a reasonable hypothesis that even in the smallest settlements some supernatural protection would be considered desirable, and where the population was large enough a permanent temple might be expected. The names of some forts may indicate the deities worshipped (pp. 17–19), though we can know nothing of the ritual; and the occasional evidence for temples of Roman date seems to imply continued sanctity, even after the general population had moved away. On the other hand, solid proof is hardly obtainable. The early shrines were not necessarily structurally different in any way from ordinary dwellings, so that even where almost all the building foundations survive, as at Garn Boduan, there is no way in which one can be picked out as a probable temple. Even excavation may not provide conclusive evidence, for the associated ritual need not have been of a kind which left recognizable traces.

Celtic sanctuaries were not always marked by buildings. The worship of springs is well attested, but is not likely to be represented within a hill-top settlement. Another type of religious structure, perhaps the oddest from a modern viewpoint, was a deep shaft, down which sacrifices could be despatched to the underworld. Examples (earlier than the ramparts) have recently been discovered at Danebury, and no doubt others have been overlooked or dismissed as wells. Again, only extensive excavations can determine how often these sacred shafts occur. The extent to which hill-forts were religious centres must for the present remain a matter for guesswork.

So far as major secular buildings are concerned, there is seldom material even for guesses. One may suppose that the greater fortresses provided for a chieftain, but superficially there is little to choose between one dwelling and another. The suggestion that a pair of buildings excavated at Hod Hill belonged to the chief is attractive, and is supported by the fact that they were the targets of attack by ballista, and that one stands in a separate compound at the end of one of the main streets of the settlement. On consideration, though, the argument does not stand. The presence of a separate compound is relatively unusual on that site, but there were other and larger examples; other buildings also are considerably larger; and since only five or six dwellings were investigated out of an original total of some five hundred or more it is impossible to maintain that the presence of the ballista bolts necessarily imples that these huts were of particular importance.

This egalitarian character of Iron Age housing seems fairly general, but as with other aspects of the subject it is unsafe to generalize. At South Cadbury some of the houses found near the temple were exceptionally large, some 10·5 metres in diameter and thus of about twice the floor area of the usual 'hut'. So it may be merely a matter of luck that the dwellings of the aristocracy have escaped recognition, at least in the regions where timber buildings were normal.

Irish traditions would imply not only a chief's dwelling but a possible separate banqueting hall. The large central round building at Clickhimin has been claimed as an example of this, and it is indeed a striking and distinctive structure, from which the associated dwellings are recognizably very different. No really satisfactory parallel has yet been claimed at any fort on the British mainland, so the southward extension of this sort of social organization must remain a matter for conjecture. It is tempting to recognize something similar in Walesland Rath, but despite, or perhaps because of, the care and completeness with which that site was excavated, its interpretation presents great difficulty.

11

The Romans and After

With the arrival of the Romans, archaeology in Britain seems to emerge from the mists of estimated dates and vague regional cultures into a clear landscape in which everything is sharp and well defined. The clarity of the view wavers a little under close inspection, but to a great extent it is genuine; there is a background of historical information, and the mass production of coins and pottery makes it possible to establish fairly reliable chronological links throughout the empire.

Hill-forts remain on the fringe of this well-systematized archaeology. In fully Romanized areas they were disused; new ones were built or old ones re-occupied only where central authority did not reach or where it broke down. Their development can sometimes be worked out in relation to the history of Roman Britain, but seldom with the same precision. Moreover, the Roman occupation was incomplete, and differed in character and duration in different regions; and its start and finish were long drawn out. To understand its influence on hill-fort building a summary is necessary, though this is unavoidably very much over-simplified.

For the Victorians, these islands entered history with the invasions of Julius Caesar. His attack, almost certainly on Bigberry in Kent, is the first record of a British hill-fort. Otherwise, archaeologically, his activities have left no structural trace as yet discovered. Full-scale invasion began nearly a century later, in AD 43. It was by no means a walkover, even though some regions, such as Sussex, willingly accepted the status of allies; but the most prosperous part of the country, south-east of the line from Severn to Trent, was under fairly secure control by AD 50. The historical record, that the general Vespasian overcame twenty towns, is vividly illuminated by the war cemetery at Maiden Castle, and the Roman fort built within the native fortress at Hod Hill. The destruction of the gateway at South Cadbury was witness to some later, unrecorded incident. These contrast strongly with the lack of anything of that kind in the downland forts of Sussex. Even in hostile regions the old hill-forts were not always forcibly cleared, but the attractions of the new Roman towns led to their evacuation within a decade or so, save perhaps for priests still tending an ancient shrine.

Further advances, mostly into wild or mountainous country, were more strongly resisted, and the whole region south of the Tyne-Solway isthmus was not brought fully under control for another thirty years, so some hill-forts north and west of the Severn-Trent line may well have remained in use for a generation after the initial invasion. After the Tyne-Solway isthmus was reached, the land to the south remained part of the empire until the end of the fourth century AD, and no hill-forts are likely to have been built or refortified there during that time, though some may have remained inhabited.

Further north, conditions were more complex. Initially, the advance continued, reaching the edge of the highlands by AD 84, when the Caledonians were defeated at the unlocated battle of Mons Graupius, but after about fifteen years the frontier was withdrawn to the Tyne-Solway line, where in about AD 120 the emperor Hadrian ordered the construction of the wall which is known by his name. After another two decades the frontier was advanced again, and a wall of turf – the Antonine Wall – built across the Clyde-Forth isthmus. Finally, in about AD 180, the troops withdrew once more to Hadrian's line, probably after treaty arrangements with the tribes between the walls. In that region, then, there were two intervals when hill-forts might be built or used; in the first by enemies to the Romans, in the second and longer period by allies.

North of the Forth–Clyde line, despite several decisive Roman victories recorded in Roman sources, the natives were never brought under the control of the invaders. No doubt evidence of slighting remains to be discovered in some hill-forts, and objects of Roman date, from trade or looting, have been found in several, showing their continued use. New types, discussed below, developed both here and further south.

The more noteworthy traces of the Roman conquest of southern Britain have already been mentioned, as at Maiden Castle and South Cadbury. Hod Hill is of especial interest, for the ramparts of the Roman fortress can still be seen superimposed on the earlier hill-fort. This conjunction is unique in Britain, and very rare anywhere. Moving further west, into the areas conquered later, evidence for massacres has been found at Bredon Hill and at Sutton Walls, but these were not certainly the work of Roman troops. Massacre of the defeated was not normal Roman practice, either because of genuine humanity or because it was wasteful to destroy financially valuable slaves; but if the heads over the gateway at Bredon Hill were those of captured Romans, the nature of the other remains found there would be explicable. The evidence which the hill-forts offer is usually less dramatic. Hod Hill, for example, displays outworks which were begun too late and never completed; but works of this kind cannot easily be identified from surface evidence.

In the north and west, where the Roman presence was primarily military, some hill-forts show indications of use for field training exercises. At Caer y Twr, above Holyhead in Anglesey, a short length of wall has been cast down; it is deliberate slighting, but could have been rebuilt in a day, and the length is far too small to have much effect on the strength of the defences. Burnswark, in Dumfriesshire, was for long believed to have been the subject of a full-scale siege. Sling bullets of baked clay have been found within the ramparts, and at the foot of the hill the regular forts of the attackers are still visible. Nineteenth-century archaeologists believed they could also trace a circumvallation, but this is now generally accepted as a misinterpretation of recent field banks.

This important site has now been re-examined by Mr Jobey, who has shown that this dramatic story was true, save for one point: the whole attack was directed against a hill-fort which had been abandoned for many years.

Still in the borders, but further east, another example of practice siege-works can be seen at Woden Law. There, genuine lines of circumvallation, apparently from two different campaigns of field exercises, would have cut off the inhabitants from any chance of escape – but again the native fort was almost certainly empty at the time.

The Britons do not seem to have practised siege warfare, so we cannot expect to find traces of their work impinging in a comparable way on Roman forts; but there is one case known, at Ruberslaw in Roxburghshire, where a Roman fortlet of some kind was demolished and replaced by a native work. The destruction was so complete that not even the plan of the fortlet can be seen, but characteristic worked stones are used in the native wall. This later work is a 'nuclear fort' (see p. 45), a type which seems to be post-Roman; so the Roman fortlet may well have been in complete ruin when the existing defences were built.

After the conquest, hill-forts in the fully Romanized zone were soon abandoned, the inhabitants moving into newly built towns. Further north and west, in areas under full control but less completely transformed socially, occupation of some forts continued, but so few have been examined that it usually remains unknown whether they remained towns or villages of their old character, or whether merely a few farms continued to exist on the otherwise abandoned site. Two examples which did survive as towns of a sort are described later: Tre'r Ceiri and Traprain Law (pp. 92–9).

The temple in Maiden Castle has been mentioned earlier (p. 79) and other examples are known; they are not in fact very numerous but more probably await discovery. One like the square temple at Maiden Castle has been recorded in Chanctonbury Ring; at Croft Ambrey there is a curious mound, best explicable as the site of a temple that was largely of wood; and a large round timber building of Roman date at Dinorben produced relics which strongly suggest that it was in fact a shrine.

The most remarkable religious establishment in any British hill-fort is that at Lydney in Gloucestershire. The site chosen was within fairly considerable ramparts, where some descendants of the original inhabitants seem to have continued to eke out a living by farming and metalworking. Some time after AD 360 an impressive temple was built, probably the finest in Britain outside a town, accompanied by a guest house and a suite of baths. The temple was a place of healing, and by good fortune inscriptions preserve the name of the deity to whom it was dedicated, Nodens. The shrine seems to have continued prosperous well into the fifth century. It is tantalizing that we can never know what spectacular cure or vision established its fame.

The end of the Roman occupation is more obscure than its beginning, and equally long drawn out. The scraps of semi-historical records cannot all be reconciled into a coherent story, and by judicious selection some can be found to support almost any desired thesis, so until much more archaeological evidence is available detailed discussion of this period is unprofitable. Basically, though, it would appear that under threat from pirates, and from looters out of the unconquered north, the authorities of Britain at the end of the fourth and beginning of the fifth centuries called in mercenaries for their defence – some from abroad, some from between the two

Roman walls, and possibly some from Ireland. Central authority collapsed, and such government as there was fell into the hands of the leaders of local war bands. In some places these were the officers of the foreign mercenaries, in others probably the descendants of legitimate local administrators. The confused traditions of battles and intrigues suggest that the former attempted to extend their rule, and the latter either to maintain their territory or to restore central government. The most successful of these last was 'King Arthur', who gained a unique position in folk memory, so that given a sufficiently uncritical approach evidence of a sort can be found for his presence in almost any part of Britain.

By the time records once more become tolerably reliable, in say the seventh or eighth centuries, the descendants of these local leaders have become royal, each ruling over his own little kingdom; there were six or seven of these in Wales alone. Everyday life must have differed little from that of the pre-Roman period, and such change as there was seems to have been for the worse. Hill-forts once again came into use. In the south-west some at least of the old earthworks were refortified, South Cadbury and probably Castle Dore being among the most notable. These were in a region which had experienced the full benefits of Roman civilization. In Wales some small forts seem to have been built at this time. That on the summit of Garn Boduan is certainly not earlier than the latter part of the Roman period, and could even have been the home of Buan, after whom the hill is named: he lived about the beginning of the seventh century.

Another much larger fort, with its defences dated fairly securely to the mid-fifth century, is Dinas Emrys. This occupies a craggy hill, naturally very strong, but the ramparts are shoddy by Iron Age standards. Its great interest comes from its traditional association with Ambrosius Aurelianus, from whom it takes its name. He was probably a genuine historical character, concerned with the defence of the remnants of Romano-British civilization, and the remarkable and rather improbable piece of fringe history which links his name to the site has been to some extent confirmed by modern excavation (see pp. 186–7). There were no dragons, but there was a pool, and at about the right period a structure had in fact been built beside it! This poses the usual problem in assessing tradition. Did Vortigern really try to build a dwelling on this rather unsuitable foundation? Or did some local storyteller make up the tale to account for what he could see at Dinas Emrys?

In Scotland several fortresses of about this time are mentioned in the chronicles. Dunadd, for example, was captured by the Picts in 736, and Dundurn was besieged in 683. Both are of the curious type known as 'nuclear forts' (see p. 45). As indicated earlier these, so far as is known at present, belong exclusively to this relatively late period. They may be a development from examples, probably earlier, where a small fort has been superimposed on a larger and more ancient enclosure, giving what is functionally the same result as a 'citadel' with base courts.

These seem to be the last structures which can be called hill-forts without straining beyond all reason the use of a term already rather overworked. The idea of a defence using the advantages of a hill top continues even up to the fortresses built round London and Portsmouth in the nineteenth century; but hill-forts can be taken to end, at latest, with the arrival of Norman influences in Britain.

12

Four Important Hill-Forts
Maiden Castle, Tre'r Ceiri, Traprain Law, Croft Ambrey

Faced with the need to select a few hill-forts of particular interest, no two archaeologists would agree; so the writer will not attempt to justify his choice. Nevertheless, there would be wide acceptance of Maiden Castle's claim to take pride of place, though there are at least four major pieces of research in progress which when fully published will threaten its supremacy. It is merely a coincidence, though a happy one, that of the four places chosen one lies in Scotland and one in Wales; the selection was made on other grounds. References to position and to published reports are given in the gazetteer.

Maiden Castle (pl. 2), near Dorchester in Dorset, was the first British hill-fort to be the subject of large-scale *scientific* excavation, and the report remains one of the foundation stones for the archaeology of the Iron Age. As its author recognized, it is not without faults, but these arose from the intervention of a major war, not from defects in method. The war also inhibited the full harvest from the planned ancillary investigations into other forts in southern England and northern France. Despite this, the work has long remained the most important study of its kind. It is only now, after a full generation, that one can look forward to this position being taken, or shared, by other sites.

The natural shape of the hill on which Maiden Castle stands is now disguised by the immense ramparts of the prehistoric town, but was originally a broad ridge with its long axis east and west, the top forming two knolls rising 5 metres or so above an intervening saddle. Occupation of the site began with a neolithic causewayed camp round the eastern knoll. Some time after this had been abandoned, people of the same or of a related culture built an enormous burial mound over the site, 540 metres long and 27 wide, between broad flat-bottomed ditches. All this took place well before 3000 BC. The interval which then elapsed before the arrival of the later fort-builders was longer than that from the final abandonment of the fort to the present day.

The new arrivals, about H 300, would have found all the neolithic structures represented by grassy mounds, the bank of the cause-wayed camp accentuating a good natural defensive line round the knoll. Along this line (fig. 11) they dug a great ditch of V profile, 11 metres wide and 6 metres deep, separated by a berm 3 metres wide from the face of the rampart. This had slightly inclined revetments of timber to front and rear (*cf.* fig. 5), a form of construction character-istic of 'Hallstatt' fortifications on the continent. The western entrance, 5 metres wide, had a pair of gates closing on a central stop, the passage being revetted in the same way as the rampart; later disturbance leaves the existence of guard houses uncertain. At the east end, the entrances were similar, but even at this stage the designer aimed at a monumental effect, building a pair of gateways separated by a 20-metre length of rampart. A space nearly 100 metres square outside this double portal was carefully paved with flint metalling. Traces of timber enclosures here suggest its use as a market-place.

These early defences were not maintained; the timbers were al-lowed to decay, and the rampart collapsed into a bank with a steeply sloping face descending unbroken into the silted ditch. This turf-covered bank may have suggested the form of rampart used when about H 200 the inhabitants decided to extend their line of wall to enclose the whole hilltop (18·5 hectares), for these later ramparts (and all subsequent reconstructions) were of the glacis type (p. 59). Excavation at the junction of the earlier enclosure and the extension not only revealed evidence for their relative age, but was rewarded by the discovery of a foundation sacrifice, the skeleton of a young man in his twenties, buried in a pit cut into the front slope of the older bank and covered (at once, for there was no weathering of the pit walls) by the material of the extension.

Either as part of the new works, or perhaps rather earlier, the eastern gateway was strengthened by a remarkable barbican (pl. 3), extending the entrance passage by a pair of hornworks and a central double bank. The ramparts forming this were not of glacis type, but had vertical faces with upright timbers, the spaces between filled not with horizontal logs or wattling but with dry-stone walling. There is thus some reason to suppose that this system of outworks may have been earlier than the enlargement of the enclosure. On the other hand

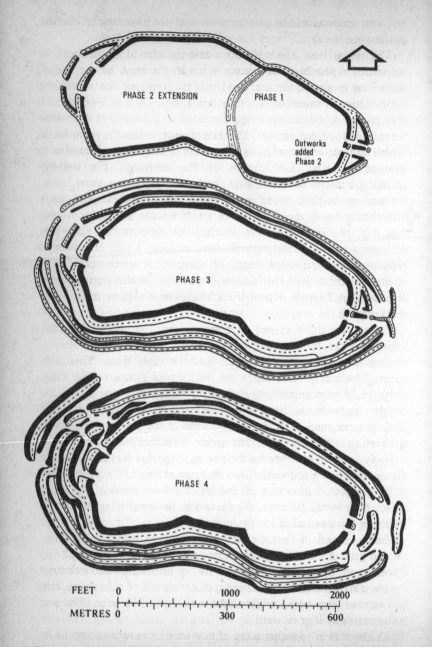

PHASE 2 EXTENSION

PHASE 1

Outworks
added
Phase 2

PHASE 3

PHASE 4

FEET 0   1000   2000

METRES 0   300   600

Fig. 11   Maiden Castle, evolution. After Sir Mortimer Wheeler.

the west gateway of the enlargement seems to have been of similar design; but the details were not worked out by excavation.

The initial Iron Age settlement, and the extension, can both be attributed to phases of the A culture, but after another half-century B influences appear on the site. The use of the sling, and the consequent introduction or invention of multiple ramparts, are to be attributed to this phase. A second bank and ditch were added round the whole circuit, and a third round the southern side, while the main bank, which had become grass-grown, was almost doubled in size rising to a broad flat top with no breastwork to front or rear. To give stability to this increased height, buried structural revetments were incorporated in the back of the rampart; the highest of these was partly exposed, giving a vertical *inner* face to the upper part of the bank. Much of the stone for these revetments was limestone brought from two miles away, and the material for the bank was largely obtained from a great quarry ditch behind the rampart. This ditch provided a sheltered site for dwellings, and the resulting accumulation of superimposed hut floors provided the archaeologist with valuable information as to the sequence of pottery and other relics. At the eastern entrance a ditch, Y-shaped in plan, its stem extending the bank between the two gateways, prevented a direct approach.

Even with this elaboration, the defences had not reached their final form. In about H 100 or H 50, the ramparts were still further enlarged, a substantial counterscarp bank being added round the whole circuit. It was at this stage that the entrance-works reached their present complexity, better understood from the reconstruction drawing (pl. 4) than from a description. In addition to the elaborate convolutions of the approach, the positioning of platforms for slingers to command their lines of approach is of interest. These defenders would have had no chance of reaching safety should an attack have reached the actual gate, and it seems legitimate to suspect that they were associated with the similarly exposed dwellings in the space just outside the main entrances.

Too little of the interior was cleared to give a detailed picture of its appearance, but at this stage in its development the settlement enclosed would seem to have been typical (see p. 236), the irregularly placed dwellings being interspersed with half-filled refuse pits and grain stores used or disused.

At about H 50, another wave of new influences arrived, Belgic or C, from the south-east. With this change can be associated the introduction not merely of new pottery styles but of coinage. More remarkable and significant was the appearance of 'a new civic discipline', to quote the report. 'The innumerable ... pits, which must have stunk to high heaven, were now everywhere filled up.' And the semi-ruinous rampart was tidied by a thick new coating of earth and provided with a rampart walk open to the front but protected along the back by a fence supported with substantial posts – interpreted by the excavator as corresponding in function to the upper section of vertical revetment which was buried by the added earth, to prevent unauthorized access to the rampart walk from the enclosure.

The security of these great defences must have given the inhabitants confidence to resist the Roman invaders; but they were self-deceived, and the town was one of the twenty which fell to Vespasian in his campaign of the mid-forties of the first century AD. Dramatic evidence of this came from the war cemetery just outside the main eastern gateway, where the remains of thirty-eight bodies were found, ceremonially buried, usually with a pot or other grave goods, in shallow graves cut through the ashes of the adjacent houses. Most of these displayed wounds; several skulls had sword cuts, and in one skeleton a Roman arrowhead was embedded in the backbone. These, no doubt, fell in battle, but others must correspond to subsequent massacre, for several show multiple injuries any one of which would have been fatal: one skull, for example, is marked by nine sword cuts, and there were at least eleven women among the thirty-eight.

After their victory the Romans were content to demolish the main gateways, but to leave the inhabitants, or most of them, in their old home. Not until twenty years later was the place finally abandoned and replaced by Durnovaria, modern Dorchester.

This was not quite the end. In the fourth century, as described earlier (p. 79), a sanctuary was established on the site. We may suspect, but cannot prove, that its priest maintained the worship of the deity who had presided over the Iron Age town from its foundation.

Tre'r Ceiri, in Caernarvonshire, offers a complete contrast to Maiden Castle. It stands 450 metres above sea level, on an exposed peak of Yr Eifl; its walls, of dry stone, still survive in places to their full height; and the footings of the dwellings remain visible. It is probably the best preserved of all the hill towns of southern Britain, and certainly can give a better idea than any other of the original appearance of a place of this kind. Unhappily, its outstanding interest led to extensive excavation before the development of modern techniques, and worse still it is a popular amusement with summer visitors to eviscerate a hut or two, presumably under the impression that in thus spoiling the appearance of the remains and destroying any surviving evidence they are 'doing archaeology'. Nevertheless, in spite of all these disadvantages, the history of the place is now tolerably clear.

The best and easiest approach is from SH 360 437, the end of a minor road north of Llithfaen, rather than by the shorter but very steep climb from the road B 4417; and the most spectacular view is given by a low westerly sun, which picks out the massive walls still standing 4 metres high in places above the dark heather among the screes and rocks. After crossing a level plateau, where ill recorded burials were found by the early excavators, the track winds steeply upwards between low tumbled walls to the ruins of the south-western gateway. The immediate interior displays only rough grass and bilberries, but continuing up the slope towards the summit – with a magnificent view – confused groups of small huts are encountered. The early excavations, by unsupervised labourers clearing through the original floors to the natural subsoil and building up the stones round about, have at least reproduced an approximation to the original height of the hut walls. These extensive clearances also produced relics, exclusively Roman, which indicate that occupation of the place continued into the fourth century AD.

Tre'r Ceiri, then, though often cited as a 'typical' hill-fort, is unique in Britain, for although occupation continued into that period, and later, elsewhere, only at this site is the complete plan of a native town of the Roman period exposed to view.

Careful examination of the remains has shown that the visible arrangement is the result of long evolution. The earliest feature on the hill is the cairn on the summit, a relic of the Bronze Age and unrelated to the fort save by the accident of position. The original enclosure is represented by the main inner wall. In several ways this is notable. Its state of preservation is exceptional, and may be the result of continued use into the Roman period so that it escaped slighting; but, whatever the cause, in places on the north it still retains the original parapet and rampart walk, as well as the sloping ramps by which these were approached. There were five gateways. The two larger are ruinous, but seem to have been unusually narrow. More interesting, perhaps, are the three 'posterns', straight-sided openings less than a metre wide; that on the north retains its lintel, perhaps the only example surviving (though precariously) in a fortress gate in southern Britain. The north-west gate and the north postern gave access to springs. Within the enclosure, the original dwellings seem to have been about twenty round houses (pl. 5), corresponding to a population of about a hundred persons.

So far, apart from being set unusually high, the hill-fort was fairly typical for the region; the present exceptional character is the result of its continued occupation during the Roman period. The changes which followed are described as if they all took place at the same time, for their sequence cannot be worked out, but in fact they may have been spread out over three centuries.

The most striking development was the alteration in the shape of the dwellings and the great increase in their number (pl. 1). In plan, they were mostly irregular or roughly rectangular, less than half the area of the earlier round houses; typologically, they could have evolved out of the D-shaped plan resulting from the subdivision of the latter. Instead of a mere score there were at least 150, so even allowing fewer inhabitants to the smaller compartments the population must have been trebled or quadrupled. The defences were reinforced by a long stretch of outer wall on the north, and by shorter lengths on each side of the western approach. Where the north wall meets the terraced track leading from the north-west gateway to the spring, an unusual out-turned gateway was built, the northern jamb crossing the older trackway, which was diverted. All round the skirts of the hill, too, except on its steepest parts, little amoeboid enclosures were constructed. Their interiors, now mostly bare scree or rubble, were formed into level terraces behind fairly well built retaining walls.

Even if this analysis of its structural development is accepted as satisfactory, this remarkable settlement still poses one problem for solution. Its general character has every appearance of a small town, permanently occupied, and the little terraced enclosures are hardly explicable save as plots for some form of cultivation. Yet today the place is decidedly inhospitable even on many days in summer, and to live there throughout the year, or to cultivate even the hardiest crop, would seem unthinkable. It seems necessary to postulate some climatic change, possibly quite small and local; this need not have been greater than the variation which may occur now, for although on many August days the hill top may be enveloped in a bitterly cold mist, by contrast one may experience warm and almost idyllic sunshine in mid-winter.

On Traprain Law (fig. 12, pl. 6), in East Lothian, the visible remains are relatively unimpressive, but the story of its occupation extends almost unbroken from the end of the Bronze Age into the early Christian period. A campaign of excavation early in this century, though crude by modern standards, demonstrated beyond doubt that the surface of this hill conceals a rich mass of information for more than a millennium of the archaeology and early history of the lowlands and northern England.

At the time of writing, this unique document is being steadily destroyed unread, for the rock on which it stands yields profit if sold for road-making. If Britain is so poverty-stricken, in outlook even if not in reality, that this inexcusable destruction cannot be stopped, it should at least be preceded by *total* scientific excavation of the area to be dug away. Areas not under threat could, and indeed should, be left alone except for limited investigations to establish the sequence of events; for excavation techniques are steadily improving, and this is a particularly difficult site.

The area cleared on the western slopes during the period 1914 to 1923 covered some 5,000 square metres, and produced a mass of material, but neither the method of excavation nor its recording were of the high standard such a site deserves, and the separate reports have never been combined to provide a definitive final account. These researches were supplemented by careful though very limited investigations in 1939 and 1947, but it remained for Mr Feachem, then on the staff of the Royal Commission on Ancient and Historical Monuments in Scotland, to prepare an accurate survey and to work out the probable development of the site (which is followed here). At the same time, Miss Elizabeth Burley (now Mrs E. Fowler) published a full study of the metalwork – over six hundred items. The glass objects and the mass of pottery have not yet been adequately described.

Five systems of defences can be distinguished on the hill, with possible faint traces of one yet earlier phase. All except the latest rampart are very ruinous, though the penultimate structure is still fairly well defined.

The doubtful earliest phase is represented by intermittent lengths of a slight scarp and lines of stones following the main axis of the hill. If this does correspond to the first defensive line, it protected an area of about 4 hectares.

The next phase, the earliest which can be recognized with certainty, was identified by Mr S. Cruden in 1939. The highest part of the hill, covering about 8 hectares, was enclosed by a rampart in the form of a terrace with an external revetment of stone. Only very small excavations have been made in this enclosure, so nothing reliable can be said as to its absolute date.

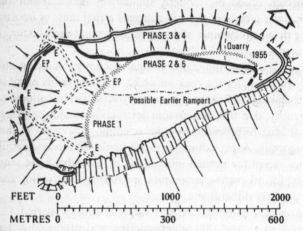

Fig. 12   Traprain Law. After R. W. Feachem.

In the second (certain) phase, a similar rampart was built to protect the lower slopes of the hill to the west, increasing the enclosed area to 12 hectares. Almost all the excavations of 1914–21 were within this area, but the discoveries cannot be related directly to the ramparts. Their significance is discussed below.

The next stage can be dated to some time within the first century AD, and the town, as it may fairly be called, now reached its greatest extent, 16 hectares. The rampart, again, was a revetted terrace, and excavation has shown that it was repaired or rebuilt in about AD 300. This was not the last of the defences, for later still a wall, 3·5 metres thick, of turf faced on both sides with stone, was built on about the same line as the second certain rampart, reducing the area once again to 12 hectares. There were thus five certain periods of rampart-building (referred to below as first to fifth without qualification) and one doubtful; the third and fourth can be dated to some time within the first century AD, and to about AD 300 respectively, and the fifth is probably post-Roman. The first and second are pre-Roman. The excavations of 1914–21 were outside the lines of the first rampart (and of the doubtful earlier one) but within all the others. The objects from these excavations which have been dated fall into three groups: the Late Bronze Age, say H 700–500; first century BC to second century AD, the last exactly dated object in this group being a coin assigned to AD 155; and third century AD to the end of the Roman period, the earliest and latest coins being of AD 253 and 408 respectively. There is a tradition of a monastery founded on the site by St Monenna in about AD 500, and a massive silver chain of about the sixth to eighth century AD was found on the hill.

Leaving aside accepted views as to the probable dates of hill-fort building, this material can be combined into a self-consistent account. The undated fifth rampart is correlated with the early Christian occupation indicated by tradition but by no relics except the silver chain. The fourth rampart, built about AD 300, corresponds satisfactorily with the occupation indicated by coins from 253 to AD 408, and other late metalwork. Similarly, some of the objects assigned to the period of the first century BC to the second century AD, with the run of coins ending at AD 155, can be related to the third rampart, built some time in the first century AD.

The Late Bronze Age objects were found within the line of the second phase rampart, but outside that of the first phase. Logically, therefore, it would seem reasonable to regard the second rampart as of the Late Bronze Age, and the first as still earlier, but even though recent work as at Ivinghoe and Dinorben would now make one period of fortification at such an early date seem plausible it is still difficult to accept two. It seems better, at least for the present, to associate the earliest material with the first rampart, as an extramural deposit. The second rampart may then be assigned to the beginning of the main pre-Roman occupation.

Pending further investigation, we cannot tell whether the people living on the hill when the Romans arrived were the direct descendants of those who utilized all the Late Bronze Age material found there, or whether there was renewed occupation in the first century BC, after a period of abandonment. The relics seem to demonstrate that in this region the Romans were welcomed. The town seems to have prospered, and the inhabitants obtained quite a lot of metal objects and pottery from the new arrivals, while continuing to make their own. They seem to have lived in round houses, but only one really satisfactory plan was recovered. This was about 6 metres in diameter, enclosed by a massive wall over 2 metres thick, of turf or cob on a foundation of slabs; there was a central hearth.

Something drastic happened soon after the middle of the second century, but again the story must remain obscure pending further excavation; tentatively, it seems likely that the town was abandoned for a generation. The Romans experienced a military setback at about this time, and withdrew from Scotland, and their friends at Traprain may also have suffered. When the place was re-occupied, it stood outside the area of direct Roman control, but within an allied client kingdom, or protectorate. Once again Roman objects are plentiful, and remain so until at least the beginning of the fifth century. One particularly notable find was a stylus, implying that some inhabitants could write.

The latest buildings seem to have had walls of mixed earth and stone, and the lines of rubble debris recorded by the excavators thus give some idea of the arrangement of the town in its final state. The dwellings were roughly rectangular, with rounded corners, the walls being 1·5 to 2 metres thick, sometimes more. Most houses consisted of a single fairly large compartment, 5 or 6 metres wide and of about twice that length; one, not fully uncovered, was more than 23 metres long. They were thus very much more commodious than the houses at Tre'r Ceiri. Almost all contained a large hearth near the middle of the floor, and some had small compartments opening off the main room. The area excavated was traversed by a road 2·5 to 3 metres wide, with cart ruts; its continuation in each direction remains visible. The houses mostly stood close together along this, but near the middle of the area cleared they were set back so as to form an irregular square about 20 metres across, which the line of the road crossed diagonally. The detail recorded does not permit an attempt at reconstruction, but they can be visualized as resembling the poorest type of cottage which still survived until recently in the remoter parts of Britain: windowless, with low walls of mud on a boulder foundation; there would be no chimney, and such peat smoke as could not escape by the doorway would seep out through the heavy rough thatch.

Only about a dozen houses were excavated, and Mr Feachem's plan shows some fifty or more platforms which could have carried others, so the richer inhabitants may have had more impressive dwellings. One man, at least, seems to have hoped to become more prosperous, for beneath the floor of one of the compartments south of the square was a large hoard of late Roman silver, evidently from its damaged condition – some vessels had been halved – representing one share of the loot from a successful raid. This find is often cited as evidence that the town was deserted, but its date falls within the limits of the coin sequence, and there would have been no problem in bringing it to the house, perhaps disguised as a sack of straw.

The story of St Monenna remains as yet unsupported by archaeology, but contains nothing inherently unlikely. If accepted, it implies that Traprain, under the name Dunpeldur, was still a flourishing small town at the beginning of the sixth century, and that somewhere on the hill top one of the earliest Christian churches in Britain awaits discovery – unless it has already been destroyed for road-metalling.

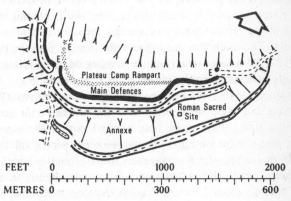

Fig. 13   Croft Ambrey. After S. C. Stanford.

Croft Ambrey (fig. 13) has been the site of one of the most important excavations in Britain. The investigation not only made it possible to recognize, for the first time, a new 'culture' in western England, but provided a more convincingly reliable chronology than any established hitherto, by considering the probable duration of the successive phases in the reconstructions which took place in the gateways; the dating is based on a thirty-year life for the posts, with controls provided by radiocarbon. The history of the site can therefore be set out in considerable detail, with fairly reliable absolute dates. The phases, in this account, follow those of the excavation report.

The position chosen was a long narrow hill, with a very abrupt scarp on the north and gentler, though still steep, slopes on the other sides. On the summit of this hill, in about 550 BC, a small dump rampart and ditch were built to protect an enclosure of 2·2 hectares. The interior was closely set with small four-post buildings regularly spaced along streets. This house pattern continued with little change throughout the six centuries of the hill-fort's life. It is discussed further below. The gateway in this first phase was a simple double portal, formed by three large posts. It was entirely rebuilt to the same design twice, and the posts were renewed twice more, giving a sequence of five successive sets of posts (covering phases one to three). No pottery, and very few relics of any kind, survived from the occupation of this earlier fort.

In the next stage (pl. 7), about 390 BC, a new and massive rampart was built, following a line mostly outside the old one. Although large, it was of simple design, being a bank with a glacis-type front running smoothly down into its single ditch. The width overall was 28 metres, and the vertical height 12 metres; the crest carried a timber breastwork. The ditch was not big enough to supply all the material for the bank, so a large quarry ditch was dug out. The filling of this quarry ditch provided a valuable series of stratified layers.

This rampart style remained unaltered for some 290 years (phases four to six), but there were changes in the design of the gateways during that time; these were best worked out at the south-west entrance. Initially (phase four) this gateway was very similar to that of the plateau camp, with a passageway nearly 7 metres wide leading to a double portal. The rampart ends were only slightly thickened, giving a passage about 5 metres long. With reconstructions, this type of gate lasted about sixty years.

In about 330 BC, the entrance was drastically replanned and strengthened (phase five). The width of the passage was almost halved, to 4 metres, and the broad double portal replaced by a single one. The gate passage was lengthened, and a pair of rectangular guard rooms provided. Sandstone, brought from the foot of the hill, was used for the lower courses of walling in this phase. The gate posts were joined by a rubble-filled trench across the entrance passage, and it seems likely, as the excavator suggests, that the opening may have been closed, in emergencies, by a temporary palisade set up in this — whether as a reinforcement to a hung gate or as an alternative cannot be decided.

This phase lasted until about 260 BC, when the system of guard rooms was given up, the gate being set at the inner end of a straight-sided passage. There was no evidence for a bridge. There were six replacements of the posts during this phase, which is estimated to have lasted some 190 years, to about 70 BC.

In the last phase (seven) the gateway arrangements were similar, save that a bridge was added across the passage in front of the gate. To this phase, also, there can probably be attributed the second bank and ditch formed outside the main bank. There was no further alteration, and the effective occupation of the hill-fort ended with the arrival of the Romans in AD 48.

All the above refers to the main enclosure. Outside this there is a relatively weak annexe, of 4·8 hectares. This was not extensively investigated, for one primary objective of the work was to throw light on the history of the adjacent hill-forts also, and annexes are rare among them; but sufficient was done to show that the lines of close-set rectangular buildings did not occur in it. Nevertheless, the annexe did contain a remarkable sacred site, which in its earliest phases consisted of a levelled terrace cut into the hillside. About AD 150 this was covered by a mound 11·6 metres square and up to 1·5 metres high, with a rough dry-stone revetment on three sides. The religious ceremonies, whatever they may have been, left much charcoal, ash and burned bone, and many fragments of broken pottery. The latest datable sherd was of the third or fourth century.

As mentioned earlier, the occupants of the first enclosure lived in little rectangular huts ranging from 2·4 by 1·8 metres to 3·6 metres square. Some essentially similar buildings were storehouses or granaries, which could be distinguished merely by such accidents as the preservation of carbonized grain. In addition to the contrast in shape and size, as compared to the dwellings in such forts as Garn Boduan or Hod Hill, there was an equally sharp contrast in arrangement, for the buildings were regularly set out in streets. Moreover, evidence was found that they had been repeatedly rebuilt on the same site; sometimes as many as six renewals of the uprights could be detected.

This barrack-like settlement differs so radically from the haphazard round house pattern that it seems impossible to avoid the conclusion that the origins of the Croft Ambrey settlers must be sought outside Britain, although Croft Ambrey itself was probably the work of descendants of the original invaders.

Another interesting result of this work is the evidence for the development of quite an extensive system of trade. In phases one to three, the plateau camp, pottery is almost absent; in later phases it becomes plentiful, and can be proved (by its mineral content) to derive from potters working in the Malvern Hills region, 30 kilometres away; the infrequency of the supply is emphasized by the discovery of a large proportion of potsherds with indications of repair by iron rivets.

Bibliography

This is not intended to be complete. Its object is to give the main sources used, and these will provide a foundation for anyone who wishes to go into the subject more deeply. Papers which deal primarily with particular sites but which also contain material of wider relevance are indicated by the hill-fort name, under which (in the gazetteer) the reference is given.

GENERAL WORKS

These are also referred to in some sections relating to separate chapters, and in the gazetteer, using the abbreviations indicated.

H F N F   Sir Mortimer Wheeler and K. M. Richardson, *Hill-forts of Northern France*, Research Report XIX, Society of Antiquaries of London (1957). Important for study of continental origins.

I A H F   D. Hill and M. Jesson (eds), *The Iron Age and its Hill-forts*, Univ. of Southampton Monograph 1 (Southampton, 1971).

I A Map   *Map of Southern Britain in the Iron Age* with introduction (Ordnance Survey, 1962). A corresponding map for northern Britain is in preparation.

I A N B   A. L. F. Rivet (ed.), *The Iron Age in Northern Britain* (Edinburgh, 1966).

P I A S B   S. S. Frere (ed.), *Problems of the Iron Age in Southern Britain*, Institute of Archaeology Occasional Paper 11 (Univ. of London, *c.* 1958).

P P   F. T. Wainwright (ed.), *Problem of the Picts* (Nelson, 1955), especially R. W. Feachem (ch. III) on fortifications.

Note also the following abbreviations: *Ant. J, Antiquaries Journal Arch. J, Archaeological Journal Preh. Scot*, R. W. Feachem, *Prehistoric Scotland* (Batsford 1963).

An important book which will provide the long needed background to the British Iron Age has been announced while this work was in its final stages of preparation: B. Cunliffe, *Iron Age Communities in Britain* (Archaeology of Britain series, Routledge, 1974).

INDIVIDUAL CHAPTERS

1 Names. The basic sources for England are the various publications of the English Place Name Society, and for Scotland W. J. Watson, *Celtic Place Names of Scotland* (Edinburgh, 1926). Names mentioned in classical sources, and thus often preserving the pre-Roman form, are discussed by I. A. Richmond, O. G. S. Crawford and I. Williams in 'The British Section of the Ravenna Cosmography', *Archaeologia* XCIII (1949), pp. 1–50, and by K. Jackson, 'Romano-British Names in the Antonine Itinerary', *Britannia* I (1970), pp. 68–82.

2 Modern Research. Most modern research appears in reports on separate hill-forts (see gazetteer) or among the more recent of the county surveys (pp. 107–11). For general works see *I A H F*, *I A N B* and *P I A S B*. Some attempts at theoretical or numerical analysis are given in *I A H F*, pp. 59–64, 114–24.

3 The Background. For the Hawkes–Piggott framework see C. F. C. Hawkes, *P I A S B*, pp. 1–16, and S. Piggott, *I A N B*, pp. 1–15. Revised evidence for date: in the Welsh Marches, S. C. Stanford in *I A H F*, pp. 42–3; also under Credenhill, Croft Ambrey, and H. N. Savory under Dinorben; in Scotland, E. W. MacKie, *Antiquity* XLII (1969), pp. 15–26.

For Celtic life in general: T. G. E. Powell, *The Celts* (Thames and Hudson, London, 1958); J. Filip, *Celtic Civilization and its Heritage* (English trans. by R. F. Samsour, Prague, 1962); S. Piggott, *Ancient Europe* (Edinburgh, 1965), pp. 168 ff. (chs 5 and 6). A. Ross, *Everyday Life of the Pagan Celts* (Batsford 1970).

Economics: in *I A H F*, B. Cunliffe (cultural environment) pp. 53–9; R. Bradley (economic change) pp. 71–83; J. Collis (markets and money) pp. 97–103; also R. Bradley, 'Stock Raising and the Origins of the Hill-Fort on the South Downs', *Ant. J.* LI (1971), pp. 8–29.

4 Function. See generally under places named in chapter, also *I A H F*, as under chs 2 and 3. For size distribution see under Croft Ambrey and (for Wales) A. H. A. Hogg in *Prehistoric Man in Wales and the West* (ed. F. Lynch and C. Burgess, Adams and Dart, Bath, 1972), pp. 293–307. On function (and population) in the Welsh Marches, S. C. Stanford, *ibid.*, pp. 307–20. See also under ch. 5.

5 Distribution and Regional Types. The south-western wide-spaced multivallate type: A. Fox in *P I A S B*, pp. 35 ff., and *Arch. J.* CIX (1952), pp. 1–22.

Scottish and Northumbrian forts: R. W. Feachem, in *I A N B*, pp. 59–88, and G. Jobey, *ibid.*, pp. 89–109.

Territories: J. F. Dyer, 'Dray's Ditches, Bedfordshire, and E.I.A. Territorial Boundaries in the E. Chilterns', *Ant. J.* XLI (1961), pp. 32–43.

For discussion of a particular region, see *The Iron Age in the Irish Sea Province* (ed. C. Thomas, CBA, London, 1972), especially A. H. A. Hogg (pp. 11–24), S. C. Stanford (pp. 25–36) and (summing up) L. Alcock (pp. 99–111).

6 Origins, Attack and Defence. General discussion with numerous references: C. F. C. Hawkes in *I A H F*, pp. 5–18. See also S. Piggott, *Ancient Europe* as under ch. 3.

Chevaux-de-frise: P. Harbison, 'Wooden and Stone *C.-de-f.* in Central and Western Europe', *Proc. Preh. Soc.* XXXVII (1971), pp. 195–225. This valuable paper, in conjunction with other refs given in it, makes *all* the evidence readily available.

Caesar's descriptions of warfare in Gaul and Britain: complete discussion with summaries and corrections of some current mistranslations, A. L. F. Rivet in *I A H F*, pp. 189–202.

7 Building the Hill Fort. R. W. Feachem's discussion of unfinished hill forts (in *I A H F*, pp. 19–39) is of primary importance. See also A. L. F. Rivet in *P I A S B*, pp. 29–34, and under Ladle Hill, Bindon Hill, Harding's Down and Overton Down.

8 The Ramparts. Palisaded enclosures: R. W. Feachem in *I A N B*, pp. 59–65; A. Ritchie, 'Palisaded Sites in N. Britain', *Scottish Arch. Forum* (1970), pp. 48–68.

Quarry ditches: A. L. F. Rivet in *P I A S B*, pp. 29–34.

Galleried duns, etc.: see under Clickhimin.

Timber lacing: M. A. Cotton, 'British Camps with Timber-laced Ramparts', *Arch. J.* CXI (1954), pp. 26–105; and on *muri gallici*, *H F N F*, pp. 159–225.

Satellite forts: J. Forde-Johnston, 'Earls Hill Pontesbury and Related Hill-forts', *Arch. J.* CXIX (1962), pp. 66–91.

9 The Gateways. See generally under places named.

Chronology (in Welsh Marches): S. C. Stanford in *I A H F*, pp. 42–5.

10 The Interior. See under places named. Also (for nature of post settings) A. Ellison and P. Drewett, 'Pits and Post-holes in the British Early Iron Age', *Proc. Preh. Soc.* XXXVII, 1 (1971), pp. 183–94.

11 The Romans and After. Distribution of forts in the south, defended and not defended against Roman attack: B. Cunliffe in *I A H F*, p. 67.

Later fortifications: R. W. Feachem in *P P*, pp. 66–86 and (modifying earlier views) in *I A N B*, pp. 82–5. Also R. B. K. Stevenson, *Proc. Soc. Ant. Scot.* LXXXIII (1948–9), pp. 186–97. And see under Dinas Emrys, Dunadd, Dundurn and Ruberslaw.

GENERAL TOPOGRAPHICAL INFORMATION

The following works include, among other material, useful summary descriptions of many hill-forts.

N. Thomas, *A Guide to Prehistoric England* (Batsford, London, 1960).

R. W. Feachem, *Prehistoric Scotland* (Batsford, London, 1963).

C. H. Houlder, *Wales, an Archaeological Guide* (Faber and Faber, London, forthcoming).

J. Dyer, *Southern England, an Archaeological Guide* (Faber and Faber, London, 1973).

For most British counties there are more or less complete accounts of the hill-forts, either in the relevant volume of the *Victoria County History* (*V C H*) or in a county *Inventory* (*Inv.*) published by Her Majesty's Stationery Office for one of the three Royal Commissions on Ancient and Historical Monuments, for England, Scotland or Wales and Monmouthshire, as appropriate. Most of these publications are fully illustrated with plans unless otherwise noted; but allowances must be made for the difference in standards between (say) 1908 and 1968. In the following list the termination 'shire' is usually omitted for brevity.

ENGLAND

Two important recent publications deal with the Iron Age in full, not hill-forts only, for regions covering parts of several counties. These are D. W. Harding, *The Iron Age in the Upper Thames Basin* (Oxford, 1972), and C. Saunders, 'The Pre-Belgic Iron Age in the Central and Western Chilterns', *Arch. J.* CXXVIII (1971), pp. 1–30. Both are concerned with parts of Berks. Bucks. and Oxford.

Bedford	*V C H* I (1904), pp. 267 ff.
Berks.	*V C H* I (1906), pp. 251 ff., supplemented by M. A. Cotton, *Berks. Arch. J.* LX (1962), pp. 30–52 (no plans). And see above before list of counties.
Bucks.	*Inv.*, 2 vols (1912–13), supersedes *V C H* II (1908), pp. 21 ff. And see above before list of counties.
Cambridgeshire	Inventories: West, 1968; North-east 1972; remainder forthcoming.
Cheshire	J. Forde-Johnston, *Trans. Lancs. and Cheshire Arch. Soc.* LXXII (1962), pp. 9–46.
Cornwall	*V C H* I (1906), pp. 451 ff. (not as complete as most *V C H*), supplemented, for cliff castles, by M. A. Cotton, *West Cornwall Field Club* II, 3 (1958–9), pp. 113 ff. (no plans).
Cumberland	*V C H* I (1901), p. 232. Map only, no descriptions or plans. Refs with no descriptions or plans: *Archaeologia* LIII (1893), pp. 485–538.
Derby	*V C H* I (1905), pp. 357 ff.
Devon	*V C H* I (1906), pp. 573 ff. Also C. Whybrow, *Proc. Devon Arch. Soc. No. 25* (1967), pp. 1–18. Discussion, with plans, of nine forts in north-west of county.
Dorset	*Inv.*, 3 vols in 6 parts, 1952–70.
Durham	*V C H* I (1905), pp. 343 ff.
Essex	*Inv.*, 4 vols (1916–23), superseding *V C H* I (1903), 275 ff.
Gloucester	No adequate account of county's hill-forts.
Hants.	J. P. Williams Freeman, *Field Archaeology as Illustrated by Hampshire* (London, 1915). An excellent work, fully illustrated with plans.

Hereford   *Inv.*, 3 vols (1931–4), superseding *V C H* I
                  (1908), pp. 199 ff.

Herts.   *Inv.* (1910), superseding *V C H* II (1908), pp.
                  103 ff.

Hunts.   *Inv.* (1926); also *V C H* I (1926), pp. 281 ff.

Kent   *V C H* I (1908), pp. 389 ff.

Lancs.   J. Forde-Johnston as for Cheshire; also *V C H* II
                  (1966), pp. 507 ff.

Leicester   *V C H* I (1907), pp. 243 ff.

Lincoln   C. W. Phillips, *Arch. J.* XCI (1934), pp. 101–2,
                  gives a brief account of the few hill-forts in the
                  county. One air photo but no plans.

Middlesex   *Inv.* (1937); but county contains no hill-forts.

Norfolk   R. R. Clarke, 'Iron Age in Norfolk and Suffolk',
                  Arch. J. XCVI (1939), pp. 48–9, gives a brief
                  account of the few hill forts, with small-scale
                  plans.

Northants.   *V C H* II (1906), pp. 397 ff.

Northumberland   G. Jobey, *Arch. Aeliana* 4 ser XLIII (1965), pp.
                  21–64.

Nottingham   B. B. Simmons, *Trans. Thoroton Soc.* LXVII
                  (1963), pp. 9–20, describing the five known forts,
                  with plans. Largely supersedes *V C H* I (1906),
                  pp. 289 ff.

Oxford   No general account of hill-forts, but see above
                  before list of counties.

Rutland   *V C H* I (1908), pp. 107 ff., but no hill-forts
                  recorded.

Shropshire   *V C H* I (1908), pp. 351 ff.

Somerset   *V C H* II (1911), pp. 467 ff.

Staffs.   *V C H* I (1908), pp. 331 ff.

Suffolk   *V C H* I (1911), pp. 583 ff., and see R. R. Clarke
                  as for Norfolk

Surrey   *V C H* IV (1912), pp. 379 ff.

Sussex   *V C H* I (1905), pp. 453 ff.

Warwick   *V C H* I (1904), pp. 345 ff.

Westmoreland   *Inv.* (1936).

Wilts.   The collection of plans in R. Colt Hoare, *Ancient
                  Wiltshire* I (1812), has now been supplemented
                  and partly superseded by *V C H* I, pt 1 (1957)

for bibliography, pt 2 (1974) for valuable discussion by Professor Cunliffe with three aerial views and eleven new plans (to various irrational scales).

Worcester *V C H* I (1901), pp. 184 ff.; inferior to other *V C H* volumes.

Yorks *V C H* II (1912), pp. 1 ff.

SCOTLAND (mainland only)

Although several counties have not been treated in detail the whole country has been at least partly covered by D. Christison, *Ancient Earthworks and Camps of Scotland* (Edinburgh, 1898).

Aberdeen No separate account.

Angus D. Christison, *Proc. Soc. Ant. Scot.* XXXIV (1899–1900), pp. 43 ff.

Argyll D. Christison, *Proc. Soc. Ant. Scot.* XXIII (1888–9), pp. 368 ff. (NW); *ibid.* XXXVIII (1903–4), pp. 205 ff. (Mid). The latter is supplemented and partly superseded by M. Campbell and M. L. S. Sandeman, *ibid.* XCV (1961–2), pp. 39–60, with good summary descriptions and full references but no plans. Also *Inv.* for Kintyre (Argyll vol. I, HMSO, 1971).

Ayr D. Christison, *Proc. Soc. Ant. Scot.* XXVII (1892–3), pp. 381 ff.

Banff No account.

Berwick *Inv.* (2nd edn 1915).

Caithness *Inv.* (1911).

Clackmannan See *Fife Inv.*

Dumfries *Inv.* (1920).

Dumbarton No account.

Fife *Inv.* with Kinross and Clackmannan (1933).

Inverness No account of any value.

Kincardine D. Christison, *Proc. Soc. Ant. Scot.* XXXIV (1899–1900), pp. 43 ff.

Kinross See *Fife Inv.*

Kirkcudbright	*Inv.* (1914).
Lanark	D. Christison, *Proc. Soc. Ant. Scot.* XXIV (1889–90), pp. 281–352 (Upper Ward only).
Lothian, East	*Inv.* (1924).
Lothian, Mid and West	*Inv.* (1929).
Moray	No account.
Nairn	No account.
Peebles	*Inv.*, 2 vols (1967).
Perth	D. Christison, *Proc. Soc. Ant. Scot.* XXXIV (1899–1900), pp. 43 ff.
Renfrew	No account.
Ross and Cromarty	No account.
Roxburgh	*Inv.*, 2 vols (1956).
Selkirk	*Inv.* (1957).
Stirling	*Inv.*, 2 vols (1963).
Sutherland	*Inv.* (1911).
Wigtown	*Inv.* (1912).

WALES

Anglesey	*Inv.* (1937, reprinted 1970).
Brecknock	H. N. Savory, *Bulletin of Board of Celtic Studies* XIV.1 (Nov. 1950), pp. 69 ff. Addenda, XV.3 (Nov. 1953), pp. 230 ff. List with reference and discussion but little detail and no plans. Further discussion with small-scale plans, *Brycheiniog* I (1954), pp. 119–25.
Caernarvon	*Inv.*, 3 vols (1956–64).
Cardigan	A. H. A. Hogg, *Bulletin of Board of Celtic Studies* XIX.4 (May 1962), pp. 354 ff. (List as for Brecknock.)
Carmarthen	*Inv.* (1917) and *County History* vol. I (1935), pp. 70–90, contain some material but greatly need revision. They are partly supplemented by H. N. Savory, *Bulletin of Board of Celtic Studies* XVI.1 (Nov. 1954). (List as for Brecknock.)
Denbigh	*Inv.* (1914) requires revision and largely superseded by Ellis Davies, *Prehistoric and Roman Remains of Denbs.* (Cardiff, 1929).
Flint	*Inv.* (1912) requires revision and largely superseded

	by Ellis Davies, *Prehistoric and Roman Remains of Flints.* (1949).
Glamorgan	*Inv.* forthcoming. Pending publication see H. N. Savory, *Bulletin of Board of Celtic Studies* XIII.3 (Nov. 1949), pp. 152 ff. Addenda XV.3 (Nov. 1953), pp. 229 ff. (List as for Brecknock.)
Merioneth	*County History*, Vol. I (Dolgellau, 1967). Very fully illustrated with good plans.
Monmouth	H. N. Savory, *Bulletin of Board of Celtic Studies* XIII.4 (May 1950), pp. 231 ff. Addenda XV.3 (Nov. 1953), pp. 229 ff. (List as for Brecknock.)
Montgomery	*Inv.* (1911) requires revision.
Pembroke	*Inv.* (1925) requires revision, and supplemented by D. W. Crossley, *Bulletin of Board of Celtic Studies* XX (May 1963), pp. 171 ff. (List as for Brecknock.)
Radnor	*Inv.* (1913) requires revision, and supplemented by H. N. Savory, *Bulletin of Board of Celtic Studies* XV.1 (Nov. 1952), pp. 73 ff. (List as for Brecknock.)

ADDENDUM

Two important works have been announced while this book was in page proof:

J. Forde-Johnston, *Hill-forts of the Iron Age in England and Wales: a survey of the surface evidence* (Liverpool University Press, 1975). This is a detailed scientific study, the scope of which is indicated by the title.

D. W. Harding (Editor), *Hill-forts: Later Prehistoric Earthworks in Britain and Ireland* (Academic Press, 1975). This contains sixteen articles, including detailed reports on Almondbury, Mam Tor, Ravensburgh and Salmonsbury; and re-assessments of the evidence from St Catherine's Hill and Traprain Law.

Gazetteer

This has two main objectives: to describe a representative sample; and to give fuller details, including the main references, for all those which are mentioned in the text, so as to avoid interruption by footnotes or descriptions which may be irrelevant in the immediate context. The arrangement is strictly alphabetical, so it provides an index to all places named.

Selection, out of the 2,500 or so hill-forts on the British mainland, proved difficult; it is hoped that an explanation of the principles adopted may mitigate readers' annoyance at discovering the omission of places which they regard as of particular interest or importance.

The original plan was to include at least one fort, if such existed, in each quarter of every 100-kilometre square of the National Grid, together with every excavated site. The list proved impossibly long, and had to be cut drastically. In doing this, major weight has been given to the need to keep a fairly even distribution. One of the chief faults of British archaeology is its localized bias, especially towards the south and east, and if full attention had been paid to the classic sites of the southern chalklands the north and west would have been badly under-represented. It is for this reason that many impressive structures have been left out in favour of such places as Am Baghan Burblach or Ashie Moor; others, though retained, have been given briefer treatment than they deserve. Further, for reasons given earlier, hill-forts recently or currently under excavation, and for which a report is pending, have in general been excluded; at a few the interim reports have yielded information of such interest that some mention is unavoidable. When, as at Craig Phadrig, work has begun since the text was drafted, the entry has usually been retained essentially unaltered.

The British forts described are shown on the three maps (figs 14–16) indexed by 100-kilometre squares. The descriptions, including foreign sites, are arranged in strict alphabetical order. Each entry gives the name, followed by the figure reference if any, then the historic county, the National Grid reference, and the approximate average height in metres above ordnance datum. The page references which follow indicate where there is further information about the site; mere mentions of the name are not indexed. The sheet numbers of the 1-inch OS map and of its successor the 1/50000 are given in the index to the gazetteer (pp. 114–21).

The accompanying text summarizes the main features of the hillfort, but does not attempt either a minutely detailed description of the remains or a discussion of the various alternative interpretations which are usually possible. Only the most important references are given in the bibliographical notes.

The plans have been derived from many different sources (see p. vi) and have been redrawn to a standard set of scales and conventions (fig. 17). The need to redraw has often been a matter for regret, for some of the originals are works of art; but it is hoped that any aesthetic loss will be counterbalanced by the advantages of uniformity. Since the chief object is to illustrate the principles used in the design of hill-forts, an attempt to show the exact form of the present ruins could often be confusing rather than helpful, and a really definitive representation would require a much larger scale than is possible here. The plans are therefore essentially diagrammatic. Modern features are usually omitted and the effects of recent disturbances eliminated where this can be done with fair certainty. In the appended acknowledgements, 'after' implies a direct copy of the outline, and 'based on' indicates that there have been some modifications, generally from an examination of the remains by the writer. When the scale is shown as 'approximate' the plan is usually a sketch from a pace-and-prismatic survey, or one of similar accuracy.

Almost all the hill-forts included here are on private land, and although most can be reached without much difficulty *in general the public has no legal right of access*. Where there is any doubt, permission should be sought. Further, the visitor is most strongly urged not to disturb the remains *in any way*. This is not merely because to do so might well render him liable to a fine or even imprisonment under the laws protecting national monuments, but because such activities hasten the decay of the structures and may destroy important evidence.

For a few sites, important new information has been published very recently. This has been incorporated in the gazetteer, but no alteration has been made elsewhere. There may therefore be occasional discrepancies, as for example in the discussion of the original name of Almondbury.

Index to Gazetteer

					1 inch sheet	1/50000 sheet
NC	1	Duchary Rock	851	050	15	17
ND	1	Garrywhin	313	413	16	12
NG	1	Am Baghan Burblach	832	199	35	33
NH	1	Ashie Moor	600	316	28	26
	2	Craig Phadrig	640	453	28	26
	3	Dunearn	933	406	28	27
NJ	1	Burghead	109	691	29	27
	2	Durn Hill	571	638	30	29
	3	Barmekin of Echt	725	070	40	38
NM	1	Dun na Ban-Oige	837	048	52	55
NN	1	Bochastle	601	075	54	57
	2	Dundurn	707	233	54	51
NO	1	Dunkeld	009	430	49	53
	2	Castle Law, Forgandenny	100	155	55	58
	3	Castle Law, Abernethy	183	153	55	58
	4	Dunsinane	214	316	49	53
	5	Barry Hill	262	504	49	53
	6	Finavon	506	556	50	54
	7	White Caterthun	548	660	50	44
	8	Brown Caterthun	555	668	50	44
	9	Maiden Castle, Arbroath	669	420	50	54
NR	1	Dunadd	837	936	52	55
NS	1	Dumbarton	400	745	60	63
	2	Dumyat	832	973	54	57
	3	Arbory Hill	944	238	68	72
NT	1	Dreva	126	353	69	72
	2	Castle Law, Glencorse	229	638	62	66

NT	3	Dunsapie	282	731	62	66
	4	Eildon Hill North	555	328	70	73
	5	Ruberslaw	580	155	70	73
	6	Traprain Law	581	746	63	67
	7	Bonchester Hill	595	117	70	73
	8	Woden Law	768	125	70	80
	9	Edinshall	772	603	63	67
	10	Hownam Rings	790	194	70	74
	11	Camp Tops, Morebattle	860	180	70	74
	12	Yeavering Bell	928	293	71	74
NU	1	The Ringses, Doddington Moor	014	327	71	75
NW	1	Kemp's Walk	975	598	79	82
NX	1	Mull of Galloway	143	307	79	82
	2	Barsalloch Point	347	413	79	82
NY	1	Burnswark	185	785	75	78
	2	Carrock Fell	342	336	83	90
NZ	1	Lordenshaws	054	993	71	81
	2	Stanwick	180	115	85	92
	3	Maiden Castle, Durham	283	417	85	88
	4	Eston Nab	568	183	86	93
SD	1	Skelmore Heads	274	751	88	96
	2	Ingleborough	741	747	90	98
SE	1	Almondbury	152	140	102	110
	2	Grimthorpe	816	535	98	106
	3	Staple Howe	898	749	93	100
SH	1	Castell Odo	187	284	115	123
	2	Caer y Twr	219	829	106	114
	3	Dinllaen	275	416	115	123
	4	Carn Fadrun	280	352	115	123
	5	Garn Boduan	310	393	115	123
	6	Tre'r Ceiri	373	446	115	123
	7	Dinlle	437	563	115	123
	8	Dinorwig	550	653	107	115
	9	Dinas Emrys	606	492	107	115
	10	Pen-y-Gaer, Llanbedr-y-Cennin	750	693	107	115
	11	Conway Mountain	760	778	107	115
	12	Caer Caradog	968	479	108	116
	13	Dinorben	968	757	108	116

SJ	1	Moel Hiraddug	063	785	108	116
	2	Foel Fenlli	163	601	108	116
	3	Llanymynech Hill	265	220	117	126
	4	Old Oswestry	296	310	118	126
	5	Maiden Castle, Bickerton	498	528	109	117
	6	The Wrekin	629	082	118	127
SK	1	Mam Tor	128	838	111	110
	2	Carlwark	260	815	111	110
	3	Caesar's Camp, Scholes Coppice	395	952	103	110
	4	Breedon-on-the-Hill	406	234	121	129
	5	Honington	954	423	113	130
SM	1	St David's Head	722	279	138	157
	2	Walesland Rath	912	170	138	157
SN	1	Moel Trigarn	158	336	139	145
	2	Trelissey	175	078	152	158
	3	Castell Nadolig	298	504	139	145
	4	Pen Dinas, Aberystwyth	584	804	127	135
SO	1	Ffridd Faldwyn	217	969	128	161
	2	Caer Caradoc	310	758	129	149
	3	Croft Ambrey	445	668	129	148
	4	Credenhill	450	445	142	148
	5	Caer Caradoc	477	953	129	137
	6	Sutton Walls	525	464	142	149
	7	Lydney	616	027	156	162
	8	Bredon Hill	958	400	144	150
SP	1	Salmonsbury	173	208	144	163
	2	Chastleton	258	282	144	151
	3	Rainsborough	526	348	145	152
	4	Hunsbury	738	583	133	152
	5	Ivinghoe Beacon	960	168	147	165
SR	1	Bosherston	971	948	151	158
SS	1	Clovelly Dykes	311	234	174	190
	2	Harding's Down	437	906	153	159
	3	Mynydd Bychan	963	756	154	170
ST	1	Hembury Castle	112	031	176	192
	2	Membury	282	028	177	193
	3	Worlebury	314	625	165	182

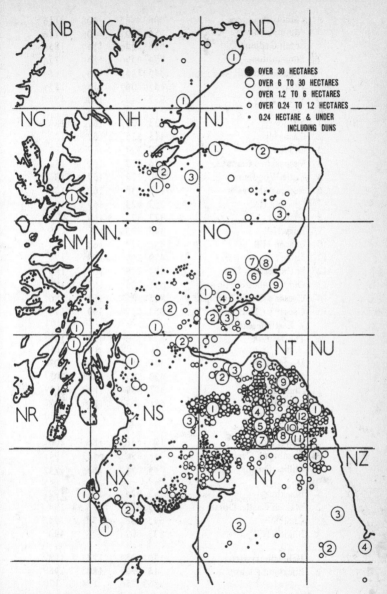

Fig. 14   Index to Gazetteer (for key see pp. 114–20).
Based upon the Ordnance Survey Map with the
sanction of the Controller of Her Majesty's
Stationery Office, Crown copyright reserved.

ST	4	Llanmelin	460 925	155	171
	5	Almondsbury	596 833	156	172
	6	South Cadbury	628 252	166	183
	7	Bathampton	774 650	156	172
	8	Hambledon Hill	845 126	178	183
	9	Hod Hill	857 106	178	183
	10	Winkelbury	952 217	167	184
SU	1	Yarnbury	035 403	167	184
	2	Casterley	115 535	167	184
	3	Old Sarum	137 327	167	184
	4	Vespasian's Camp	146 417	167	184
	5	Little Woodbury	150 279	167	184
	6	Figsbury Rings	188 338	167	184
	7	Quarley Hill	262 423	167	184
	8	Danebury	323 376	168	185
	9	Bury Hill	346 435	168	185
	10	Beacon Hill	458 572	168	174
	11	Ladle Hill	479 568	168	174
	12	St Catherine's Hill	484 276	168	185
	13	Old Winchester Hill	641 206	168	185
	14	Caesar's Camp, Farnham	825 500	169	186
	15	Caesar's Camp, Easthampstead	863 657	169	175
	16	The Trundle	877 110	181	197
SW	1	Maen Castle	347 257	189	203
	2	Gurnard's Head	433 387	189	203
	3	Chun Castle	405 339	189	203
	4	Carn Brea	686 407	189	203
SX	1	Tregeare Rounds	033 800	185	200
	2	Castle Dore	103 548	186	200
	3	Cranbrook Castle	738 890	175	191
	4	Milber Down	884 698	188	191
SY	1	Blackbury	187 924	176	192
	2	Maiden Castle, Dorset	669 885	178	194
	3	Chalbury	695 838	178	194
	4	Bindon Hill	835 802	178	194
SZ	1	Hengistbury Head	170 908	179	195
	2	Buckland Rings	314 968	180	196
TF	1	Warham	944 409	125	132
TL	1	Ravensburgh	099 295	147	166
	2	Caesar's Camp, Sandy	179 490	147	153

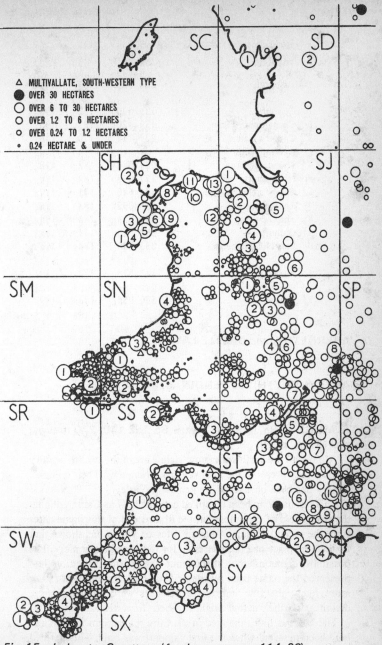

Fig. 15 Index to Gazetteer (for key see pp. 114–20).
Based upon the Ordnance Survey Map with the
sanction of the Controller of Her Majesty's
Stationery Office, Crown copyright reserved.

TL	3	Wandlebury	493 534	148	154
	4	Clare	769 459	149	155
TM	1	Tasburgh	200 960	137	144
TQ	1	Cissbury	139 080	182	198
	2	Chanctonbury Ring	139 120	182	198
	3	Caesar's Camp, Wimbledon	224 711	170	176
	4	Thundersbarrow	229 084	182	198
	5	Hollingbury	322 078	182	198
	6	Caesar's Camp, Keston	421 640	171	177
	7	Ranscombe	438 092	183	198
	8	The Caburn	444 089	183	198
	9	Oldbury	582 566	171	188
	10	East Hill, Hastings	833 099	184	199
TR	1	Bigberry	117 575	173	179
TV	1	Beltout	560 956	183	199

ABERNETHY, *see* CASTLE LAW.

ABERYSTWYTH, *see* PENDINAS.

ALMONDBURY (fig. 18; Yorks., SE 152 140; 270 metres; pp. 17, 18, pl. 8).

Almost all the earthworks now visible are of the twelfth century AD, but they preserve the lines of earlier ramparts. Their complex history has been unravelled by Professor Varley.

This hill has long been identified convincingly as Camulodunon, the stronghold of Camulos; but the first record of this name dates from the second century AD and Professor Varley has shown that by then the place had been deserted for two centuries or more. The possibility remains that throughout this period tradition had preserved the name used by the original builders, but it is rather more likely that the impressive defences were attributed to a divinity after their actual origin had been forgotten.

The hill was first inhabited in the third millennium BC, but had long been deserted when the first rampart was built. This, termed the univallate enclosure to distinguish it from later more powerful works, took in 1·1 hectares on the south-western half of the hill

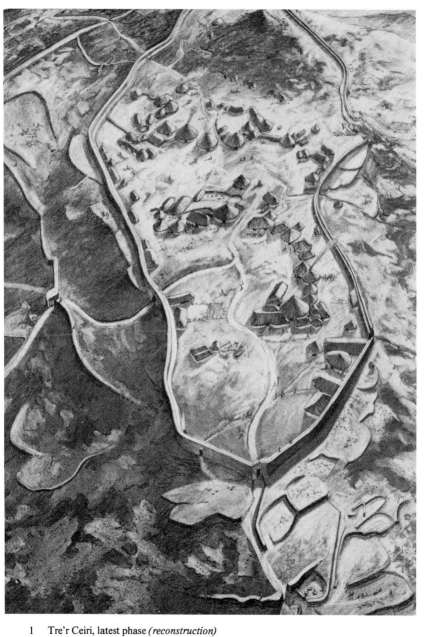

1   Tre'r Ceiri, latest phase *(reconstruction)*

2　Maiden Castle from south-east

3　Maiden Castle, East Gateway, phase II *(reconstruction)*

4   Maiden Castle, East Gateway, final phase *(reconstruction)*

5   Tre'r Ceiri, early phase *(reconstruction)*

6 Traprain Law

7   Croft Ambrey, early third century BC *(reconstruction)*

8   Almondbury

9   Arbory Hill

10 Barmekin of Echt

12 Bonchester Hill

11   Beacon Hill

13 Bredon Hill

14　The Brown Caterthun

15 Caer Caradoc, Church Stretton

16 Caer Caradoc, Clun

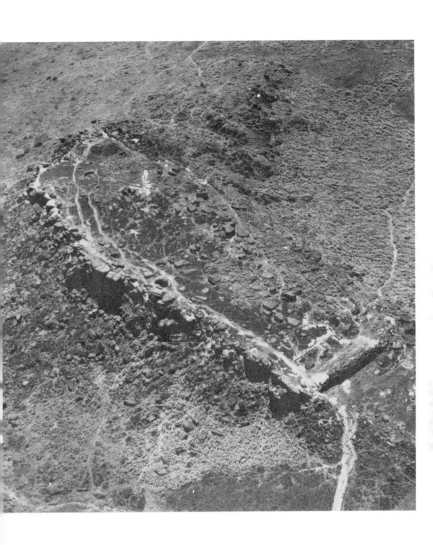

17 Carlwark

18 Casterley

19 Castle Dore

20 Chalbury

21 Cissbury

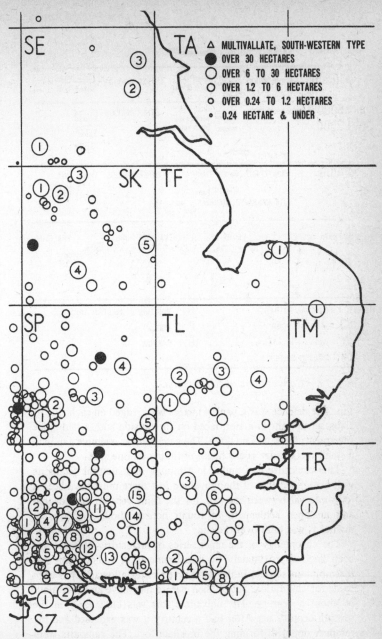

Fig. 16 Index to Gazetteer (for key see pp. 114–20).
Based upon the Ordnance Survey Map with the
sanction of the Controller of Her Majesty's
Stationery Office, Crown copyright reserved.

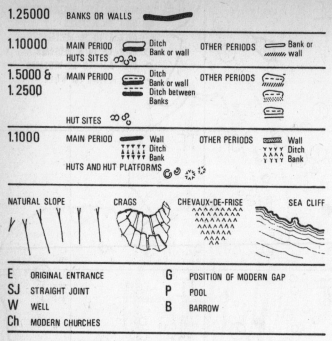

Fig. 17   Conventions used on plans.

top. The defence was a bank 4 metres wide, edged on each side by slabs set upright in a slot, faced on the outside with a laid stone revetment; there was no ditch. The gateway was a simple gap with a small rectangular guard house of timber on one side.

This enclosure was undated. Although in structural details its wall resembled that of the univallate fort there must have been a long interval between the two, for the ruins became turf-covered and an open settlement, of round houses about 6 metres in diameter, was built over the site.

The chronology of the main series of prehistoric defences has been fixed approximately by measurements of radiocarbon and thermoluminescence. In the dates given below allowance has been made for calibration, but by their nature they have an uncertainty of about a century. The univallate fort was built early in the seventh century BC. After half a century it was extended and the rampart doubled, forming the bivallate fort. The ramparts were again doubled for part of the circuit a century or so later, and outworks added. The resulting multivallate fort was burned in the latter half of the fifth century, and the site remained deserted until

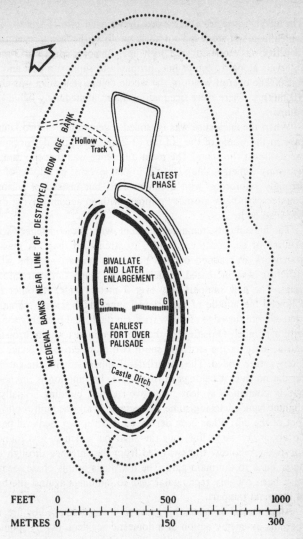

Fig. 18 Almondbury. After W. J. Varley.

the twelfth century AD, when the earthworks were incorporated in those of a castle.

The defences of the univallate fort followed the same line as those of the univallate enclosure, and comprised a counterscarp bank and a ditch separated by a narrow berm from the rampart. This was closely similar to its precursor, but rather more elaborate.

The clayey core was reinforced by an axial pile of stones, from which layers of stone led out horizontally to the facing revetments. The top was stone-covered with upright posts spaced at 3-metre intervals along its centre line, probably to support a post and rail fence. The overall width of the whole defensive system was about 10 metres. There were occupation floors immediately behind the rampart.

When the enclosure was extended a generation or two later to take in the whole of the hill top (2·2 hectares), the defences used were almost the same. The main difference was that the rampart was only 3 metres thick and the lowest layer of its fill was of turf strongly reinforced with a timber raft; but instead of a simple counterscarp bank an outer rampart with an accompanying ditch was also built.

The inhabitants remained content with these defences for a century or so, and then decided to strengthen them. A mass of stonework was added outside the inner rampart and the whole structure was increased in height, with much timber reinforcement. The new rampart was over 7 metres wide. Its outer face followed the middle of the original inner ditch, rising perhaps 4 metres from the edge of a new rock-cut ditch, and probably topped with a parapet. Outside this the second rampart was refurbished, and at least on the east and south two more close-set banks and ditches were added. The quadrilateral annexe outside the gateway on the north-east belongs to this phase. Its function is unknown, but it contained at least one two-roomed building. Finally, a slighter bank enclosing some 13 hectares in all was built round the foot of the hill; it has been destroyed to form two medieval banks on about the same line, but the shelf on which it was founded survives. A hollow trackway led from the entrance through this outer bank to the main gate. The dwellings in this phase seem to have been roughly rectangular lean-to buildings against the back of the main rampart.

After several decades, this great wall was destroyed by fire, not it seems by enemy action or a domestic accident, but by spontaneous combustion, much as an ill-ventilated haystack may burst into flame. The evidence for this is that burning was restricted to the core of the wall; the facing stones were unaffected. Presumably the conditions for this disaster developed slowly over the years as the decaying wood formed a natural tinder and ventilation was reduced by silting. The inhabitants could well have regarded this disconcerting event as a manifestation of supernatural malice (perhaps by Camulos?), but whatever the reason they abandoned their fortress, which remained uninhabited until Henry de Laci built his castle there in about AD 1150.

W. J. Varley, *Castle Hill, Almondbury. A Brief Guide...* (Huddersfield, 1973), supplementing and correcting *Arch. J.* CV (1948), pp. 41–66 *passim*. The final report is in preparation (1974).

ALMONDSBURY (Gloucester, ST 596 833; 85 metres; p. 18).

The village takes its name from the hill-fort in Knole Park, an elongated oval enclosing about 2·8 hectares within a single rampart. It is now partly built over and damaged.

AM BAGHAN BURBLACH (fig. 19; Inverness, NG 832 199; 90 metres; p. 35).

The summit of a small oval knoll projecting from the mountains on the north side of Glenelg has been fortified by a stone wall, now ruinous but originally nearly 3 metres thick. The single entrance, at the east end, is 1·5 metres wide, and on the south of the gap the wall is thickened so that the line of its outer face runs nearly a metre outside that on the north. The enclosed area is only 0·12 hectare. It contains the stone-built foundations of a hut about 8 metres in diameter, and traces of two smaller rings; these may well

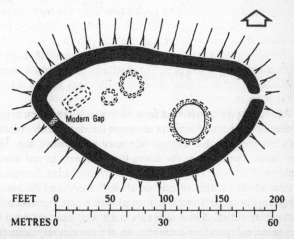

Fig. 19 Am Baghan Burblach. Scale approximate.

be contemporary with the defences. At the west end, the ruins of an oblong building and an adjacent break in the rampart are much more recent.

L. Bogle, *Proc. Soc. Ant. Scot.* XXIX (1894–5), p. 182 (rough plan).

ARBORY HILL (fig. 20; Lanark, NS 944 238; 430 metres; pl. 9).

This interesting and well preserved fort consists of three widely separated ramparts, very nearly circular and concentric, but perhaps representing two or three periods of construction, though their relative age cannot be deduced.

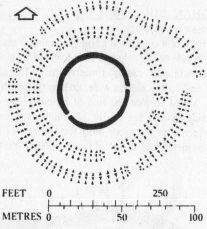

FEET   0   250

METRES 0   50   100

Fig. 20   Arbory Hill. Based on D. Christison.

The inner ring is protected by a stone wall about 3 metres thick, enclosing 0·2 hectare with entrances on the east and on the south-west, simple gaps 1·5 metres wide lined with small slabs. There are vague markings in the interior which may be the sites of buildings.

The other two rings of defence are both banks and ditches. The inner encloses 0·4 hectare. It is pierced by three entrances, to north, east and south-east. The outermost ring is similar, enclosing 0·9 hectare. It has four entrances. At the eastern, the rampart on the north side stands 4 metres further out than that on the south.

As in other Scottish forts, the entrance system seems puzzling. The only reasonably direct access to the centre is from the east, and one of the outermost entrances has not even a corresponding gap in the middle rampart.

D. Christison, *Proc. Soc. Ant. Scot.* XXXIV (1899–1900), p. 302 (plan).
Preh. Scot., p. 134.

ASHIE MOOR (fig. 21; Inverness, NH 600 316; 250 metres).

This little fort, of only 0·08 hectares, stands on an outcrop in wet heather-covered waste overlooking Loch Duntelchaig. Its plan

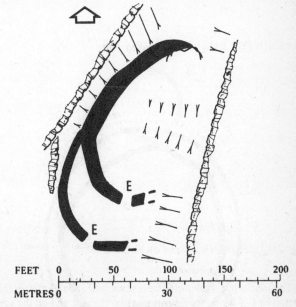

FEET	0		50		100		150		200
METRES	0				30				60

Fig. 21 Ashie Moor. Scale approximate.

is simple, a wall about 3 metres thick forming the main defence, with a thinner wall forming an arc outside the entrance, on the south-west. The east face of the outcrop is precipitous, and requires no artificial defences.

Some good facing, of large blocks, is visible in places, but there is not now enough material to build the walls up to any considerable height; they have probably been pillaged to build the adjacent roads. No detail survives at the entrances.

> *Trans. Inverness Sci. Soc.* VIII (1912–18), p. 130 (Dun Riachie; poor plan).
> *Preh. Scot.*, p. 126.

AVARICUM (Bourges, France; p. 64).

The term 'Avaricum type' is used to describe the 'true' *murus gallicus* (see p. 64), since the classical description by Caesar refers to the rampart there.

> M. A. Cotton, *Arch. J.* CXI (1954), pp. 27–9.

BAENINTES BURY, *see* Bredon Hill.

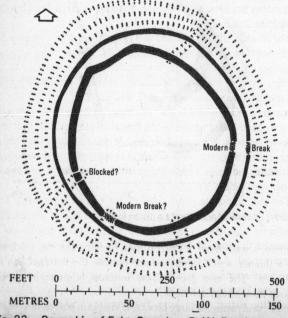

Fig. 22   Barmekin of Echt. Based on R. W. Feachem.

BARMEKIN OF ECHT (fig. 22; Aberdeen, NJ 725 070; 270 metres; p. 36 p. 10).

Five ramparts, following the general outline of the hill, protect an almost circular enclosure of 1·0 hectare. The fort is a good example of the use of multiple entrances.

Two periods of construction are evident, though excavation might show this to be an over-simplification. The earlier is represented by the outer three banks, which are now grass-grown and must have been largely of earth. Their inner revetments, of large upright slabs, can still be seen in places; they were probably revetted on the outer face also. They are pierced by four entrance passages, one on the north and three close together on the south; the fifth gap, on the east, is a modern break made when an observatory was built on the hill. These passages are slightly sunk, and their sides are revetted. There are other transverse walls on the south-east, but they are modern and have been omitted from the plan.

The second period of building now appears as the ruins of two stone walls, within the line of the earlier banks and roughly concentric with them. The outer wall was about 1·5 to 2 metres thick, the inner perhaps 2·5 metres, but they are very ruinous. There does not seem to be enough material to allow for a height of more than 2 metres.

The finished structure offers two problems. First, that in its final form there seems to have been no entrance at all to the inner enclosure. The outer of the two walls is continuous, apart from modern gaps, and although the inner wall is interrupted opposite the middle one of the three southern entrances, this has every appearance of a modern break. The most westerly of the three does seem to have had a properly constructed entrance, but this seems to have been built up in antiquity. Whether there were narrow entrances through the walls which have been obscured by collapse, or whether the walls were crossed by steps, can only be solved by proper excavation.

The second puzzle is provided by the entrance passages. These shallow linear depressions can all be traced to within the line of the innermost wall, that is to some 20 metres inside the line of the presumed first period defences; but, as stated above, the wall is uninterrupted. Such extensions seem to have no function unless there were additional defensive lines, belonging to the first period, and now concealed beneath the stone walls. An alternative possibility is that there were dwellings set round the enclosure during the first period, leaving a central open area primarily for cattle. Conjectures of this kind can only be tested by excavation.

W. D. Simpson, *Proc. Soc. Ant. Scot.* LIV (1919–20), p. 45, and *The Province of Mar* (Aberdeen, 1943), p. 16 (inaccurate plan).
R. W. Feachem in *I A N B*, fig. 9, p. 73 (good plan).
Now see also J. K. St Joseph, *Antiquity* XLVIII (1974), p. 52 and pl. VII (air photo).

BARRY or BARRA HILL (fig. 23; Perth, NO 262 504; 210 metres; pp. 20, 45).

The most prominent feature on this site is the ruin of a very large and strong wall, originally timber-laced and now partly

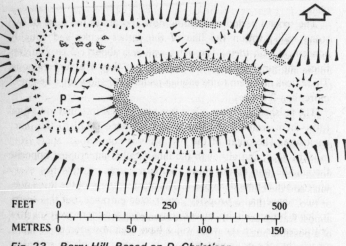

FEET   0   250   500
METRES 0   50   100   150

Fig. 23   Barry Hill. Based on D. Christison.

vitrified, forming an enclosure of regular plan with parallel sides and semicircular ends, area about 0·2 hectares. There is apparently no entrance. Outside it are some additional enclosures which can best be understood from the plan. These suggest that the vitrified fort has been built over the remains of an earlier structure. Essentially, this seems to have been protected mainly by natural crags on the north, and on other sides by a huge bank, mostly built up with material from a large quarry ditch set some way behind it, but also using a natural hump at the east end. The entrance was between this and the top of the crags. At the west end the irregularity of the ground combined with the superimposition of the stone fort makes it impossible to work out the arrangements from surface investigation; there may have been another entrance about here through the south bank. The artificial pool is outside the defences, for the banks which enclose it are very slight.

> D. Christison, *Proc. Soc. Ant. Scot.* XXXIV (1899–1900), pp. 93–6 (plan).
> *Preh. Scot.*, pp. 146–7.
> This is probably the 'Doun-bervie' where, according to a sixteenth-century chronicle, Queen Guinevere was imprisoned after King Arthur's death. Metrical Chronicle of Scotland, *Rolls Series* VI, pt II, p. 261.

BARSALLOCH POINT (Wigtown, NX 347 413; 30 metres).

This fort stands on the edge of a cliff from which the sea has receded. The A747 from Stranraer towards Whithorn runs on the former beach. The structure is in guardianship, but unlike most such is not clearly signposted. The direct approach from the road, up the muddy and overgrown slope of the old cliff, will make clear to the visitor why this side needed no artificial defences.

The scarp edge forms the straight south-western side of a D-shaped enclosure of about 0·1 hectare. The rest of the circuit is protected by two substantial banks rising nearly 3 metres above the ditch between them; their overall width is about 20 metres. There is no obvious entrance, but it was almost certainly at the north-west angle of the enclosure, between the ends of the ramparts and the cliff-top, which has probably been eroded for a metre or two. Near this point outside the fort is a spring. The interior is almost featureless, and may have been ploughed, but there is a hint of a possible hut floor about 6 metres in diameter against the inner bank on the north-east.

> *Wigtown Inv.* (1912), No. 199.
> *Preh. Scot.*, pp. 159–60.

BATHAMPTON DOWN (Somerset, ST 774 650; 200 metres).

This fort is unusually large, but not very strongly sited or defended. A single rampart and ditch enclosed an area of about 32 hectares, of irregular rounded oblong plan. The defences are mostly obliterated or badly damaged except on the west.

The ditch was originally 4·1 metres wide and about 1·5 to 2 metres deep, with nearly vertical sides and a flat bottom. It was separated from the rampart by a berm 3·5 metres wide. The rampart itself was 2·9 metres wide, revetted at the back with a single row of upright slabs, and at the front by a double row with laid masonry above, set at a slight batter. The interior was not examined, but occupation with early A-style pottery preceded the ramparts. The whole area of the fort has been covered by a system of small square fields, probably of the pre-Roman Iron Age, but certainly later than the defences.

G. J. Wainwright, *Trans. Bristol and Gloucester Arch. Soc.* LXXXVI (1967), pp. 42–59.

O. G. S. Crawford and A. Keiller, *Wessex from the Air* (Oxford, 1928), pp. 144–7, fig. 34, pl. 23 (air photo).

BEACON HILL (fig. 24; Hants., SU 458 572; 260 metres; pl. 11).

This finely situated fort is accessible to the public as an open space. It is protected by a bank, ditch and counterscarp bank, of

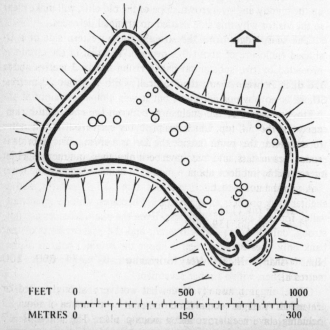

| FEET | 0 | | 500 | | 1000 |
| METRES | 0 | | 150 | | 300 |

Fig. 24   Beacon Hill. After J. P. Williams Freeman.

fairly uniform profile, some 55 metres wide overall. The area enclosed is 3·6 hectares. About twenty round hut platforms can be traced. There is one entrance, opening onto a ridge which forms a natural line of approach. Here the main rampart is inturned and linked to the counterscarp bank, and further protection is given by two slight crescentic banks, arranged as though to form a barbican with no banks lining the entrance passage.

J. P. Williams Freeman, *Field Archaeology* [in] ... *Hampshire* (London, 1915), p. 356 (plan).

BELTOUT (Sussex, TV 560 956; 60 metres).

Most of this fort has been lost by erosion. It must originally have been very large, though the single bank and ditch which protect it are of no great strength. It occupies the highest point of the down, and now forms an enclosure of lenticular plan, 1080 metres along the cliff edge and 320 metres across at its widest point, of 27 hectares.

VCH (Sussex) Vol. I (1905), pp. 455–6 (plan).

BICKERTON, *see* MAIDEN CASTLE.

BIGBERRY (fig. 25; Kent, TR 117 575; 60 metres; pp. 41, 66, 82).

This is almost certainly the place captured by Caesar in his expedition of 54 BC. Unfortunately, the north half is heavily wooded and the south planted with orchards; the banks are eroded, gravel pits have been opened in the interior, and the site is intersected by modern roads.

A single bank and ditch encloses about 10·7 hectares, and a slighter bank protects an annexe of 3·1 hectares, where a re-entrant valley forms a point of weakness. Even the main defences are not strong, only 9 metres wide overall, and the present crest of the bank only rises about 3 metres above the original bottom of the blunt V-shaped ditch; it may originally have been perhaps 1·5 metres higher, with a timber revetment.

Gravel digging has revealed what were probably rich Belgic graves, as well as occupation material, with much ironwork, including slave neck irons and a piece of a fire-dog, and agricultural implements. The published accounts record some Belgic C

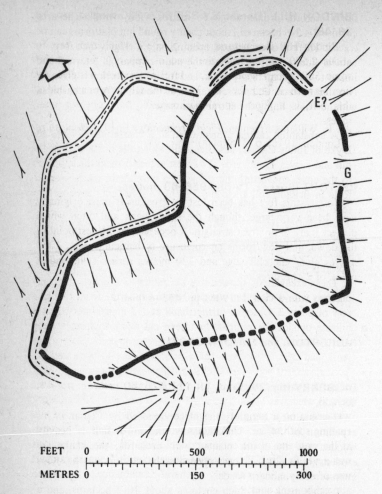

FEET   0   500   1000

METRES 0   150   300

Fig. 25   Bigberry. After R. F. Jessup.

ware from beneath a rampart; but the work as a whole must be of
more than one period, for a recent excavation at the east entrance
produced pot exclusively of Iron Age A (H 400?) from the bottom
of the ditch (*ex inf.* Frank Jenkins). This entrance proved to be
original.

R. F. Jessup, *Arch. J.* LXXXIX (1932), pp. 87–115 (description of site and finds); and with N. C. Cook, *Arch. Cantiana*
XLVIII (1936), pp. 151–68 (excavation report).

BINDON HILL (Dorset, SY 835 802; 160 metres; pp. 18, 36, 48).

Bindon Hill is a natural ridge of chalk which runs east for about 2,500 metres from the head of Lulworth Cove; a belt some 500 metres wide of fairly level arable and pastoral land lies between it and the sea. The cove, at the western end of this belt, is a good natural harbour, the only one for many miles.

A substantial rampart, mentioned in a charter of 1279 as the Dyke of Julius Caesar, has been built along the north edge of the hill and curves southwards at its west end to protect the approach to the cove, converting the whole area into one of the largest hill forts in Britain, still enclosing 114 hectares despite erosion. The total length of the rampart is 2,800 metres. The entrance, about 1,800 metres from the east end, is approached by a terraced roadway, and the ramparts are inturned. It is unusually wide. Excavations in 1950 did not reveal any guard chambers, nor any uprights for the gate.

These excavations showed that the rampart had been originally planned with a close-set wooden revetment at the front tied to a row of posts 3·7 metres further back at 1·3-metre intervals; the hillside outside the rampart had been cut away to form a steep scarp above a small ditch with a counterscarp bank. Before this work had been completed, there was a change in plan, and the front revetment was given up, the rampart being formed as a bank of earth behind a revetment formed of horizontal timbers placed behind what was to have been the rear row of posts. Later, work was begun on a rampart at right angles to the main defence and running south to the coast, which would have cut off 12 hectares at the west end of the enclosure, including the harbour; but this was never finished. The pottery associated with the main rampart was of A style, but with only a general resemblance to that found at neighbouring sites.

The excavator demonstrated that, without allowing for the cutting and transport of timber and using modern tools, sixty men could have completed the whole rampart in about a fortnight; but the evidence now available from the experimental earthwork (p. 56) suggests that with the tools available in the Iron Age the time needed would be at least twenty times as long for that number of workers. He considered the enclosure to be a 'beach-head' for an Iron Age invasion. An alternative solution would be to regard the work as intended to protect a trading post, for an appreciable amount of pottery was found, although investigation was restricted to four cuts through the rampart, and the area near the cove has not been examined.

Sir Mortimer Wheeler, *Ant. J.* XXXIII (1953), pp. 1–13 (plan).
Dorset Inv. II (1970), pt 3, pp. 489–92 (plan).

BLACKBURY CASTLE (fig. 26; Devon, SY 187 924; 180 metres; p. 71).

The enclosure straddles a narrow ridge, so that approach is easy from east or west but steep on north and south. The original entrance was to the south, the three gaps towards the other cardinal points being modern. The site was excavated during 1952–4, attention being concentrated on the entrance.

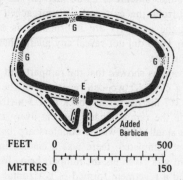

Fig. 26   Blackbury Castle. After K. M. Richardson.

The main rampart, enclosing 1·3 hectares, was built round a fairly long established settlement (of late A culture) soon after the arrival of B influences, about H 200. It consisted of a glacis-type bank with a blunt V-shaped ditch, the whole measuring 20 metres wide and 6 metres high overall; there may have been a flint breastwork. At the entrance, certainly on its east side and probably on both, the bank projected in a bastion with a vertical timber revetment. The gateway was 2·5 metres wide, between two pairs of posts. Each pair stood in a single large post pit 1·3 metres long from north to south; the arrangement probably supported a narrow bridge.

Not long after the main defence had been built the entrance was strengthened by the addition of a barbican, similar in many ways to the more elaborate structure in the second Iron Age phase at

Maiden Castle. This barbican, never quite finished, provided an elongated entrance passage, closed at its outer end by gates, presumably of two leaves, in an opening 4·5 metres wide between two large posts.

Not much of the interior was cleared, but within the main rampart near the gateway a group of post holes indicated a rather lightly built hut, 3 metres square with a porch. Pottery and sling stones were plentiful throughout the site.

A. Young and K. M. Richardson, *Devon Arch. Exploration Soc.* V. 2 and 3 (1954–5), pp. 43–67 (with plan from survey by J. V. Ramsden).

BOCHASTLE (fig. 27; Perth, NN 601 075; 180 metres; p. 45).

This little fort is exceptionally well preserved. It is almost circular enclosing 0·2 hectare, and protected by four massive ramparts with intervening ditches; the outermost bank has no accompanying ditch, but is too large to be described as merely a counterscarp bank. There are no artificial defences on the east side, for the ground there falls away almost precipitously.

The only certain entrance is from the north. The approach is by a gap between the main outer rampart and the end of a relatively weak bank, with an internal quarry ditch which protects a plateau of nearly level ground. The fort itself is then reached by a path between the ends of the ramparts and the top of the natural slope.

At the southern end there is a puzzling elaboration of the plan, with a gap left in the outermost main bank and a small space outside protected by a scarp; there is also a break, which could be ancient, in the line of the innermost bank. The two intermediate banks, though, are continuous, and there is nothing to indicate that they were ever interrupted. Various explanations are possible, but cannot be tested by surface evidence.

The interior is featureless except for a well.

'Bochastle' refers to a Roman fort near the farm of that name. The hill fort is known merely as Dunmore, the 'big fort'.

D. Christison, *Proc. Soc. Ant. Scot.* XXXIV (1899–1900), p. 63 (plan).
Preh. Scot., p. 147.

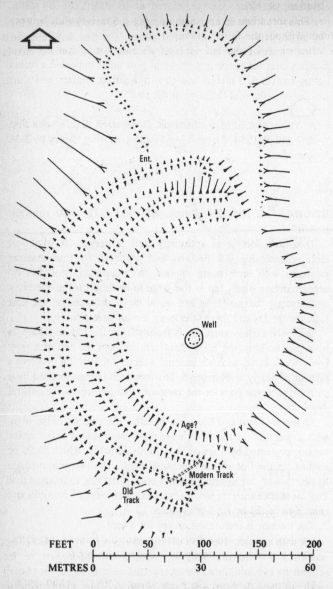

Ent.

Well

Age?

Modern Track

Old
Track

FEET   0   50   100   150   200
METRES 0   30   60

Fig. 27   Bochastle. Based on D. Christison.

BONCHESTER HILL (fig. 28; Roxburgh, NT 595 117; 310 metres; pl. 12).

This fort seems to have had a history similar to Hownam Rings, but without the initial palisaded phase. The first and innermost structure was protected mainly by a single bank some 3 metres

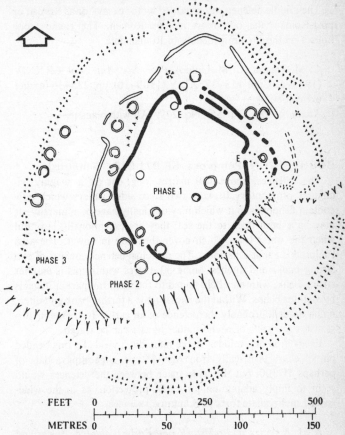

Fig. 28 Bonchester Hill. After C. M. Guido.

thick with a rough revetment of large stones on the outer face. This enclosed 0·7 hectare, and was supplemented for part of the circuit by two additional banks revetted on both sides; the overall width of these defences was 16 to 20 metres. They may be dated to H 100.

Two further rampart systems encircled the hill. The middle

defence was faced with upright slabs trigged with spalls, with laid stones above, and enclosed 2·4 hectares. The outermost comprised a pair of earth and rubble banks heaped up from deep steep-sided quarry ditches on their *inner* sides, the inner bank having a double palisade of stakes on the top. The area enclosed was 2·6 hectares, with an annexe of a further hectare.

The middle defence was regarded by the excavator as Roman or post-Roman, the outermost as post-Roman. The round stone houses on the site are probably of Roman date.

C. M. Piggott (C. M. Guido), *Proc. Soc. Ant. Scot.* LXXXIV (1949–50), pp. 113–37; XLIV (1909–10), pp. 225–36 (earlier excavation).
Roxburgh Inv. I (1956), No. 277. (All with plans.)

BOSHERSTON (Pembroke, SR 971 948; 15 metres).

The defences, about 180 metres long, cut off a roughly tri-angular promontory between two steep-sided valleys which now contain fishponds, but which may originally have been marshy, or may have been open to the sea; they are exceptionally beautiful when the water lilies which cover them are in flower. The area enclosed is about 2 hectares. The principal defence consists of two strong banks and ditches. Some 30 metres within this is another strong bank, with no ditch, joined to the main rampart at its ends by slighter banks. Within the enclosure is a further bank and ditch, much eroded, probably the defence of an earlier fort. One or two slots for the walls of round timber houses can be traced.

Excavation of a midden in the main ditch yielded a ring-headed pin of characteristically Iron Age A type, suggesting a date of perhaps H 300, but the wide space between the defences would seem to imply adaptation for cattle protection, as in the wide-spaced multivallate forts of B culture.

A. H. A. Hogg in *Prehistoric and Early Wales* (ed. Foster and Daniel (Routledge & Kegan Paul, London, 1965)), p. 134 (plan).
T. C. Lethbridge, *Arch. Cambrensis* LXXXIII (1928), p. 177 (note on excavation).

BOURGES, *see* AVARICUM.

BREDON HILL (figs. 9, 29; Gloucester, SO 958 400; 290 metres; pp. 17, 49, 69, 73, 84, p. 13).

The north end of this hill has been converted into a strong fortress by the construction of two ramparts. The site was well excavated in 1935–7. The interpretation offered here differs from that of the excavator in regarding the outer rampart as the earlier (see end).

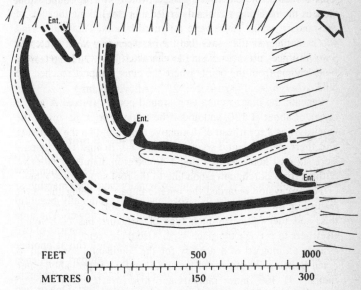

Fig. 29   Bredon Hill. After T. C. Hencken.

The first defence measured 30 metres overall, comprising a V-shaped rock-cut ditch originally about 10 metres wide and 4·5 deep, a berm 6·3 metres wide, and a bank 13·5 metres wide and still 2·4 metres high; the bank had a sloping back, but was revetted in front with a dry-built wall which still stood more than a metre high where examined. The enclosed area was about 7·1 hectares. No entrances survive, but they were presumably between the rampart ends and the cliff edge, and have been destroyed by landslips. Some pottery and other objects belonging to the last phase were found on top of the bank, but nothing contemporary with its construction.

The inner rampart was of glacis construction with a V-shaped ditch, and measured 33 metres wide by 11 high overall; it probably had a timber breastwork. It enclosed almost exactly half the area within the outer bank. There was a single entrance near the middle. This showed three phases of construction, the first being a simple overlapping of the rampart ends; the timber details had been destroyed. In the two later phases, this was converted to a passage nearly 40 metres long and 7·5 metres wide between inturned rampart ends (fig. 9). There were three post holes for a gate at the inner end, and two upright posts set 3 metres apart halfway along the entrance passage, which with uprights set in slots in the revetting walls had carried a bridge linking the ends of the rampart walk. There were no guard houses. The final period was essentially similar, save that the passageway was straightened. Two inturned entrances of similar character, but even longer, were built leading from the points where the outer rampart reached the cliff.

Beneath the inner rampart was found pottery (mixed A and B style), of about H 100, and under the second period paving of the gateway was a spearhead of distinctive type found on the continent and there dated to mid-second century BC. Behind the rampart were six post holes set in a ring 3·5 metres in diameter, with two outliers for a porch, corresponding to the roof supports of a hut.

The excavator regarded the outer rampart as being the latest feature on the site, but the evidence of the report does not require this, and the wall-berm-ditch type of structure has been found elsewhere to precede the glacis type. Also there seems no reason to assume an interval of a century for the continental spearhead to reach Britain. The history of the site, therefore, is probably: outer rampart H 300; inner rampart and first (overlapping) gateway H 150; successive gateways perhaps H 100 and H 50 or later; final destruction early in the first century AD, or perhaps rather earlier.

The destruction of the fortress had left macabre and dramatic evidence in the gate passage. Clearance revealed the remains of at least sixty-four human bodies, which had been literally hacked to pieces and left where they fell. To quote one short extract from the report: 'Thus at 18 feet from the gate, two human trunks were found with but one arm and forearm between them, and neither legs nor head . . . At 41 feet from the gate there was a pair of legs and a lower jaw; 5 feet from these legs was a hand with all the small bones intact and in position.' This furious massacre is attributed by the excavator to Belgic invaders rather than Romans. Reason for this apparently barbarous behaviour may be supplied by the discovery at the gateway itself of the remains of six heads lying roughly in line among burned timber, as though they had been displayed above the gate. Were they perhaps from captives taken by the inhabitants?

T. C. Hencken, *Arch. J.* XCV (1938), pp. 1–111.

BREEDON-ON-THE-HILL (Leicester, SK 406 234; 120 metres; p. 17).

This large fort, of 9·2 hectares, encircles the summit of the hill on which the church stands. It is of a rather pointed pear-shaped plan, about 410 metres north to south by 270 metres, protected by a single bank and ditch with a counterscarp bank. The eastern two-thirds is being rapidly destroyed by quarrying, and has been the subject of two campaigns of rescue excavation which have produced a considerable quantity of A pottery, and have shown that the defences include work of two periods. The only certain entrance was from the west, along the present lane south of the church. It was deeply inturned.

There was some occupation before the erection of the defences (H 250). The first rampart was revetted in front by a palisade of posts about 0·25 metre in diameter, set in a palisade slot and spaced at 0·7-metre centres. The rear had a revetment, or perhaps merely a kerb, supported by similar posts spaced nearly twice as far apart, set in separate post holes. From this the bank sloped up to a wall walk probably about 3·5 metres above ground level. The front of the rampart was separated by a berm 2·5 metres wide from a broad flat-bottomed ditch, 8 metres wide and 2 deep, with a small counterscarp bank.

This rampart was reconstructed, after what may have been no more than half a century, by stabilizing the back with a turf layer and building a wall of the same material in front, capping the whole with a dry-stone breastwork.

K. M. Kenyon, *Trans. Leicester Arch. Soc.* XXVI (1950), pp. 17–82.

J. S. Wacher, *Ant. J.* XLIV (1964), pp. 122–42.

BROWN CATERTHUN (fig. 30; Angus, NO 555 668; 287 metres; pl. 14).

This is less impressive than its neighbour the White Caterthun, but is one of the finest specimens of the forts with multiple entrances, having no less than nine through its main defences. The whole structure seems undisturbed, and its character can easily be followed on the ground. This and the White Caterthun are readily accessible, and both are under the guardianship of the Department of the Environment.

The defences fall into three groups. The central enclosure, probably the earliest, was protected by a single wall, now so heavily robbed as to be scarcely traceable. It encloses 0·4 hectares. Near

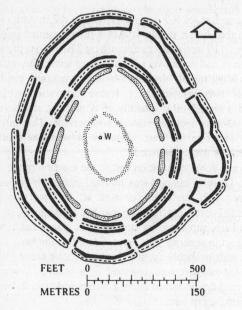

Fig. 30   The Brown Caterthun. After R. W. Feachem.

the middle is a small artificial water hole which may well be contemporary. From the traces of the wall, the ground falls gently to the second rampart system, enclosing 2·2 hectares. This consisted of a fairly substantial stone wall, now mostly a grass-covered bank. Separated from this by some 8 or 10 metres, and at a lower level, but running roughly parallel, is an earthen bank accompanied by an external ditch with a very slight counterscarp bank. There are nine entrances through this system. All seem to be original. They show no elaboration, being simply gaps in the ramparts with accompanying causeways across the ditch.

Outside this ring the ground falls fairly steeply to the outermost line of defences, which is probably also the latest, though it could be contemporary with the second line. This also consists of a bank,

probably originally mainly of stone, accompanied by a second
bank with an outer ditch. The spacing is less uniform than in the
second ring, and in one place on the east the two lines of bank
diverge considerably. There are eight entrances through this
system. At all except the two on the west the inner and outer lines
are linked by slight transverse banks defining the entrance passages. The fact that the inner entrances do not correspond exactly
to the outer ones does not necessarily imply that they are of
different dates, for the detours involved are not large. It may be
noted that the outer system follows very closely the upper edge of
what would be dead ground to an observer on the second rampart.

D. Christison, *Proc. Soc. Ant. Scot.* XXXIV (1899–1900),
p. 105 (plan p. 102).

R. W. Feachem in *I A N B*, p. 74 (plan).

Now see also J. K. St Joseph, *Antiquity* XLVIII (1974), pp. 53–
4 and pl. VIII (air photo); he regards the second rampart system
as being of two phases.

BUCKLAND RINGS (fig. 31; Hants., SZ 314 968; 15 metres).

A roughly trapezoidal enclosure of 3 hectares, strongly
defended by two banks and ditches with a counterscarp bank, and
perhaps a third ditch in places, the whole measuring about 43
metres overall. The inner rampart was revetted by an inner and

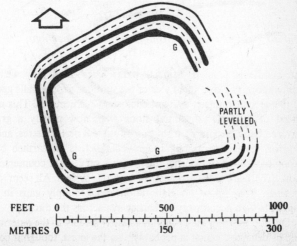

Fig. 31   Buckland Rings. After C. F. C. Hawkes.

outer line of posts, the middle had an outer revetment only. The entrance was deeply inturned, the cheeks of the passage being revetted with turf. There had been a pair of posts at the inner end, 3 metres apart, but no guard houses. Pottery was sparse, in the style of A with admixture of B, and slight C influence. The fort may have been dismantled by the Romans. Date of occupation perhaps H 50 to AD 43.

C. F. C. Hawkes, *Proc. Hants. Field Club* XIII (1935–7), pp. 131–64.

BURGHEAD (fig. 32; Moray, NJ 109 691; 10 metres; p. 63).

Until the beginning of the last century this must have been one of the most impressive fortresses in Scotland, but the then land-owner decided to establish a small sea port here and destroyed most of the defences. Two pieces of good fortune mitigate this disaster. A fairly accurate survey was made before the destruction; and most of the interior remains unbuilt-over, and is thus available for future scientific investigation. What remains shows how note-worthy the original works must have been.

In surface appearance the fortress must have seemed a fairly normal promontory fort, though the great size of its defences

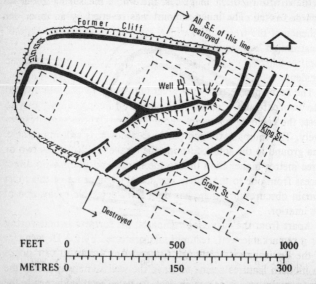

Fig. 32   Burghead. Based on W. Roy.

would have been exceptional for this region, and would have seemed more appropriate to southern Britain. Nevertheless, successive excavations have shown that so far as present knowledge goes the place is unique, probably a Pictish capital.

The evidence for this comes from three radiocarbon determinations using charcoal from the rampart, which shows that the earliest possible date of construction is in the latter half of the Roman period; that is, in this region, after their latest recorded intrusion. The work could even be as late as the seventh century AD.

The ramparts seem originally to have been 7 or 8 metres thick and to have stood at least 6 metres high. Their outer faces were formed by a solid stone revetment, and the inner was well built of laid sandstone slabs, nearly vertical but stepped back slightly at intervals of rather less than a metre. In places, long well-hewn oak planks were intercoursed with these slabs, forming part of the wall face, and occasionally, at irregular intervals, planks or logs were set at right angles to the wall. These did not penetrate more than 1 or 2 metres, but projected from the face of the wall. Excavators in the last century found that these were joined to the longitudinal timbers by iron spikes, but none of these was found during the more recent work. Pending full publication, it must remain an open question whether the projecting beams formed steps for access to the rampart walk. These works were for a long time regarded as the only British example of true *murus gallicus*, on the evidence of the iron spikes which are diagnostic for that type of construction on the continent. The radiocarbon evidence now implies that the resemblance is no more than a remarkable accident.

The space protected by the great multiple defences was divided into two parts by a substantial rampart running almost east to west; the enclosed areas are about 1·2 and 1·6 hectares respectively. The rampart, though partly cast down, is still impressive. The ground to the south, forming the smaller enclosure, is two or three metres higher than that to the north, and there is no direct access from one to the other. The social significance of this must remain obscure until there has been some scientific excavation of the interior.

Apart from the surviving ramparts, the fortress is noteworthy for a remarkable well, restored and protected by the Department of the Environment. Although General Roy's plan superimposed on modern features seems to leave the well some way inside the lower enclosure, it seems in fact to have been underneath the actual bank. Indeed, the appearance of a semicircular bastion on Roy's plan may be a representation of the crater left by the collapsed roof before excavation. In any case, the approach would have been from within the fort, and there seems to be no need to regard it as anything other than the inhabitants' water supply, though it has been variously described as Roman, early Christian or medieval, and as a well, a bath and a baptistry.

The most notable objects known from the site are carved stones, especially some with incised figures of bulls. Other relics, at least those which have been adequately recorded, are sparse, but range from the Roman to the Viking period, so the place may well have been inhabited for some centuries, though the evidence is not at all conclusive. There can be no doubt that it was destroyed by fire, for the timberwork reinforcing the ramparts was extensively burned.

Burghead cannot be identified with any place known from historical records, but the size of its defences and the number of incised slabs mark it out as one of the main centres of Pictish power, and thus of primary importance for their history. It contrasts strongly in many ways with such 'documented' fortresses as Dundurn. One must earnestly hope that the appropriate local authorities fully appreciate the importance of what survives, and that when the western part of the nineteenth-century town requires to be rebuilt the opportunity to investigate the remains of the destroyed ramparts will not be overlooked.

W. Roy, *Military Antiquities of the Romans in N. Britain* (1793), pl. XXXIII. This plan is not quite accurate in detail.

J. Macdonald, *Proc. Soc. Ant. Scot.* IV (1860–62), pp. 2–51.

H. W. Young, *ibid.* XXV (1890–91), pp. 435–7; XXVII (1892–3), pp. 86–91.

A. Small, *Scottish Arch. Forum* (1969), pp. 61–8 (recent excavation).

I. Henderson, *The Picts* (London, 1967), pls 14 (air photo) and 32 (bull).

Preh. Scot., p. 138.

BURNSWARK (fig. 33; Dumfries, NY 185 785; 280 metres; p. 84).

Burnswark (or Birrenswark) is one of the most important hill-forts in south-west Scotland, but is even more noteworthy for its remains of Roman siege-works. These latter were fairly thoroughly investigated as long ago as 1898, and an excellent report published, but proper examination of the hill-fort did not take place until recently.

The siege-works consist of two Roman forts, fairly typical though rather irregular in plan. The north fort is about 300 metres long, and had six gateways (four can still be traced), of which three were protected by the characteristic device of a short length of

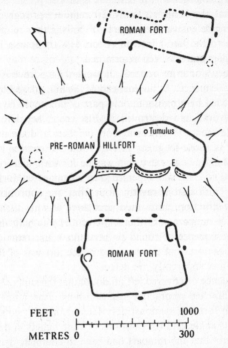

Fig. 33 Burnswark. After D. Christison and J. Barbour.

bank and ditch set in advance of the gateway. The south fort is more regular, about 260 by 200 metres. There is a gateway in the middle of each of the east, south and west sides, protected as in the north fort, but in the north rampart there were three entrances, one facing each of the hill-fort's gateways, and each with a large circular mound about 3·5 metres high set in front of it. These large mounds are convincingly interpreted as bases for stone-throwing engines.

There is a small enclosure, an earlier Roman fortlet, in the north-east corner of the south fort. A bank, which once linked the two Roman forts round the base of the hill, was formerly regarded as part of the siege-works, but is now generally accepted as a relatively recent field boundary. Other small earthworks at the base of the hill are also probably the sites of farmsteads unconnected with the major earthworks.

The hill-fort plan suggests two periods, in one of which only the western summit was defended, but where this rampart crosses the interior of the larger fort it is very slight. The recent excavations showed that the bank was only 30 centimetres high, though it gained some defensive advantage by following the top of a natural scarp. Up to the latest interim report (1970) its relation to the main rampart had not been determined.

Mr Jobey's interim reports, however, have revealed a very interesting sequence. At the east end of the hill, all visible defences were preceded by a palisade; only part of this could be traced, as the later works had destroyed it. Elsewhere, beneath the main rampart, evidence was found for (another?) double palisade, composed of close-set posts in two rows 3 metres apart; radio-carbon dating indicates that this was built within a century either way of 500 BC. This was superseded by a bank of scraped-up earth and rubble with a stone revetment in front; the outer bank was of similar construction, unrevetted, and there was no ditch. Finally, on the main rampart, a further bank of turf was built up. Within the fort, a sequence of round timber-built houses was identified. The small enclosure at the west end of the fort was of Roman or later date, and apparently not defensive.

The evidence discovered left no doubt that the supposed Roman siege was directed as practice against a long-disused hill-fort. The large south fort was demonstrably later than the second-century fortlet in its angle, and the positions of sling bullets in the hill-fort left no doubt that the rampart had been in complete decay at the time of the 'attack'. Surprisingly, at the two gateways examined, the remains of the pre-Roman entrance were found buried beneath a later pavement set on a slightly different line, and apparently not part of a defended gate. The excavator suggests, convincingly, that these later structures correspond to a Roman practice firing range.

D. Christison and J. Barbour, *Proc. Soc. Ant. Scot.* XXXIII (1898–9), pp. 198–242.

G. Jobey in *Discovery and Excavation in Scotland* (1966) p. 21; (1967) p. 23; (1968) p. 20; (1970) p. 21 (interim reports).

BURY HILL (Hants., SU 346 435; 95 metres).

This fort is one of those investigated as part of the important planned series of excavations by C. F. C. Hawkes (p. 25).

It occupies a bold spur of chalk jutting out to the north-west. The defences comprise two periods. The earlier rampart now appears as a scarp about 2·5 metres high, forming an oval 370 metres from north-west to south-east, by 330 metres, enclosing 9 hectares. It was originally a bank and ditch 16 metres wide overall. The associated pottery was of late A style, H 300.

After an interval of at least a century, the site was refortified with a bank, ditch and counterscarp bank, 36 metres wide overall; these still remain well preserved. There were two entrances, to the north-west and south-east, both simple gaps. This enclosure was almost circular, 250 metres in diameter, its circumference coinciding with that of the earlier work on the south-east. The pottery showed some B influence.

Finally, about H 50, the place came under the control of the Belgae.

C. F. C. Hawkes, *Proc. Hants. Field Club* XIV.3 (1940), pp. 291–337.

O. G. S. Crawford and A. Keiller, *Wessex from the Air*, p. 94, pl. XIa (air photo).

THE CABURN (fig. 34; Sussex, TQ 444 089; 150 metres.

This is one of the South Downs group, but smaller than most, enclosing only 1·1 hectares. In its present form it is defended in part by a double bank and ditch, but this is the result of long development.

The much larger but unfinished fort at Ranscombe stands a short distance away to the north-west, but although both are of A culture conventional dating seems to indicate an interval of perhaps two centuries after the abandonment of that site before the Caburn hill was settled; this may be placing too great reliance on the precise dating for pot of this period.

The Caburn was excavated in 1937–8, and the results indicated an initial occupation as an unfortified village, starting H 300 and continuing to H 100. The inner rampart, of simple glacis type with no revetment, was then built. The entrance passage was revetted with timber between slightly inturned ramparts, the gate being supported by two posts at the inner end. On the north of the entrance the bank had an end T-shaped in plan, the outward

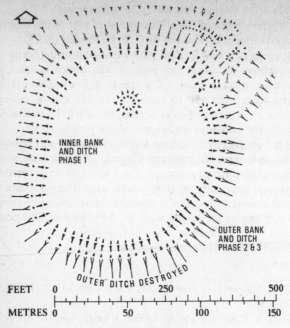

INNER BANK
AND DITCH
PHASE 1

OUTER BANK
AND DITCH
PHASE 2 & 3

OUTER DITCH DESTROYED

FEET	0		250		500
METRES	0	50	100	150	

Fig. 34   The Caburn. After A. E. Wilson.

projection being perhaps intended to give command of the approach.

After a considerable time, a second rampart was built outside the earlier line, accompanied by a broad shallow ditch, resembling the type of defence found at Fécamp in France and at Oldbury in Kent. This development is regarded as a reaction to the Roman invasion. The rampart was revetted along the front by a line of posts set very regularly at 34-centimetres centre to centre and at the back by a palisade. These were linked by horizontal timbers. Near the entrance this second rampart filled the inner ditch and its width was greater than elsewhere, a mass of chalk being built up in front of the close-set posts. The gateway at this stage was through a rectangular setting of four posts.

If these defences were intended to resist the Romans, they did not succeed, for the place seems then to have been deserted for two or three centuries at least. Subsequently the ramparts were again strengthened, which by analogy with events at Cissbury may have been late in the Roman period. Finally, in the twelfth century AD, the defences were again made effective, probably as an adulterine earth and timber castle in the anarchy of Stephen's reign.

A. E. Wilson, *Sussex Arch. Coll.* LXXIX (1938), pp. 169–94; LXXX (1939), pp. 193–213 (plans, excavation).
C. F. C. Hawkes, ibid. LXXX (1939), pp. 217–66 (discussion of pottery).

CAER CARADOC, CHURCH STRETTON (fig. 35; Shropshire, SO 477 953; 450 metres; p. 21, pl. 15).

This is the most impressively situated of the three forts assigned (wrongly) to Caratacus. It occupies a steep-sided ridge. The space

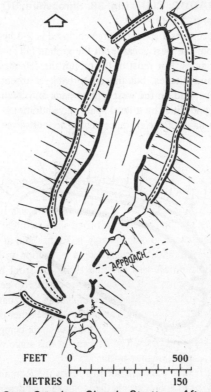

APPROACH

FEET 0   500
METRES 0   150

Fig. 35   Caer Caradoc, Church Stretton. After Victoria County History.

enclosed is an irregular oval 380 metres long, area 2·6 hectares. Its surface is irregular, and falls some 30 metres from north to south. The main rampart was a stone wall following the crest of the slopes, and utilizing some stretches of natural crag. About 25 metres from this, for part of the circuit, there is an additional bank thrown down from an internal quarry ditch. The entrance is located so that it is commanded by a natural outcrop on the south as well as by the slope of the hill on the north; the ramparts are slightly inturned. A well engineered terrace way leads up the hill to it from the north-east. Many hut platforms exist within the enclosure.

VCH Shropshire I (1908), p. 361 (plan).

CAER CARADOC, CLUN (fig. 36; Shropshire, SO 310 758; 400 metres; p. 21, pl. 15).

The fort occupies a spur; the area enclosed is 2·3 hectares. The approach from the west is easy, but the ground falls away steeply on the other sides. For most of the circuit the defences consist of two banks and ditches, but the outer bank is absent along the southern slope, and on the west a third bank and ditch, separated from the second ditch by a level space, give additional protection on the south flank of the entrance. There are entrances at the east

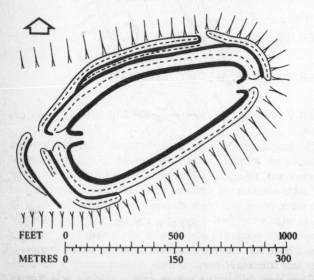

FEET   0   500   1000

METRES 0   150   300

Fig. 36   Caer Caradoc, Clun. After Victoria County History.

and west ends, both inturned. Half a dozen round hut platforms exist near the east end, and near the middle of the enclosure is a collapsed shaft, perhaps a well.

This fort was known as Caer Caradoc before 1700.

VCH Shropshire I (1908), pp. 362–3 (plan).

CAER CARADOG (Denbigh, SH 968 479; 380 metres; p. 21).

This is a simple oval enclosure, 125 × 150 metres, area 1·5 hectares, defended by a single strong bank and a ditch. The bank is of dump construction, perhaps of two periods. The entrance, a simple gap, was on the east; there are several other breaks in the bank, probably recent.

Excavations in 1963–4 by R. G. Livens yielded no relics and no traces of timberwork even at the entrance. A slight inner bank is probably recent, not an earlier line of defence.

The name Caer Caradog is not recorded before 1800.

Ellis Davies, *Prehistoric and Roman Remains of Denbighshire* (Cardiff, 1929), pp. 234–6 (plan).
R. G. Livens in *Archaeology in Wales* 3 (1963) No. 7, and 4 (1964) No. 8, gives a summary note on the excavation.

CAER HELEN, *see* PEN-Y-GAER, LLANBEDR-Y-CENNIN.

CAER OGYRFAN, *see* OLD OSWESTRY.

CAER Y TWR (fig. 37; Anglesey, SH 219 829; 220 metres; p. 84).

The irregular rocky summit of Holyhead Mountain has been protected on its more accessible sides by a single substantial masonry wall, to enclose 7 hectares. The entrance, on the north-east, takes advantage of a natural cleft in the rock to give the effect of a short inturn, but is not otherwise elaborated. The wall is 4 metres wide where best preserved, and has a stepped back, the parapet walk being 1·3 metres wide and about 1 metre above ground level, the front rising at least 1 metre higher. In places the outer face still stands 3 metres high. A short stretch of the north wall has been deliberately thrown down, possibly as a Roman military exercise. No hut sites can be identified in the interior. The

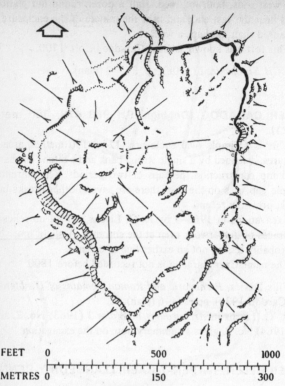

FEET   0   500   1000

METRES 0   150   300

Fig. 37   Caer y Twr. After W. Gardner.

fort takes its name from a square tower of mortared masonry,
probably Roman, which formerly existed on the summit; it is now
hardly traceable.

The remains are in official guardianship.

W. Gardner, *Arch. Cambrensis* (1934), pp. 156–73.
See also *Anglesey Inv.* (1937, reprinted 1970), pp. 24–5.

CAESAR'S CAMP, EASTHAMPSTEAD (fig. 38; Berks., SU 863 657; 130 metres; p. 21).

This is a large univallate fort, of 7·8 hectares. It is notable,
apart from its size and fictitious association with Caesar, for its
curious oak leaf plan, which results from the rampart following the
edges of small natural valleys which have cut back into the sandy
plateau which it occupies. Two of these re-entrants have been

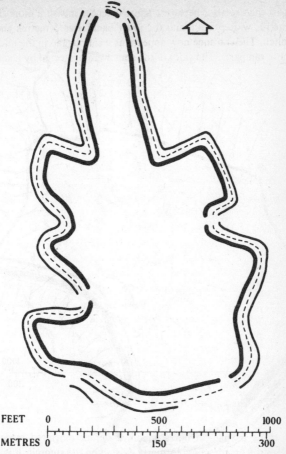

FEET 0 ⊢⊢⊢⊢⊢⊢⊢⊢⊢⊢⊢⊢ 500 ⊢⊢⊢⊢⊢⊢⊢⊢⊢⊢ 1000
METRES 0 150 300

*Fig. 38 Caesar's Camp, Easthampstead. After Victoria
    County History.*

adapted to form entrances, and there seem to be two more, to
north and south. Superficially, they seem to be simple gaps, but the
site has never been excavated.

VCH Berks. I (1906), pp. 256–7.

CAESAR'S CAMP, FARNHAM (fig. 39; Hants., SU 825 500; 180 metres; p. 21).

The end of a steep-sided spur projecting from a level gravel
plateau has been fortified by a double bank and ditch across the

neck to enclose 10·2 hectares. These defences measure more than 40 metres wide overall, and the inner bank rises 5 metres above the ditch. The entrance now appears as a simple gap in the middle of these ramparts. The sides of the spur were protected by a single

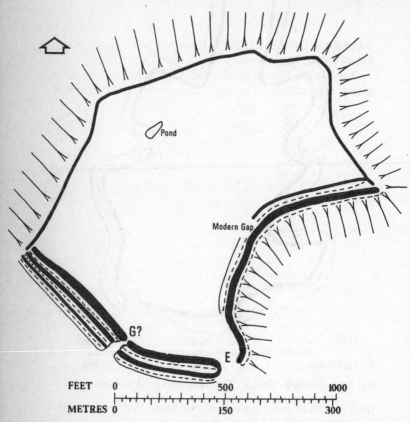

Fig. 39   Caesar's Camp, Farnham. After Victoria County History.

bank which has mostly been reduced to a scarp, but on the south-east the bank, ditch and counterscarp bank survive. The interior shows no trace of dwellings, but contains a pond, and a spring breaks out just outside the rampart on the north-east.

J. P. Williams Freeman, *Field Archaeology* [in] . . . *Hampshire* (London, 1915), p. 366 (plan).

CAESAR'S CAMP, FOLKESTONE (Kent, TR 214 379; 130 metres above OD; p. 21).

This is a twelfth-century earthwork castle.

A. H. L. F. Pitt-Rivers, *Archaeologia* vol. 47 (1883), pp. 429–65.

CAESAR'S CAMP, KESTON, Holwood Hill (fig. 40; Kent, TQ 421 640; 120 metres; p. 21).

Only interim reports on this fort are available as yet, work having been interrupted by the untimely death of the excavator,

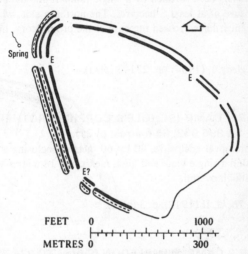

Fig. 40   Caesar's Camp, Keston. Based on Vetusta Monumenta.

but it is such an important and interesting site that some description must be included here.

Much of the circuit was destroyed more than a century ago, but a plan exists showing that the area enclosed was 16·8 hectares, protected by a double bank and ditch, with a counterscarp bank in places. Their overall width, including the counterscarp bank, amounted to 42 metres, the main inner and outer banks being now 17 metres wide by 2·5 high and 7 by 1·2 metres respectively, the ditches 9·8 by 4·5 metres original depth, and 6·7 by 2·5 metres. The inner bank had reached this form in three stages, all associated with pottery of B style. The west gateway, which used a natural gulley to form an inturn, had an entrance passage 26 metres long, with a massive revetment of flint walling between timber uprights; all had been burned *in situ*.

Mrs N. Piercy Fox, *Arch. Cantiana* LXXI, pp. 243–5; LXXII, xlviii, lxiii; LXXIII, xlviii.
Vetusta Monumenta vol. IV (1815), pl. X (plan).

CAESAR'S CAMP, SANDY (Bedford, TL 179 490; 45 metres; p. 21).

A spur has been fortified by a single rampart and ditch to give an enclosure of at least 3 hectares. The northern side, where the rampart must have crossed the base of the promontory, has been destroyed.

VCH Beds. I, (1904) pp. 271–3 (plan).

CAESAR'S CAMP (SCHOLE'S COPPICE), ROTHERHAM (Yorks., SK 395 952; 85 metres; p. 21).

A simple oval enclosure, 80 by 60 metres, enclosing 0·3 hectares within a single bank and ditch measuring 18 metres wide by 5 metres high overall.

VCH Yorks. II (1912), p. 3 (plan).

CAESAR'S CAMP, WIMBLEDON (Surrey, TQ 224 711; 45 metres; p. 21).

The fort, formerly called Bensbury, is almost circular in plan, slightly flattened on the north side, with a single rampart enclosing 4·3 hectares. Its defences have been partly levelled by a nineteenth-century builder; happily he was prevented from completing the destruction.

A section cut for a water main in 1937 showed that the rampart had been of gravel between timber revetments front and rear, 9 metres apart, and separated by a berm 3 metres wide from a ditch about 10 metres wide by at least 3 metres deep. The pottery was of A style, H 250. There was no indication of more than one period of use.

A. W. G. Lowther, *Arch. J*. CII (1945), pp. 15–20.

CAESAR'S CAMP, WOLLASTON (Shropshire, SJ 324 120; p. 21).

This is a twelfth-century earthwork castle.

CAESAR'S HILL, *see* CISSBURY.

CAMELOT, *see* SOUTH CADBURY.

CAMP TOPS, *see* MOREBATTLE.

CARLWARK (Derby, SK 260 815; 370 metres; p. 58, pl. 17).

Photo. Page 307 Backcover

This well preserved and accessible fort occupies an oblong plateau with steep scarps on all sides except the north-west. The area enclosed measures about 170 metres north-west to south-east by 50 metres wide (0·9 hectares). The steep sides are strengthened by a revetment wall joining the intervals between the crags, and the accessible west end is defended by a large bank of turf 8·5 metres wide revetted in front by a wall of large blocks standing 2·5 metres high. This must be nearly its original height, for owing to the consolidation of the turf the upper courses have tilted backwards instead of falling into ruin. The gateway, about 1·5 metres wide, is close to the southern end of this rampart; the revetment wall curves back on each side of the entrance passage, which is approached by a natural gully cutting into the steep slope.

Slight excavations by F. G. Simpson in 1950 revealed the construction of the rampart but produced no evidence of date. Mrs Guido, in her discussion, draws attention to the use of turf in the known post-Roman defences at Traprain Law, but does not regard this as secure evidence for the date of Carlwark.

C. M. Piggott (C. M. Guido), *Antiquity* XXV (1951), pp. 210–11 (plan).

CARN BODUAN, *see* GARN BODUAN.

CARN BREA (fig. 41; Cornwall, SW 686 407; 225 metres).

This hill is one of the most important and interesting archaeological sites in southern Britain, but has never even been

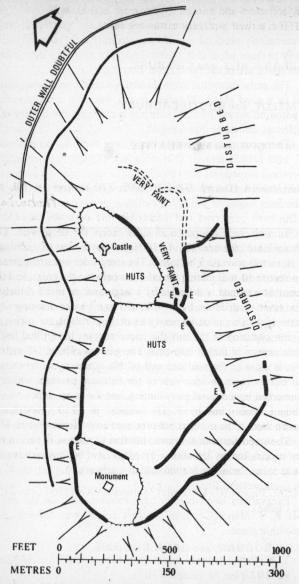

OUTER WALL DOUBTFUL

DISTURBED

VERY FAINT

VERY FAINT

Castle

HUTS

E   E

E

HUTS

E

DISTURBED

E

E

E

Monument

FEET   0   500   1000

METRES 0   150   300

Fig. 41   Carn Brea. Based on S. Hill and H. O'N Hencken;
scale approximate.

adequately planned as a whole, and has suffered much disturbance by collectors and miners. (But now see note at end.)

The earliest occupation was neolithic, and nineteenth-century excavations indicated that it was unusually rich; some of the huts may perhaps be of this period, but more probably they, like the ramparts, are of the pre-Roman Iron Age.

The early excavator accompanied his report with what appears to be a good plan of the western end, but until a really accurate contoured survey of the whole hill is available the history of the defences cannot be disentangled.

The accompanying plan is based on a combination of those by S. Hill (1895) and H. O'N. Hencken (1932), supplemented by personal inspection, but should only be regarded as a sketch. The monument and castle are shown for convenience of reference. The southern slopes of the hill are thickly overgrown and much disturbed.

Tentatively, at least four stages may be recognized in the evolution of the remains. In each the rampart was a substantial stone wall, now much robbed. The earliest was probably the small enclosure (0·6 hectares) round the summit on which the monument now stands. An extension – eastward, as in all subsequent additions – added another 3 hectares to the area, stopping a little west of where the castle now stands. The next phase took in the castle site, adding a further 2 hectares; the double wall on the south-east side of this may imply two periods of work. Finally, the whole hill was fortified, increasing the total area to about 14 or 15 hectares. Again, the double wall may indicate two periods. Of the numerous round dwellings whose foundations can still be traced, some probably belong to each period; several grouped near the castle seem to have obliterated the supposed earliest rampart.

The importance of this great hill-fort is emphasized not merely by its size but by the discovery of a hoard of at least seventeen gold coins, dating from about 50 BC; such coins are extremely rare in south-western Britain.

Excavations have recently been recommenced on the site (by Mr R. J. Mercer), though the first season was devoted to the neolithic phase.

T. C. Peter, *Journal Royal Inst. Cornwall* XIII.1 (1895), pp. 92–102 (plan by Sampson Hill).

H. O'N. Hencken, *Cornwall and Scilly* (County Archaeologies, Methuen, 1932) *passim*, plan fig. 36, p. 128.

Recent work: R. J. Mercer, *Cornish Archaeology* IX (1970),

pp. 53–61. (The final report, with a new plan, is now in preparation. The results do not support the evolution suggested above.
ex inf. R. J. Mercer.)

CARN FADRUN (fig. 42; Caernarvon, SH 280 352; 370 metres; p. 43).

The remains of this interesting fort have mostly escaped disturbance, and are free from vegetation. Its ruins indicate a long
history.

Initially a fairly level plateau of about 5 hectares was protected
by a strong stone wall, and the area was later doubled by building
a similar defence to take in the upper slopes of the hill. A spring
was also included; when this was improved to form a well is not
known. In both periods there seem to have been two gateways
(now much damaged), opening to north and south, and in the
second phase these were approached by deliberately engineered
zigzag terraced roadways; that to the south is particularly well
preserved. Only nine or ten round houses can be traced within the
enclosure, but about ninety more exist on the slopes of the hill
outside the defences (the area of the plan does not include all
these).

These round houses, and the two main ramparts, may be
accepted as pre-Roman. In addition a great many small irregular
huts have been built, mostly in the ruins of the inner ramparts.
These are accompanied by irregular enclosures; by analogy with
Tre'r Ceiri they are probably late Roman, and slight irregular
ramparts, one forming a small annexe on the north and another
isolated stretch on the south-east, may be associated with them.

The actual summit of the hill is occupied by a very small
fortress, some 90 by 30 metres, protected by a dry-stone wall
which still retains its parapet walk in places. Although the
defences look far too primitive for a medieval structure, they can
be identified as a 'stone castle' recorded as newly built by Giraldus
Cambrensis writing in 1188.

Caernarvon Inv. III (1964), No. 1650 (plan).

CARROCK FELL (fig. 43; Cumberland, NY 342 336; 660 metres).

The steep sides of an irregular double summit have been fortified by a single substantial stone wall about 2·7 metres thick

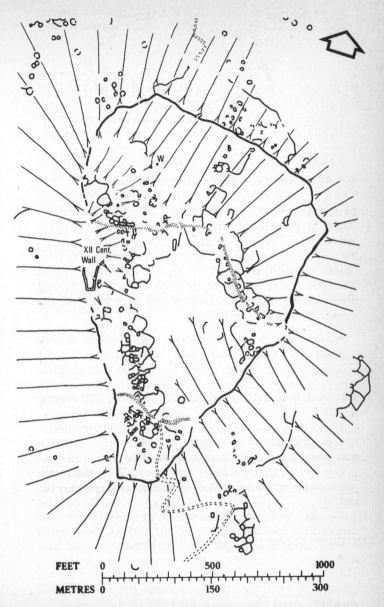

Fig. 42   Carn Fadrun. After Royal Commission on Ancient
Monuments (Wales).

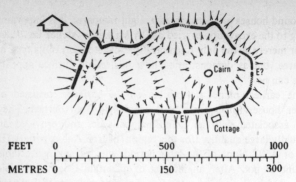

FEET   0   500   1000

METRES 0   150   300

Fig. 43   Carrock Fell. After R. G. Collingwood.

forming an irregular oval enclosure of about 2·1 hectares, the largest in the region. There is a robbed cairn on the eastern summit but no huts can be traced. The wall is interrupted by a number of gaps, but only two, on the west and south, are certainly original entrances, though a narrow gap at the east end may be. The other breaks seem to be the result of deliberate slighting, presumably by the Romans, though whether in an actual campaign or as training remains uncertain.

R. G. Collingwood, *Cumberland and Westmorland Soc. Trans.* XXXVIII (1938), pp. 32–41 (plan).

CASTELL NADOLIG (Cardigan, SN 298 504; 210 metres; p. 18).

One of the most northerly of the 'wide-spaced multivallate' type of fort; unfortunately its ramparts are entirely incorporated in field banks. The enclosures are oval, that in the centre 115 by 60 metres (0·5 hectare), the outer (concentric) 220 by 180 metres, with a crescentic annexe 140 long by 40 metres wide on the north-east.

Two decorated bronze spoons of Iron Age type have been found here (*Arch. Cambrensis* (1870), pp. 201, 205–6). These objects normally occur in pairs, and seem to have had some ritual function.

CASTELL ODO (Caernarvon, SH 187 284; 140 metres).

This little 'fort', occupying the summit of a low ridge in the Lleyn peninsula, gives the impression of a simple village of nine or ten round houses protected by two slight ramparts. It is important owing to the excavation carried out by Mr Leslie Alcock in 1958–9, not merely as the only scientifically excavated fort of its type in the area, but as demonstrating how misleading surface appearances can be.

The earliest phase, not visible on the surface, consisted of timber houses (probably round) which had been burned. They were associated with an unfinished palisade, and provided an unusually large quantity (for this region) of Iron Age A pottery (H 400 or 450). None of the later periods yielded any appreciable amount of pot. After an interval of uncertain length, a simple unrevetted bank, only about 2·5 to 3 metres wide and 1·5 metres high, was heaped up to form an almost circular enclosure of 85 metres diameter, 0·5 hectares in area. There were probably round stone houses within, but they were almost all destroyed in later phases.

In the third phase the bank was given revetments on each face and enlarged, and a similar revetted bank built concentric with it, forming a smaller inner enclosure of 55 metres diameter. The gateway in each bank was a simple gap with a pair of posts to carry the gate, about 1·7 metres wide. Some of the visible round houses, about 6 metres in diameter, belong to this period.

These revetted banks were some 3 metres thick and probably no more than 1·5 metres high – not much larger than modern field banks in the neighbourhood, as Mr Alcock emphasizes. Nevertheless, in the next phase they were deliberately slighted, though the occupation of the village continued, for more dwellings were built over the ruins. This event is attributed, with strong probability, to the Roman conquest. The fact that they considered it worthwhile to slight the defences must imply (*pace* Mr Alcock) that the new arrivals considered that these rather insignificant banks had some military value.

L. Alcock, *Arch. Cambrensis* CIX (1960), pp. 78–135.

CASTERLEY (fig. 44; Wilts., SU 115 535; 160 metres; pl. 18).

This curious site is not a typical hill-fort, but may illustrate the nature and functions of *some* large enclosures. It has recently been discussed by Mr Feachem.

The area enclosed is nearly 25 hectares, protected by a single bank and ditch. These are not of uniform profile, and are unfinished, the indications being clearest in the salient at the north end. Excavation of a good section on the south showed that the defences measured 17 metres wide overall and that the present crest stood 6·5 metres above the original ditch bottom, so that when completed it would have been quite a formidable rampart.

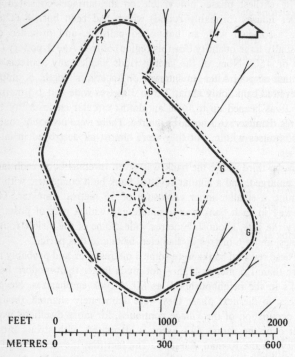

Fig. 44 Casterley. Based on R. W. Feachem and B. H. Cunnington.

Nevertheless, the position is defensively poor, astride a spur over-looked from the west, and the line was not chosen so as to make the best use of natural slopes. The salient on the north looks like a change in plan made during building in order partly to remedy this defect.

There were three entrances. That to the south was excavated. It was approached by a causeway 5 metres wide leading to a gateway 2·5 metres wide between two pairs of posts set 1·2 metres apart back to front. The line of ramparts was slightly staggered, but otherwise there was no elaboration of the plan.

Casterley escaped cultivation until modern times, and traces survived of a system of ditched enclosures near the middle of the 'fort'. These have been excavated, and found to date from the immediately pre-Roman Iron Age, with use continuing into the Roman period. Some of the ditches were earlier than the enclosing rampart. Dr Feachem has drawn attention to the presence of a large pit in the oval enclosure, which contained four human skeletons and the emplacement of a very large upright post, and he suggests convincingly that these central enclosures were ritual sites. It would seem that their presence dictated the choice of the otherwise unsuitable position for the defences.

Mr and Mrs B. H. Cunnington, *Wilts. Arch. Mag.* XXVIII (1914), pp. 53–105.
R. W. Feachem in *I A H F*, pp. 35–8.
R. Bradley's discussion of hill-forts on the South Downs (*q.v.*) is relevant.

CASTLE DORE (Cornwall, SX 103 548; 120 metres; p. 86 pl. 19).

This fort is protected by two ramparts and ditches, the inner being almost truly circular, internal diameter 77 metres, enclosing 0·5 hectares. The outer rampart is set close to the inner round two-thirds of the circumference, but diverges to form a barbican with a single passage; the lateral banks were small and have been destroyed. For plan, *cf.* Tregeare Rounds.

Excavation showed that there were two structural periods in the defences, though the plan was not altered. Initially (H 150) the two banks were of about the same height, without revetments, the faces continuing the slope of the ditches. In the later period the inner rampart was heightened and given a vertical outer revetment of stone, perhaps with timber uprights; the lateral banks of the barbican entrance were levelled. Sling stones were in use at this period.

About a fifth of the interior was cleared. At least five round houses were found which belonged to the initial defences; these banks had remained unaltered long enough for some of the buildings to be demolished and replaced by others. Four other round houses and a square granary were attributed to the later period, after the inner rampart had been enlarged. All the associated pottery was of B culture.

In addition, post holes were found which could not fit the plan of these round houses, and which indicated the existence of three rectangular buildings, 27 by 12 metres, 20 by 11 metres, and 7 metres square respectively. These were not accompanied by any relics, but on the evidence of stratification and historical arguments were regarded by the excavator as the remains of an early medieval palace, probably of the King Mark of the Trystan romance, who is traditionally associated with the site.

C. A. R. Radford, *Journal Royal Inst. Cornwall*, NS I (1951), Appendix.

CASTLE LAW, ABERNETHY (figs. 6, 45; Perth, NO 183 153; 220 metres; p. 62).

This fort was partly excavated in 1896–8, and the report contains a fine photograph of the sockets left by the timber lacing. Much of the walling can still be seen, though this particularly interesting feature has collapsed.

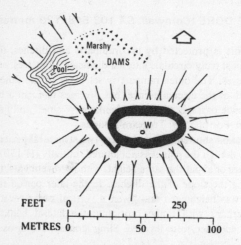

Fig. 45   Castle Law, Abernethy. After D. Christison.

The timber-laced wall, from 5·5 to 7·5 metres thick and probably 3 or 4 metres high originally, encloses a rather irregular oval of about 0·05 hectare; there is no entrance, and the only visible feature in the enclosure is a small well. On the west is a thinner outer wall, not timber-laced. The position is rather similar to that of Castle Law at Forgandenny, not far away, and here also a stream has been crossed by two dams; one of the pools still holds water. The outer wall may have protected the approach to the water, but its northern end is ruinous.

D. Christison, *Proc. Soc. Ant. Scot.* XXXIII (1898–9), pp. 13 ff. (excavation report with plan and photographs).
Preh. Scot., p. 145.
For reconstruction drawing by A. Sorrell of such a fort being built, see B. Green and A. Sorrell, *Prehistoric Britain* (Lutterworth, 1968), fig. 27.

CASTLE LAW, FORGANDENNY (fig. 46; Perth, NO 100 155; 280 metres; p. 45).

The wall faces in this fort were cleared in 1891, so that it gives a clearer impression than most other timber-laced forts of the character of the defences. The beam sockets were noted by the excavators, but little else was recorded except the plan.

The impression given by the remains is of a rather elaborate

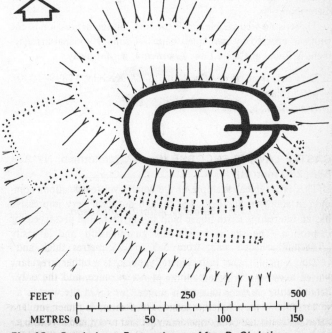

Fig. 46 Castle Law, Forgandenny. After D. Christison.

design of one period. The summit of the hillock is occupied by an enclosure of 0·2 hectare, with rounded ends and parallel sides; the wall is about 5·5 metres thick. Outside this, and separated from it by a space of 8 to 15 metres, is a further wall, 4·5 metres thick, now barely visible on the north. The two walls are connected at the east end by a wall which extends both outwards and inwards. There is an entrance to the outer enclosure, but no break in the inner wall. This arrangement suggests that the central space was for humans, who could reach it by steps or a movable ladder; cattle could be protected between the two walls. The axial wall may be compared with that at Finavon.

These timber-laced walls form the main fortifications, but there are additional works outside. On the north there is a natural shelf at a lower level; the edge of this, above the steeper hillside, is followed by a low bank. On the south the hill on which the fort stands is separated from the higher ground by a depression which carries a small stream in wet weather. The slope between this and the fort is crossed first by a ditch with a small bank on the north, then nearer the fort by a large bank and ditch towards the fort; the arrangements may be compared with Barry Hill and the White Caterthun.

There is no well visible inside the fort, but the depression to the south is crossed by two small dams. A similar unusual arrangement is found at Castle Law, Abernethy, not far away.

D. Christison, *Proc. Soc. Ant. Scot.* XXXIV (1899–1900), p. 75 (plan).
Preh. Scot., p. 145.

CASTLE LAW, GLENCORSE (fig. 47; Midlothian, NT 229 638; 290 metres).

This is a typical example of the small oval fortifications common in southern Scotland, and though not itself very impressive has an interesting earth house built in the ditch, and preserved for inspection. The site is in national guardianship, and is easily accessible.

The remains have been partly excavated, and features now buried have been 'restored' on the plan, though some of the minor details at the entrance have been omitted for simplicity.

The fort forms a fairly regular oval of about 0·3 hectares. The defences consisted of an inner rampart and two ditches, both now completely silted up. The material from each ditch had been thrown up to form a bank on its outer lip, and a fairly wide berm was left between the inner edge of each ditch and the corresponding inner bank. There were entrances at each end of the enclosure, and probably also in the south side; the gap here may be later, but the deviation in the line of rampart suggests that it is original.

Except immediately adjacent to the entrance, the inner rampart seems to have been about 2·5 metres wide, composed of a low

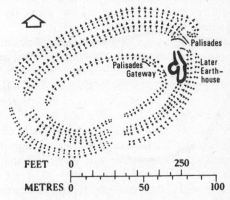

Fig. 47   Castle Law, Glencorse. Based on V. G. Childe and S. Piggott.

bank of white clay (brought from elsewhere) reinforced with brushwood laid horizontally and held in place by vertical stakes. Set in this bank about 0·5 metres from the back was a palisade; this rarely penetrated the bedrock. For about 5 metres from the actual entrance, the clay bank was built on a foundation of beams laid transversely and packed with stones, and the front was revetted with a rough wall.

The gateway was basically formed by four posts set in a square of 3-metre side, but the plan is complicated by holes which suggest that there were at least four reconstructions which were not distinguished in the earlier excavations, and it seems likely that wear caused by later use of the gap has destroyed some of the palisade trench. Outside the gateway the ditches and banks were arranged in association with lines of palisade to enforce an oblique approach.

South of the entrance, at some time after the abandonment of the fort, the inner ditch was deepened and lined with walls to form a subterranean earth house, with a side passage leading to a beehive chamber. Objects found in it show that it was in use up to the second century AD.

> V. G. Childe, *Proc. Soc. Ant. Scot.* LXVII (1932–3), pp. 362–88; *Ant. J.* XIII (1933), pp. 1 ff. (plan).
>
> S. and C. M. Piggott *Proc. Soc. Ant. Scot.* LXXXVI (1951–2), pp. 191–4.

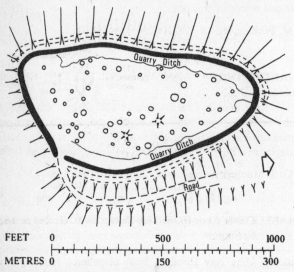

Fig. 48   *Chalbury. After M. Whitley.*

CHALBURY (fig. 48; Dorset, SY 695 838; 100 metres; p. 73; pl. 20).

This fort is of particular interest in that it preserves its interior plan undamaged. Its area is 4 hectares, defended by a single substantial ditch and bank, with a quarry ditch behind. The rampart had a kerb at the rear and was reinforced by an internal structural revetment near the back. The front had a revetment founded on large slabs set on edge. It was separated from the ditch by a berm, now 2 metres wide but originally perhaps 7 metres. The ditch was originally about 7 metres wide by 5·5 deep on its inner edge, shallower on the outer owing to the slope of the ground. The entrance was not examined, but seems to be simple; it was approached by an 'engineered' terraced roadway overlooked from the ramparts.

In the interior, seventy-three levelled platforms or hollows can still be seen. Twenty-three (not shown on plan) were probably storage pits, the remainder huts. Two huts were examined. The earlier, behind the rampart, was of wood; human bones were found scattered on its floor. The later, 10 metres in diameter, was enclosed by a low stone wall 1 metre wide by 0·5 metre high. Both yielded pot of A styles, but indicating a fairly long interval between them. The rampart, however, showed no sign of more than one period of building.

M. Whitley, *Ant. J.* XXIII (1943), pp. 98–121.

CHANCTONBURY RING (Sussex, TQ 139 120; 230 metres; p. 85).

The Ring is oval, axes 54 and 74 metres, enclosing 0·3 hectares, protected by a single bank and ditch, with an entrance, apparently a simple gap, on the west. It is of interest as one of the examples of a hill-fort within which a Roman temple was built.

G. S. Mitchell, *Sussex Arch. Coll.* LIII (1910), pp. 133–7.

CHASTLETON (Oxford, SP 258 282; 230 metres; p. 18).

This fort stands on the end of a broad spur, so that although the adjacent ground is fairly level it commands an extensive view. It is almost circular, 125 metres in diameter (1·2 hectares) protected by a substantial bank with no visible ditch. Slight excavation in 1928–9 showed that the bank was revetted on its inner face by a well preserved wall of large blocks. Plentiful pottery, of A style, was recovered, and hearths and paving were noted, but the plans of the associated buildings were not worked out.

On the ancient name, Susibre, see p. 18.

E. T. Leeds, *Ant. J.* XI (1931), pp. 382–98.

CHUN CASTLE (fig. 49; Cornwall, SW 405 339; 210 metres; p. 36, 71).

This interesting little fortress stands on a gently rounded hill with fine views. It has attracted the attention of antiquaries since 1769, when W. Borlase published a plan. Some excavations were carried out by E. T. Leeds in 1925 and 1930.

The remains are still impressive, but in Borlase's time must

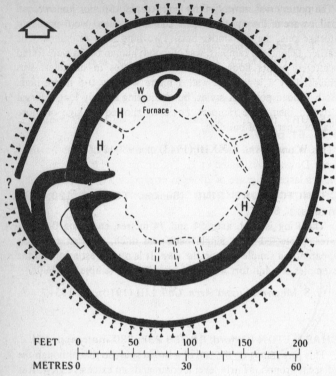

Fig. 49   Chun Castle. After E. T. Leeds.

have been very remarkable indeed, with the main wall standing 4·5
metres high, and of equal thickness at the base. In plan it is almost
(but not geometrically) circular, 50 metres in diameter, reinforced
by a slight outer wall, and beyond it a shallow ditch. The gateway
is approached by a zigzag, but a blocked opening in the outer wall
shows that the original entranceway was straight. The main passage, through the inner wall, tapers to a pair of stone gateposts
about 1·5 metres apart, and then widens again between two
inturned horns.

Within the enclosure an irregular ring of roughly rectangular
enclosures is set against the rampart. They are lightly built, and
excavation has shown that they are secondary. The original dwellings were round, about 5 metres in diameter, set near the rampart;
there may originally have been ten or a dozen, but only three were
examined. A well existed on the northern side of the enclosure, and
just south of it was a furnace, probably for tin smelting.

The pottery was mostly of the Iron Age, H 150, but some post-Roman ware of the eighth or tenth century AD was also found.

E. T. Leeds, *Archaeologia* LXXVI (1926–7), pp. 205–40; LXXXI (1931), pp. 33–42. For the late pot, see *Ant. J.* XXXVI (1956), p. 76.

CISSBURY (fig. 50; Sussex, TQ 139 080; 180 metres; pp. 21, 61, pl. 21).

This is one of the most important of the line of forts on the Sussex Downs investigated by E. C. Curwen and his helpers.

It is a large enclosure of 20 hectares protected by a strong bank and ditch with a counterscarp bank, originally about 25 metres

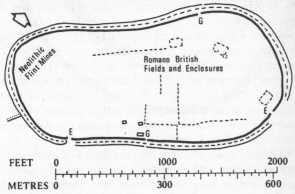

Fig. 50   Cissbury. After E. C. Curwen.

wide overall. The ditch had been cut over 3 metres deep into the chalk, and was of unusual profile, being flat-bottomed with a central ridge. The main rampart still stands 2·5 metres high, and had been revetted with upright timbers set in a continuous slot. The associated pottery was 'La Tène I', that is early in the middle phase of the Iron Age. Sling stones were numerous. The gateways now appear as simple gaps, and were not excavated.

During the Roman period, the enclosed area was ploughed, and some small rectangular cottages were built. Finally, late in the Roman period or subsequently, the defences were reinforced.

The deep pits scattered over the western part of the site are the remains of neolithic flint mines, far earlier than the fort.

The ancient name of the fort was 'Sieberie' (meaning unknown).

The present form is probably due to sixteenth-century attempts to associate it with the Saxon King Cissa. In the 1695 edition of Camden's *Britannia* it is called Caesar's Hill.

E. C. Curwen and R. P. Ross-Williamson, *Ant. J. XI* (1931), pp. 14–36 (plan) (*q.v.* for earlier references).

CLARE (Suffolk, TL 769 459; 55 metres; p. 41, pl. 22).

On Clare Common, immediately north-west of the town, substantial defences enclose 2·6 hectares. Where best preserved, on the south-west, the massive inner bank and ditch are accompanied by a small outer bank and ditch, but round most of the circuit this outer defence has been destroyed. The plan is roughly that of a quarter of an ellipse, the south and east sides being straight. The only surviving entrance is in the southern half of the east side. It is now a simple gap about 6 metres wide, the rampart to the south being set 5 metres further out than that to the north. The ramparts may have been inturned, but two hollow trails through the gap have obscured the details. These trails may correspond to original roadways inside the enclosure, but the surface has been very much disturbed. There may also have been an entrance at the west end, but the rampart there has mostly been levelled.

The regular plan and almost level site make this a very uncharacteristic 'hill-fort', and no evidence for date has been found, so it may in fact be later. On the other hand, there are very few early forts in the area, so there is no local material for comparison.

VCH Suffolk I (1911), p. 588 (plan).

CLICKHIMIN (Shetland, HU 465 408; p. 81). See End Paper

Shetland falls outside the range covered here, but the monograph on Clickhimin is of primary importance, not only for the details of the excavation of the small fortress, but because it sets out a convincing hypothesis as to the nature and origins of the 'vitrified' forts of the Scottish mainland.

J. R. C. Hamilton, *Excavation at Clickhimin, Shetland* (HMSO, Edinburgh, 1968).

CLOVELLY DYKES (fig. 51; Devon, SS 311 234; 210 metres; p. 44, pl. 23).

This is one of the finest of the south-western type of fort with wide-spaced multiple ramparts, although the banks now form field boundaries. The innermost enclosure is of 1·2 hectares, but the defences contain 9·6 hectares in all. It stands on almost level

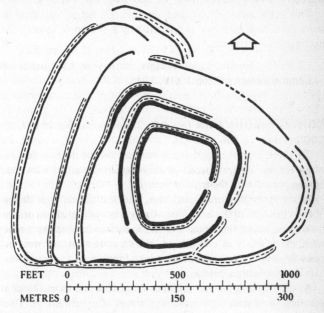

Fig. 51   Clovelly Dykes. After Lady Fox.

ground, at the junction of three ridges, each of which is followed by an ancient trackway.

The work seems to be of at least two periods, probably more. The innermost enclosure is the earlier, with two ramparts widely separated but roughly parallel; the outer is the more substantial. The entrance was on the east, the gaps in the two ramparts being slightly offset.

To this nucleus three more ramparts were added, the outermost again being the strongest. These formed three strip-like enclosures on the west, and a roughly semicircular one on the east. There is an entrance through this last on the line of the gaps leading into the inner enclosure. The others, on the west, were entered through gaps between their northern ends, the approach being strengthened by an additional stretch of bank and ditch. Most entrances have the rampart ends slightly knobbed, but are otherwise simple gaps.

A. Fox, *Arch. J.* CIX (1952), pp. 12–14 (plan).

COLCHESTER (Essex, 149, TL 987 253; pp. 17, 31).

This is the most fully studied example of a Belgic '*oppidum*' in Britain. A large territory is protected by a system of dykes connecting natural features.

C. F. C. Hawkes, *Camulodunum*, Society of Antiquaries of London Research Report XIV, 1947.

CONWAY MOUNTAIN (fig. 52; Caernarvon, SH 760 778; 250 metres; pp. 46, 69, 77).

This well preserved and accessible fort has the unusual feature of an entirely separate small inhabited enclosure at the west end, contemporary with the main structure.

Apart from the small enclosure, the fort seems a perfectly normal example of the local type. A single rampart encloses nearly 3 hectares, containing about fifty hut foundations; so far as can be seen, the work is of one period. Near the western end was the gateway, with a roughly square setting of four posts to support the gate and probably a bridge.

At the extreme end the southern rampart forks, to mark out a separate small enclosure containing traces of six dwellings. This enclosure has a single gateway opening to the south. There is no direct access to the main fort, and indeed the approach from that side is provided with an additional protection by a bank and ditch set in front of the wall.

What now appears as the south wall of the small enclosure proves on examination to be a modification of an earlier and more elaborate defence. Further south there appear ruinous traces of a wall accompanied by a ditch and following a zigzag course so that each section is commanded from an adjacent stretch set at an angle. This earlier rampart was penetrated by an impressive entrance, the passage being nearly 6 metres wide and 7 long, the sides faced with very large upright slabs, some almost 'megalithic' in character. This entrance had been deliberately blocked after one side had partly collapsed; this blocking was probably done when the present south rampart was built. Another small gateway, now barely traceable, existed further east.

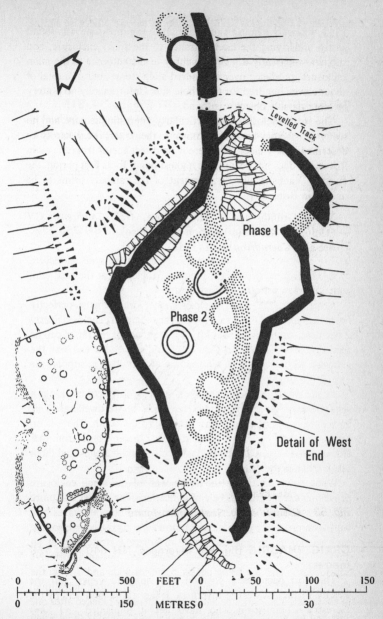

Fig. 52   Conway Mountain. After Royal Commission on Ancient Monuments (Wales).

Some of these details were worked out by slight excavations in 1951, when four house sites were also examined; one was found partly underlying the later entrance to the small enclosure, and another, apparently a guard chamber at the entrance to the main enclosure, produced over a hundred sling stones, out of a total of about eleven hundred for the whole site. Unfortunately no pottery or other datable object was found.

The small enclosure is a particularly interesting feature, and no really satisfactory parallel is known to the writer. It can hardly be described as a 'citadel', for there is no direct access from the main fort and it does not occupy the highest point. In its first period, the curious 'Vaubanesque' arrangement of the rampart seems to be unique in Britain.

W. E. Griffiths and A. H. A. Hogg, *Arch. Cambrensis* CV (1956), pp. 49–80 (excavation report, plan).

See also *Caernarvon Inv.* I (1956), No. 201.

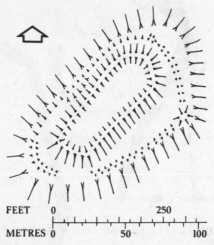

FEET   0   250

METRES 0   50   100

Fig. 53   Craig Phadrig. Scale approximate.

CRAIG PHADRIG (fig. 53; Inverness, NH 640 453; 150 metres).

This fort occupies a position with splendid views over the Beauly Firth, just west of Inverness. It lies within land held by the Forestry Commission who have left it unplanted and have provided an attractive woodland walk leading to it, with a parking space.

The ramparts are now grass-grown, but both are known to be heavily vitrified. The inner is very massive, standing nearly 4 metres high externally and a metre internally, its ruins spreading to a width of 10 metres. No entrance can be seen. The outer rampart is much slighter. The mound on the east may be natural. The interior, of 0·2 hectares, contains several hollows, probably mostly the result of recent disturbance, though a well would not be unlikely in a fort of this type.

Preh. Scot., p. 126.

A radiocarbon measurement on material from the rampart indicates a date in the mid-fourth century BC. (*Discovery and Excavation in Scotland* (1971), p. 23.) This discovery is the first fruit of excavations which have just been started.

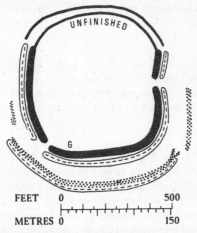

Fig. 54   Cranbrook Castle. After J. Collis.

CRANBROOK CASTLE (fig. 54; Devon, SX 738 890; 330 metres).

The substantial rampart which is such an obvious feature of this fort is clearly unfinished, but examination when the vegetation is low shows that it is superimposed on a larger enclosure, complete but much slighter. Some excavations in 1900 threw light on the construction of the ramparts and produced sling stones and pottery of B culture (H 50). The excavators, working in summer, overlooked the greater part of the outer rampart, and regarded the structure as an unfinished bivallate work.

Both enclosures were roughly circular. The earlier contained nearly 4 hectares, and was defended by a glacis-type bank and ditch only about 9 metres wide overall and now, even where best preserved, with the original ditch bottom only 2·5 metres below the present crest. At the entrances the line of rampart on one side was set back from that on the other. The later work as planned was smaller, only 2·8 hectares, but much more strongly defended. The rampart was 11·5 metres wide at its base, with a stone revetment on its outer face; parts of this are still visible, and it probably stood more than 3 metres high originally. This was separated by a berm 3 metres wide from a ditch 8 metres wide and 2·3 metres deep. Both this and the earlier ditch were flat-bottomed. Round the southern side of the enclosure, the earlier rampart was retained as a counterscarp bank. This new rampart, however, was never built round the northern third of the circuit, and the two entrances through it, to north-east and south-west, seem never to have been finished, though the ends of the banks are thickened and slightly inturned.

S. Baring-Gould, *Trans. Devon Assoc.* XXXIII (1901), pp. 131–5, with plan by R. H. Worth.
But now see a new survey and description by J. Collis, *Proc. Devon Arch. Soc.* XXX (1972), pp. 216–21.

CREDENHILL (fig. 55; Hereford, SO 450 445; 210 metres).

This fort, twice as large as any other in the county, was partly excavated by S. C. Stanford in 1963, before afforestation of the interior. The results are especially important as the first published discussion of a defended settlement where the dwellings seem to have been small rectangular buildings regularly arranged, as contrasted with the random scatter of round houses which seems more usual in some regions. See also Ffridd Faldwyn and Croft Ambrey.

The position chosen was the summit of a steep hill well suited to defence, and round this there was built a substantial rampart with an accompanying ditch, enclosing 20 hectares. Two entrances survive, both with the ramparts inturned to give a long approach passage, probably with guard chambers.

Excavation was restricted to an area behind the rampart just south of the east gate, and revealed evidence for small rectangular buildings set at regular intervals of about 6 metres in parallel rows 8 metres apart – centre to centre. The buildings were represented by holes for four corner posts, and were of two sizes, about 2·5

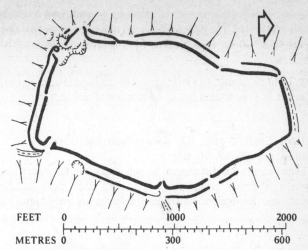

Fig. 55   Credenhill. After S. C. Stanford and Royal Commission on Historic Monuments (England).

metres square and 2·5 by 3·5 metres. Most were rebuilt six times, to the same plan and on the same site. The excavator demonstrates that the buildings must have had raised wooden floors, and argues convincingly that they were dwellings. He estimates a population of about four thousand for the settlement, and suggests that the fort may have been in effect the political capital of the region.

The occupation seems to have ended on the arrival of the Romans, about AD 60, and by making certain reasonable assumptions as to the life of the buildings the first construction of the fort would be about 390 BC, agreeing well with evidence from Croft Ambrey.

> S. C. Stanford, *Arch. J.* CXXVII (1970), pp. 82–129 (excavation report).

CROFT AMBREY (fig. 13; Hereford, SO 445 668; 300 metres; pl. 7).
For description see pp. 92–102; also pp. 31, 45–6, 66, 77, 85.

> S. C. Stanford, *Croft Ambrey* (Hereford, 1974).

DANEBURY (Hants., SU 323 376; 140 metres; p. 80). *Photo Page 2.*
This splendid and complex fort, of 5·3 hectares, is at present (1972) being excavated under the direction of Professor Barry

Cunliffe. It will therefore not be discussed here, though it is very well worth a visit. The two entrances are of particular interest, that on the west having been blocked by a later modification of the ramparts.

B. Cunliffe, *Ant. J.* LI (1971), pp. 240–52 (first interim report); in *I A H F*, p. 65 and fig. 17 (discussion of entrance).

DINAS EMRYS (fig. 56; Caernarvon SH 606 492; 130 metres; pp. 20, 53, 55, 86).

Dinas Emrys is a picturesque hillock, rocky and wooded, which forms a landmark rising above the valley floor close to Llyn Dinas, near Beddgelert. Its artificial defences are not impressive,

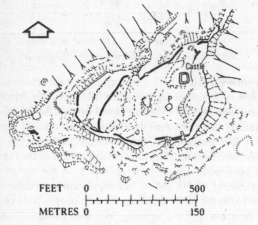

Fig. 56   Dinas Emrys. After Royal Commission on Ancient Monuments (Wales).

but are of interest as one of the rare examples of a wholly post-Roman hill-fort. The hill, moreover, is one of those places which seem to attract legends. It is impossible to list them all, but the oldest must be summarized. It appears in Nennius's *History of the Britons*, a disjointed collection of material first assembled early in the ninth century.

The wicked King Vortigern, so the story goes, decided to build a citadel here. The work, having been begun, vanished completely in one night. After this had happened three times, Vortigern's wise men advised him to sacrifice a child, and Ambrosius (Emrys in Welsh) was brought to be put to death.

Ambrosius, however, revealed that the pavement on which Vortigern was building covered a pool. In this pool were two vases, containing a red and a white serpent, symbolizing respectively the British and Saxon people. All this was confirmed by digging; the red serpent attacked the white one, and drove him away. Vortigern, impressed by this revelation, assigned the city to Ambrosius.

There is in fact a pool within the fort, which has long been regarded as that mentioned in the legend, but when the place was excavated by Dr H. N. Savory in 1954–6 it was rather surprising to discover evidence that the fortification was of about the right date and that there was in fact a platform above the pool! Here the agreement between fact and legend breaks down, for this platform was, so far as could be determined, much later than the time of Vortigern, though there seem to have been buildings of about his time near the pool. Was there really some recollection that the place was a fifth to sixth-century stronghold? Or did some storyteller, perhaps two centuries later, compose a tale to fit the visible remains, and hit on a suitable date by accident? These questions are unanswerable.

Turning to the facts proved by excavation and survey, the defences, where best preserved, were stone walls from about 2·5 to 3 metres thick and still standing a metre high in places, making use of every irregularity in the craggy hill-top and forming an irregular inner enclosure of about 1 hectare. Access was by a steep ascent from the west, the edges of two lower shelves on the hillside being defended by additional walls; the present approach from the north-east does not seem to be original. The gateways seem to have been simple gaps, with a single post to support the gate; the outermost gives the impression of an elaborate obliquely inturned plan, but this is probably merely an adaptation to the irregularities of the rocky hillside. Thanks to the discovery of an occupation layer which contained late Roman and early post-Roman material and which extended under the innermost wall, the fortifications can be dated to the sub-Roman period, probably the fifth or sixth century AD, about the time of Vortigern and Ambrosius. The pool, which proved to be an artificial cistern, is of about the same date. In fact, whether it belonged to Ambrosius or not, the whole site represents the fortress of some local chieftain during the barbaric period which followed the departure of the Romans.

Excavation of the area round the cistern unravelled a sequence of structures showing that the site had been occupied, though unfortified, from before the Roman period; it is not necessary to describe them in detail here, since although of great interest in themselves they were too fragmentary to add much to our knowledge of the interior arrangement of the fort.

The rectangular tower, the base of which is the most conspicuous object on the hill, is the remains of a twelfth-century castle; it lacks any history, but was probably built by the Welsh.

Caernarvon Inv. H (1960), No. 742 (plan).

H. N. Savory, *Arch. Cambrensis* CIX (1960), pp. 13–77 (excavation report).

DINLLAEN (Caernarvon, SH 275 416; 30 metres; p. 19).

The prominent headland which this fort occupies overlooks the only good natural harbour west of Caernarvon. The enclosed area is about 5·7 hectares, and was protected by two banks with ditches, spaced about 60 metres apart across the neck of the promontory. These are now badly mutilated. The site is of interest for its name, the 'fort of the Leinstermen' (p. 19).

Caernarvon Inv. III (1964), No. 1567.

DINLLE (Caernarvon, SH 437 563; 30 metres; pp. 18, 191).

The fort occupies a low knoll partly cut into by the sea. To judge from aerial photographs, the reclaimed marsh to the north may originally have been penetrated by a creek which would have provided a sheltered landing place.

The enclosure was originally oval, about 145 by 110 metres (1·2 hectares), protected by two banks with an intervening ditch, measuring 55 metres wide overall. The inner (larger) rampart rose at least 11 metres above the bottom of the ditch; the section exposed in the cliff face shows that it was revetted with a double facing built up of large boulders. There is a single entrance, to the south-east, which now appears to be a simple gap.

The cliff section shows a depth of nearly a metre of discoloured sand, but this has yielded nothing contemporary with the fort except pebbles which have been used for rubbing or pounding. Roman coins and potsherds of the second century and later have been found within the enclosure, and the slight and ill defined hollows which can be seen in its eastern half may be traces of structures of that period.

Caernarvon Inv. II (1960), No. 1211 (plan).

DINORBEN (figs. 7, 8, 57; Denbigh, SH 968 757; 170 metres; pp. 29, 30, 46, 48, 63, 69, 73, 85).

This hill fort has a number of claims to distinction. It is protected by very impressive defences, penetrated by a gateway with massive and well preserved stone-built guard chambers. The occupation of the site started at the beginning of the first millennium BC and continued for some fifteen centuries. It was first investigated in 1912–22 by the pioneering excavations of Dr

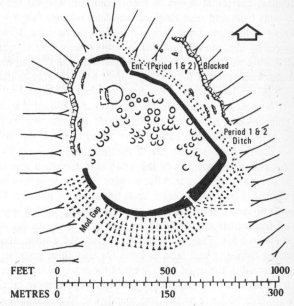

Fig. 57   Dinorben. After H. N. Savory.

Willoughby Gardner, conducted with a technique well in advance of his time. Dr H. N. Savory has published the results of these excavations, supplemented by additional research of his own in 1956–61 and 1965, in two monographs which together form a major contribution to the study of hill-forts. The rock forming the promontory is of such enormous economic importance that the whole site will be quarried away.

In the fort's final state the promontory was defended by three ramparts across the neck, with accompanying ditches, traversed by an entrance on the south-east. The inner defence, which was very massive, continued in a slighter form round the steep sides of the promontory, except where they became precipitous. Within the enclosure, of 2·5 hectares, some fifty platforms were visible, for dwellings mostly of 6 to 7 metres in diameter.

The excavations showed that these remains were the result of long evolution starting with an unfortified village. The defences comprised work of five periods, and there was at least one further phase of occupation after they had fallen into ruin. Hut platforms had been built in all these phases.

The earliest defence ('phase one') was of clay reinforced with continuous horizontal layers of timber and with vertical timber revetments front and rear. Radiocarbon dates indicate that it was probably built some time during the ninth century BC. It was destroyed by fire, and not replaced for some three centuries, when the first stone rampart was built, associated with a simple gateway, having a framework of four upright posts and probably bridged (fig. 7). A similar gateway, near the north end of the enclosure, showed a sequence of changes, having first been reduced in width and then blocked. Some time during the life of these defences (in phase two) a rather flat bastion was added west of the main entrance, extending over the line of the ditch, and a second ditch was cut round at least part of the south side, though it was not traced as far as the entrance. After another century or so the place was refortified on a much larger scale (phases three to four). The entrance, moved a short distance westward, was provided with a pair of rectangular guard chambers, with a bridged gateway immediately in front. The gate seems to have closed against stones projecting from the wall face, as holes for only three posts were found, instead of the usual four. West of the entrance the defence was a simple bank of glacis design, probably with a timber breastwork, though no trace of this was found. The bank ended at the gate passage with a vertical revetment wall. East of the gateway the rampart was faced with a stone revetment, probably because the ground here falls away steeply, and glacis construction would have been very extravagant in material. A ditch accompanied this rampart on both sides of the entrance.

The modifications of phase four were obscured by later work, but seem to have comprised the addition of a second bank west of the entrance, and some reconstruction of the stone revetment to the gate passage.

Finally, in phase five, a rampart west of the entrance was enlarged and given a stone breastwork and a terraced back; the breastwork was continued eastward past the entrance as a vertical wall. A further outermost ditch with an accompanying bank was constructed in front of the existing works, and west of the entrance an inner ditch was cut, partly into the face of the glacis rampart. The gate passage was also extended and given a second setting of four posts, so in its final form there may well have been two bridges and two sets of gates. The guard houses were retained but reduced in size (fig. 8).

These impressive defences were partly demolished, probably by the Romans, and the site was then deserted. After some two centuries it was re-occupied, but not refortified. The main structure was a very large round building 20 metres in diameter. The excavator regarded this as a dwelling, but it yielded the bronze head of a wand or sceptre, and may have been a temple. The coins found indicate use from about AD 260 to 330. Very nearby, finds from a poorly constructed rectangular building carry the occupation on into the fifth century. The suggestion has been made that there was actual continuity between this site and the medieval manor of Dinorben; but there seems little evidence to support this hypothesis.

The early date for the initial fortification is of particular interest, for the quarry long ago yielded a remarkable collection of Late Bronze Age horse harness decorations. These can now be accepted as derived from the occupation of the fort.

W. Gardner and H. N. Savory, *Dinorben* (Cardiff, 1964).

H. N. Savory, *Excavations at Dinorben 1965–9* (Cardiff, 1971).

DINORWIG (fig. 58; Caernarvon, SH 550 653; 170 metres; p. 19).

The defences of this little fort are exceptionally strong for this district. The inner bank rises about 6 metres above the ground outside it, the outer nearly 9 metres above its accompanying ditch; there is also a counterscarp bank. On the south-west, where they run parallel, this rampart system measures about 38 metres wide overall, but on the east the outer and inner ramparts diverge, and at the north end the outer rampart bends outwards to enclose an annexe. The internal area is about 0·9 hectare, that of the annexe a further 0·3 hectare. Details of the relation between the annexe and the main enclosure are obscured by the existing farm; the plan suggests as a possibility that the inner rampart may be later than the outer, but they are linked at the entrance, which is a fairly straight passage giving access to the interior from the west.

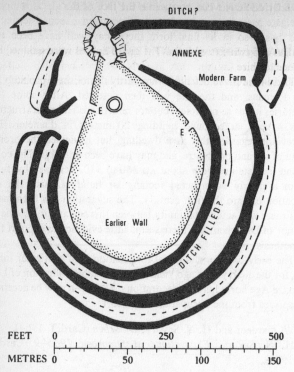

Fig. 58   Dinorwig. After W. Gardner and Royal Commission on Ancient Monuments (Wales).

Whatever the relative dates of the two earthen ramparts, the remains of an earlier wall (enclosing 0·7 hectare) can be traced close to the rear of the inner bank. Its face was of large boulders (partly rebuilt on the north-east), and it was penetrated by two entrances. One, to the west, opens in the same direction as the later approach; the other, to the north-east, must have been rendered useless by the construction of the inner bank. Most of the interior has been cleared, but one hut circle survives.

The name (p. 19) – the 'fortress of the Ordovices' – preserves that of the tribe which occupied this region during the Roman period and earlier.

W. Gardner, *Arch. Cambrensis* XCIX (1947), pp. 231–48 (plan).

See also *Caernarvon Inv.* II (1960), No. 1170 (plan).

DODDINGTON MOOR, *see* **THE RINGSES.**

DREVA (fig. 59; Peebles, NT 126 353; 270 metres).

Peeblesshire is very rich in forts, which have been well described in the Inventory. That at Dreva is particularly notable for

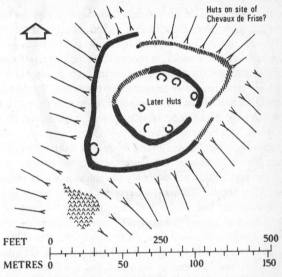

Fig. 59   Dreva.   After Royal Commission on Historic Monuments (Scotland).

the presence of *chevaux-de-frise*, and has the added interest of two well preserved later unenclosed settlements near the fort, and two more not far away.

The fort itself consists of a stone wall about 4 metres thick enclosing the top of a rocky knoll (area 0·2 hectare). The entrance is by a natural gully, passing through a simple gap between the rampart ends. Another similar wall follows the foot of the knoll, and to the south of this the line of easiest approach along the ridge is defended by a broad belt of *chevaux-de-frise*; more than a hundred of the upright stones still remain in position. There may have been a similar belt to the north, destroyed by the later settlement.

Peebles Inv. I (1967), No. 275 (plan).
Preh. Scot., p. 143.

DUCHARY ROCK (fig. 60; Sutherland, NC 851 050; 230 metres; pp. 46, 66).

The fort occupies a long narrow ridge with precipitous sides which require no additional defence. At the north-west and south-east ends of the enclosure massive stone walls link the points where the cliffs give way to steep slopes. The area enclosed is 2·4 hectares.

To the south-east, the ground falls fairly steeply, and the wall is 3·6 metres thick. Near the middle is an entrance 1·3 metres wide, which seems to have been blocked in antiquity. The north-western wall, where access is easier, is more substantial, nearly 5 metres wide, and still stands more than a metre high in places. It was penetrated by at least two entrances, perhaps four. Starting from the west, the first of these occurs about 18 metres from the cliff. The masonry of the adjacent rampart is very massive, and the gate passage has been blocked in antiquity, using rather smaller stones. The second gateway occurs after a further 14 metres; the passage is now filled with stones, but there seems to be no built facing across the gap, so this was probably the entrance which remained in use. After another 18 metres, beyond a modern gap, a straight joint crosses the line of the wall; this may be the east side of another blocked gateway. Finally, 27 metres further on, the 5-metre wall ends with a built face, which may be the west side of yet a fourth entrance. The two certain entrance passages are about 2 metres wide, and like that at the south end are lined with large slabs set upright. Thinner walls continue the line of the north-western rampart for some distance, where the sides of the ridge are not impregnable. The interior is peat-covered with rock outcrops, and no structures are visible.

The Inventory description records a second slighter wall running parallel to the main wall and about 5 metres outside it in front of the two northern entrances; also a chamber in the wall west of the southern entrance. These features are no longer obvious.

Sutherland Inv. (1911), No. 29.
Preh. Scot., p. 158.

DUCLAIR (Seine-Inférieure, France; p. 26).

A promontory fort of 10 hectares, on the right bank of the Seine, 16 kilometres west-north-west of Rouen; one of the sites investigated by Sir Mortimer Wheeler during 1938–9.

H F N F, pp. 75–83.

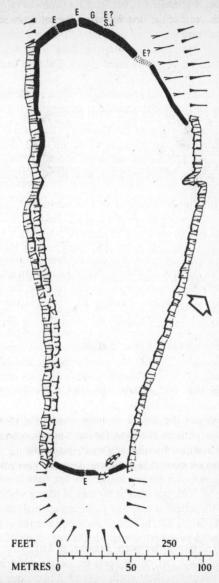

Fig. 60   Duchary Rock. Scale approximate.

DUMBARTON ROCK (Dumbarton, NS 400 745; p. 19).

The rock is spectacular, but later buildings have destroyed all traces of the 'fort of the Britons' which the name shows must once have existed here.

Preh. Scot., p. 118.
P P, pl. 2 (air photo).

DUMYAT (Stirling, NS 832 973; 300 metres; p. 19).

This name — the 'fort of the Maeatae' — has been transferred to the mountain itself, but the actual structure stands on a projecting shoulder some 120 metres below the summit. There seem to be two main phases of construction, with possible traces of a third not discussed here.

The earlier phase consisted of two substantial walls 5 to 15 metres apart, forming the west side of an oval enclosure measuring 100 metres east to west by 60 metres (0·5 hectares); the east side is protected by natural cliffs. The walls, which show traces of vitrification, are completely ruinous. There is an entrance 6 metres wide in the west side, and outside this opening slight walls only a metre thick form an enclosure on each side of the approach.

The later phase is a small oval fort, about 30 by 15 metres (0·03 hectares), roughly concentric with the main enclosure.

Stirling Inv. I (1963), No. 68 (plan).

DUNADD (fig. 61; Argyll, NR 837 936; 50 metres; pp. 45, 87).

Although not the largest or most impressive of the 'nuclear forts' this is perhaps the most famous and interesting. It is also under national guardianship and easily accessible.

The position chosen is a typical irregular rocky boss, in this case rising out of a former marsh. At one time it was probably accessible by boat, but there is no way of telling whether this was so during its period of use. The fortifications are restricted to the upper parts of the hill, but there are broad shelves at lower levels which seem to have been occupied. On one, south of the fort and near what seems to have been the main ascent, there are the foundations of a large rectangular building; but its date is quite uncertain. There is also a slight wall forming a large enclosure outside the main defences. Both these features are outside the area of the plan.

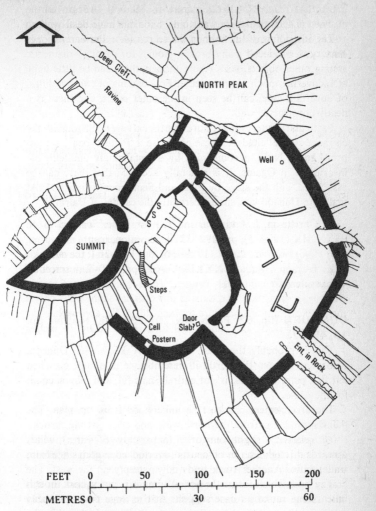

Fig. 61   Dunadd. After D. Christison.

The fortress proper makes skilful use of the irregularities of the hill, and the summit is reached by passing through a series of courts at different levels. The 'citadel' on the summit could have originally formed an isolated structure, but the arrangement of the remains seems to suggest that the system of defences was planned as a whole. The outer entrance, cut through rock, is impressive, and the outermost wall must have been quite substantial, but the others are relatively slight; indeed, the natural strength of the position is such that there was no need for much artificial work.

The interior was dug over in the search for relics early in this century; it produced many broken moulds for casting ornaments, among other objects. As a result, though, there can be little hope of recovering much interior detail. Foundations of two buildings, of uncertain date, can be seen in the outer court, and there is a neatly constructed well.

Particularly interesting features are the carvings (SSS) outside the entrance to the 'citadel'. These comprise a 'Pictish' boar, a 'footprint' and a basin, accompanied by a tantalizingly unintelligible inscription in Ogams. It is generally accepted that these can be associated with the siege by Picts and Scots recorded in 683. At that time Dunadd was almost certainly the capital of Dalriada.

D. Christison, J. Anderson and T. Ross, *Proc. Soc. Ant. Scot.* XXXIX (1904–5), pp. 292–322 (excavation, plan).

J. H. Craw, *ibid.*, LXIV (1929–30), pp. 111–26 (excavation).

K. Jackson, *Antiquity* XXXIX (1965), pp. 300–2 (inscription transliterated).

DUNDURN (fig. 62; Perth, NN 707 233; 150 metres; pp. 18, 45, 87).

This is probably the finest 'nuclear fort' known (*cf.* Dunadd, Ruberslaw). From the north, its resemblance to a huge clenched left fist, palm upwards, is not entirely fanciful, and may account for the name.

The arrangement can best be understood from the plan. The main approach is from the north-west, and after passing through some relatively slight outworks (apparently of earth) winds upwards through a series of 'courts', overlooked at each stage from walls above. Another track leads down steeply on the west. The craggy boss which forms the actual summit is not walled, though fallen stone round its base suggests that its edge may have been protected by a relatively slight breastwork. There is a well in the uppermost court. The ramparts throughout are completely ruined, and no facing is visible, but the mass of stone present indicates that they must have been of great strength.

This fine fortress has escaped disturbance of any kind, and it is to be hoped that such a fortunate condition may long continue – though an accurate modern contoured survey is highly desirable. It has also produced no relics. There is historical evidence for its occupation in the seventh and ninth centuries AD, for a siege is

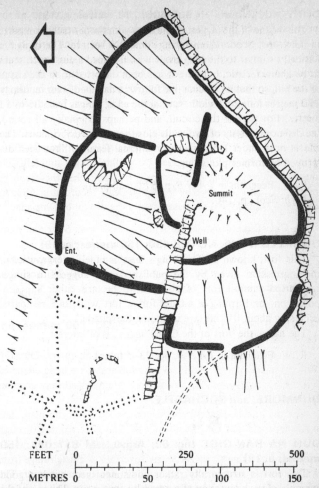

Fig. 62   Dundurn. After D. Christison.

recorded (as at Dunadd) in 683, and King Girig died there in 878.
How much its occupation extended either way beyond these dates
is quite uncertain. It may perhaps incorporate a pre-Roman
fortress, but to the writer the whole scheme gives the impression of
unitary design, though a long time would no doubt have been
needed to complete the work as planned.

D. Christison, *Early Fortifications in Scotland* (1898), pp. 208–
13, and *Proc. Soc. Ant. Scot.* XXXIV (1899–1900), p. 65 (plan).
Preh. Scot. p. 146.

DUNEARN (Nairn, NH 933 406; 240 metres; p. 19).

This is one of the largest of the forts with timber-laced ramparts in north-east Scotland, enclosing some 0·9 hectare. The design is basically similar to the long ovals with flattened sides which seem to be characteristic, but here it has been distorted to fit the shape of the hill, so that its median line follows a flattened S curve, nearly 280 metres long; the width, save at the ends, ranges from 35 to 55 metres. For part of the circuit, and perhaps originally all round, the defence consists of two walls close-set, now very ruinous. The site is now under trees, and any internal features have been destroyed by former ploughing.

R. W. Feachem in *I A N B*, p. 67 (small plan).
Preh. Scot., p. 140.

DUNKELD (Perth, NO 009 430; 150 metres; p. 19).

This fort, known as The King's Seat, is much overgrown, but the impression given by the published plan suggests a single-ramparted summit fort of about 0·06 hectare either superimposed on, or forming a citadel for, a fort with four ramparts, enclosing about 0·3 hectare including the 'citadel'.

The name, the 'fort of the Caledonians', is of interest.

R. W. Feachem in *I A N B*, pp. 73–5 (plan).

DUNMORE, *see* BOCHASTLE.

DUN NA BAN-OIGE (fig. 63; Argyll, NM 837 048; 150 metres; p. 18).

This fort is structurally rather undistinguished, but is a good example of the adaptation of a naturally strong site. The top of the hill is an irregular hummocky plateau, with sides which are precipitous or nearly so except towards the north-east, where it is separated from the adjacent ground by a small saddle, the bottom of which is some 5 to 10 metres below the level of the rampart.

On this side the edge of the plateau is followed by the remains of a substantial stone wall. This is completely ruined and has been partly rebuilt as a modern boundary, so it is difficult to estimate its original size; it may have been more than 4 or 5 metres thick originally. The only entrance was near the north-west end. No details can be made out, but its position has been chosen so that the form of the ground enables the approach to be overlooked from the rampart on each side.

The wall continues for some distance along the south-east side of the hill, though it is here only about a metre thick. At one point it turns deliberately across a natural shelf below a low crag, as if to bar the use of this line for access. There is in fact a fairly easy ascent along this route, now followed by a sheep track.

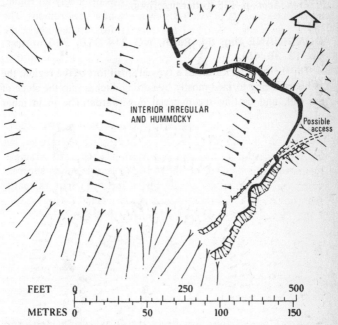

Fig. 63 Dun na Ban-Oige. Scale approximate.

The rest of the circuit seems to have been without artificial defences, though there are stones here and there which may indicate the presence of a wall. The interior (area about 1·7 hectares) is irregular, and offers many sites suitable for dwellings, but nothing likely to be contemporary with the defences is visible. There are remains of two or three turf-built structures near the centre, but they are almost certainly much more recent.

M. Campbell and M. Sandeman, *Proc. Soc. Ant. Scot.* XCV (1961–2), p. 52, No. 351. This valuable summary description and first record notes outer works to east and west and huts nearby.

DUNSAPIE (Midlothian, NT 282 731; 135 metres; p. 18).

The 'fort covered with tufts of grass' has been severely robbed, but can still be traced. The inner wall protected the south-east side of a summit with cliffs on west and north; the area enclosed was 0·5 hectares. An outer wall lies lower down the hill, and there are probable house platforms between the two.

Midlothian Inv. (1929), No. 10.
Preh. Scot., p. 135 (better description).

DUNSINANE (fig. 64; Perth, NO 214 316; 300 metres; pp. 19, 36, 45).

This is to all appearances a typical small fort of the region, the ramparts being formed mostly by cutting ditches into the slope of the hill, and casting the material downwards. The main inner

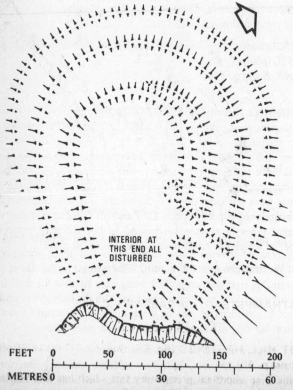

INTERIOR AT
THIS END ALL
DISTURBED

FEET	0	50	100	150	200
METRES	0		30		60

Fig. 64   Dunsinane. Based on D. Christison.

rampart is now only slightly above the level of the area enclosed, and the ditches mostly appear as terraces. The fort is egg-shaped, area 0·13 hectare; there are two banks and ditches with a counterscarp bank on most sides, increased by a third on the northeast, intermediate between the main and second bank. The entrance is by a straight passage running obliquely through all four banks from the north-east.

Traditionally, the fort is the site of Macbeth's castle; and it is in fact mentioned in an early chronicle as the place where Kenneth, King of Alban, was murdered in AD 995. These associations led to some excavations (in 1854) which are remarkably badly described even for that period. Nevertheless, the results indicate that the inner bank conceals the remains of a substantial stone wall, with inner and outer revetments of dry-built masonry, and that the interior contained buildings apparently of rectangular plan, all buried to a depth of about a metre by their own ruins. These could well have been part of the dwelling of King Kenneth, built within a partly refortified pre-Roman fort.

D. Christison, *Proc. Soc. Ant. Scot.* XXXIV (1899–1900), pp. 85 ff. (plan).
Preh. Scot., p. 146.

DURN HILL (Banff, NJ 571 638; 200 metres).

This is a good example of an unfinished hill-fort. It consists of three roughly concentric ovals, 200 by 110 metres, 204 by 140 metres and 208 by 160 metres respectively; the finished fort would have enclosed 1·7 hectares. The inner and outer markers are small ditches, while the middle line is indicated by piled stones. A little work has been done on the middle line, but construction was abandoned almost at once. Dr Feachem suggests that the two different types of marker correspond to two different projects, neither of which got much beyond the setting out stage.

R. W. Feachem in *I A H F*, pp. 27–8 (plan).

EASTHAMPSTEAD, *see* CAESAR'S CAMP.

EAST HILL, HASTINGS (fig. 65; Sussex, TQ 833 099; 90 metres; p. 48).

This is an important promontory fort which has received less attention than it deserves. It is protected by a strong bank and ditch across the base of the spur, with a sea cliff on the south and a steep natural slope on the north. The area enclosed is about 14 hectares, but some has been lost by erosion. The entrance seems to have been at the south end of the rampart, which is double for a short distance here. A further bank runs parallel to the cliff, as though there had been a long inturn, but erosion has rendered interpretation of these works uncertain.

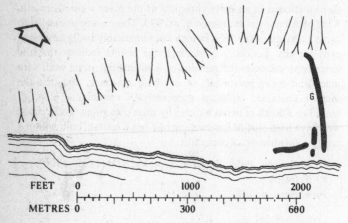

Fig. 65   East Hill, Hastings. After Victoria County History.

The particular interest of the fort comes from its close resemblance to many earthworks in France, where the *éperon barré*, a spur fortified by a single massive rampart, is a very characteristic type. The ditch at East Hill is occupied by gardens, and its form is obscured, but the fact that buildings have been erected close to the front of the rampart suggests that it may have been the broad flat-bottomed Fécamp type. East Hill may well be an important pre-Roman invasion base; the location is certainly appropriate.

VCH Sussex I (1905), p. 468.

ECHT, *see* **BARMEKIN OF ECHT.**

EDINSHALL (fig. 66; Berwick, NT 772 603; 200 metres; pl. 24).
This is a complicated structure of great interest, showing a long history of development; since there has been no recent excavation,

22 Clare

23 Clovelly Dykes

24 Edinshall

25 Figsbury Rings

26 Finavon

28 Hod Hill

27　Hambledon Hill

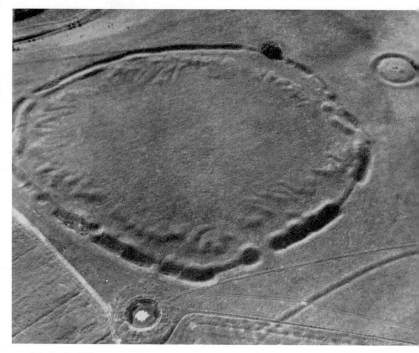

29 Ladle Hill

30 Mam Tor

31 Old Oswestry

32 Pen Dinas, Aberystwyth

33 Quarley Hill

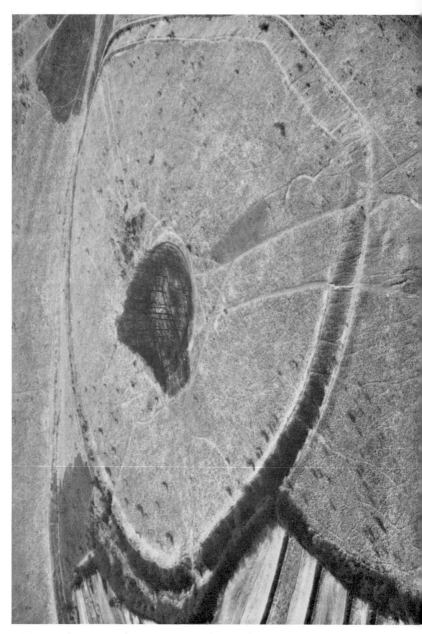

34   St Catherines Hill

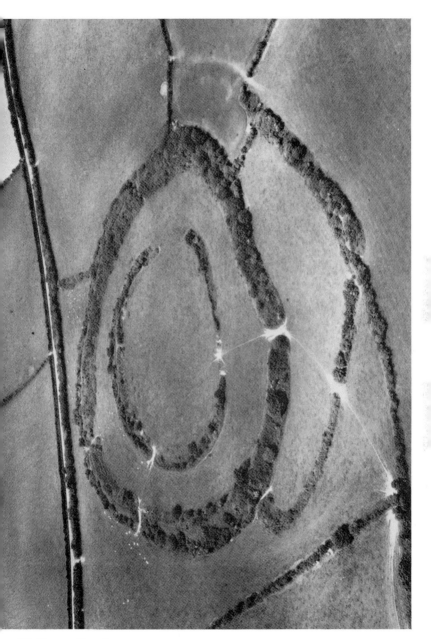

35 Tregeare Rounds

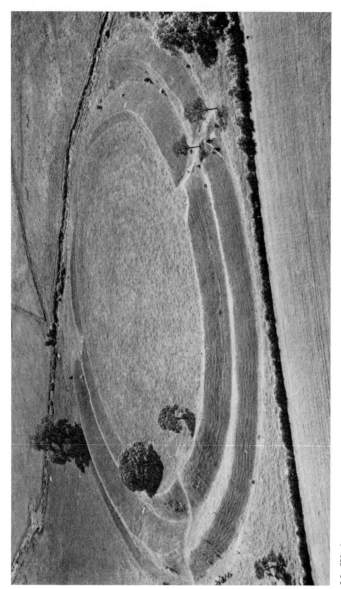

36 Warham

37 The White Caterthun

38 Winklebury

39　Woden Law

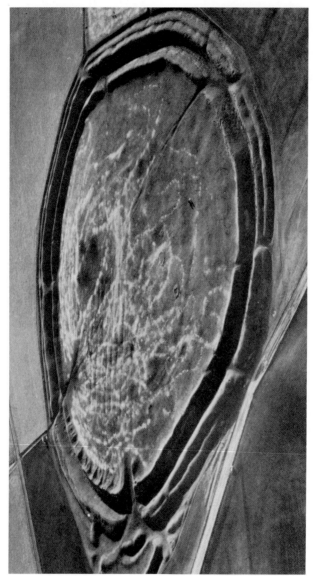

40 Yarnbury

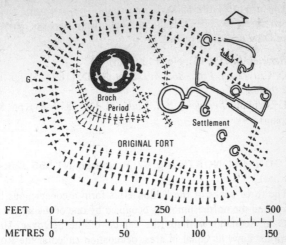

FEET   0   250   500

METRES 0   50   100   150

Fig. 66   Edinshall. After J. Turnbull and D. Christison.

the story of its evolution is not completely certain, but can be deduced fairly safely by analogy. The remains are under national guardianship.

Its earliest phase was a simple oval fort of 0·8 hectares, sited on ground not well suited to defence, but protected by two strong banks with accompanying ditches, with entrances to the east and the south-west. Within the enclosure, near the west end, are the remains of a later broch, with a wall about 6 metres thick, but now only about 2 metres high; the courtyard, an oval 15 by 18 metres, is unusually large. Three chambers exist in the thickness of its wall, in addition to the guard rooms on each side of the entrance. The bank which encloses the broch may well be contemporary with it. It is possible that the straight passage leading from the east gateway towards the broch is also of that period, but it seems more likely to be associated with the settlement of round stone houses, partly built over the destroyed ramparts of the fort on the north-east. One of these round houses, near the centre of the fort, is of quite exceptional size, being over 14 metres in diameter, within a wall 2·5 metres thick.

The site was extensively cleared in 1879, but although quite a good account was published the stratification of the few relics was not recorded. By analogy with other sites, the fort may be tentatively assigned to H 200, the broch to the early part of the second century AD (long after the abandonment of the fort), and the settlement to perhaps the third century and later.

The origin of the name is uncertain. The Inventory cites an earlier form, 'Wooden's Hall', and tentatively suggests derivation from Odin or 'Jötun' (giant).

Berwick Inv. (1915), No. 115 (plan).

D. Christison, *Proc. Soc. Ant. Scot.* XXIX (1894–5), pp. 161–2 (plans).

J. Turnbull, *Berwicks. Nat. Club* Vol. IX (1879–81), pp. 81 ff. (plan).

EILDON HILL NORTH (fig. 67; Roxburgh, NT 555 328; 400 metres).

The three peaks of the Eildon Hills form a conspicuous landmark, and the northernmost is occupied by one of the largest hill-forts in Scotland, perhaps the capital of the Selgovae. Unlike Traprain Law, its equal in area, occupation ended at the Roman conquest.

In its final form it was almost circular, enclosing 16 hectares. Within the triple ramparts, now mostly reduced to terraces, 296 hut platforms have been identified, and a hundred or so have probably been destroyed by a former plantation of trees which occupied a large shelf on the south of the enclosed area. There were four entrances, on the west, south-west, south-east and east; the ramparts are slightly incurved or otherwise modified at these gaps. A fifth opening, on the north, is modern.

The defences of the 16-hectare enclosure were the latest of three on the hill. The smallest, and probably the earliest, is barely visible on the ground but has been traced by the staff of the Scottish Ancient Monuments Commission from aerial photographs. It is a fairly regular oval, occupying 0·7 hectare and taking in the summit. The other rampart can still be traced as a terrace or very low bank. It enclosed just over 3 hectares, including some rather more comfortably habitable shelves. Both these ramparts have been cut into by hut platforms belonging probably to the 16-hectare fort.

At the Roman conquest, about AD 80, a large Roman fort was built at the northern foot of the hills, and this event almost certainly coincided with the enforced abandonment of the hill-fort. On the summit, however, a shallow ditch about 11 metres in diameter marks the position of a wooden tower built by the Romans for transmitting signals from the fort below.

Roxburgh Inv. II (1956), No. 597 (plans).

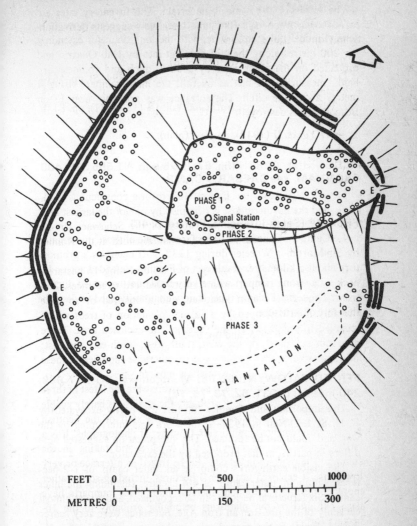

Fig. 67 Eildon Hill North. After Royal Commission on Historical Monuments (Scotland).

ESTON NAB (Yorks., NZ 568 183; 240 metres).

This strongly fortified enclosure occupies 1·1 hectares. It is semi-elliptical, 90 metres wide, with the long diameter extending for 200 metres along the cliff now cut into by Nab Quarry, and protected on the other sides by a bank, ditch and counterscarp bank, measuring 14 metres overall, the main rampart rising 4 metres above the ditch. The entrance was probably near Eston Beacon, but is destroyed.

VCH Yorks. II (1912), pp. 3–4 (plan).

FARNHAM, *see* CAESAR'S CAMP.

FÉCAMP (Seine-Inférieure, France; p. 48).

Le Camp du Canada, of 20 hectares, is one of those investigated by Sir Mortimer Wheeler during 1938–9. It occupies a promontory about 5 kilometres south-east of Fécamp, defended across the neck by a strong rampart with a very broad flat-bottomed ditch in front. The term 'Fécamp type' is now commonly used to describe this sort of structure.

H F N F, pp. 62–75, and pp. 9–11.

FFRIDD FALDWYN (fig. 68; Montgomery, SO 217 969; 240 metres; pp. 31, 62, 73, 76, 77).

This important and complex hill-fort was partly excavated by B. H. St J. O'Neil in 1937–9; the work was interrupted by the war, and could not be resumed. The interpretation suggested here differs in part from that proposed by the excavator.

The visible earthworks comprise an 'inner camp' of 1·2 hectares, within an 'outer camp' of 4·4 hectares (including the inner camp). Six structural periods can be recognized, and all are almost certainly of the pre-Roman Iron Age, but relics were very scarce indeed. Owing to the uncertainties in the analysis of this complex site, the same convention has been used for all phases.

There was some neolithic occupation of the hill-top, but the earliest defences were on the line of the inner camp, and consisted of a palisade formed by two rows, nearly 2 metres apart, of posts spaced similarly. These palisades turned inwards at a right angle to leave a passageway 11 metres wide and 6 long, at the rear of which two sets of three larger posts had formed a gateway.

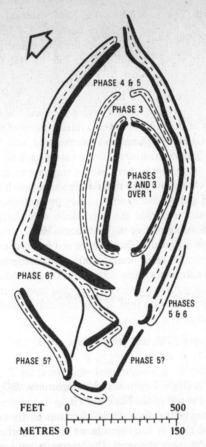

Fig. 68   Ffridd Faldwyn. After B. H. St J. O'Neil.

In the second phase, the palisade was replaced by a timber-laced wall separated by a berm from a rock-cut ditch, the whole system being about 15 metres wide. The details of the gateway were confused by later work. This rampart was destroyed by fire.

In phase three, after what seems to have been a fairly long interval, a new ditch was cut just inside the line of the original one, which was filled up, and a second ditch was made 20 metres further out. The gateway seems to have been similar in plan to that of the first phase. This enclosure was filled with rows of small square buildings, similar to those at Croft Ambrey and Credenhill. (But on the position of this phase in the structural sequence, see below.)

The remaining phases correspond to the large outer camp. Its inner rampart was built up in three stages. First (phase four) it seems to have been a simple dump, with a small ditch. Over the ruins of this was built a very substantial rampart, 7 metres wide with an almost vertical stone revetment front and rear (phase five), probably accompanied by a broad flat-bottomed ditch, the whole system being 21 metres wide and having a vertical height (from the surviving top of the bank to the excavated bottom of the ditch) of 10·5 metres. Finally (phase six) the revetted wall was buried beneath a large dump rampart. This last stage gave the impression of hurried work, and may have been a response to the arrival of the Romans. On the plan, the outer earthworks have been assigned to phases five and six, but almost entirely by conjecture.

The excavator regarded the outer ditch here described as of phase three as being part of the defences of phase two. The other structures here assigned to phases three and four were regarded as contemporary, the recut inner ditch being intended to keep animals within the inner camp.

B. H. St J. O'Neil, *Arch. Cambrensis* XCVII (1943), pp. 1–57.

FIGSBURY RINGS (fig. 69; Wilts., SU 188 338; 140 metres; p. 21, pl. 25).

The hill-fort is a simple oval enclosure, of 6·3 hectares, protected by a single large bank and ditch, now 26 metres wide overall, with the top of the bank still rising 7·5 metres above the original bottom of the ditch. Original entrances open on the east and west, and there is a modern break on the south. A roughly concentric ditch with corresponding entrance causeways can be traced about 40 metres behind the rampart, enclosing 2·6 hectares.

Excavations in 1924 showed that the existing bank had been built up in three phases. The inner ditch was also examined; in the excavator's view it was intended as a quarry ditch to provide material for the rampart, for it was very irregular. An alternative, perhaps more probable, would be to regard it as an unfinished defensive ditch.

Relics were sparse, mostly of Iron Age A culture.

At one time the site was regarded as 'Chlorus's camp' (p. 21).

M. E. Cunnington, *Wilts. Arch. Mag.* XLIII (1925), pp. 48–63 (plan p. 144 in some copies).
O. G. S. Crawford and A. Keiller, *Wessex from the Air* (Oxford 1928), p. 84, pl. IX (air photo).

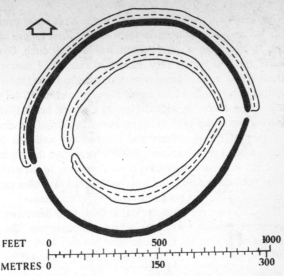

Fig. 69   Figsbury Rings. After M. E. Cunnington.

FINAVON (fig. 70; Angus, NO 506 556; 200 metres; p. 45, pl. 26).

This is a typical vitrified fort, so far as such a thing can be said to exist, and is unusually accessible. It was investigated by excavation in the early 1930s, so more details are known of its construction than of most others.

It was defended by a single massive wall, now heavily vitrified, enclosing 0·4 hectare. The plan seems to be the result of deliberate setting out, parallel-sided with semicircular ends, and pays little regard to the form of the ground. There is a further arc of walling outside the east end, linked to the main enclosure by a straight axial line of wall (*cf.* Castle Law, Forgandenny); this is now slightly lower than the ramparts which it links. There is also a horn of vitrified material projecting at the east end of the south wall. These features were not investigated. There is a rock-cut well in the enclosure, and a deep hollow which may also have been a water hole at the west end. The ramparts have been broken through by a modern track, but no ancient entrance can be identified.

Excavation showed that the wall was 6 metres thick, and it was estimated originally to have stood 3·6 metres high internally and 4·9 metres high externally, having been built on a slope. On the inner face, at a height of 2·4 metres, the wall face was set back

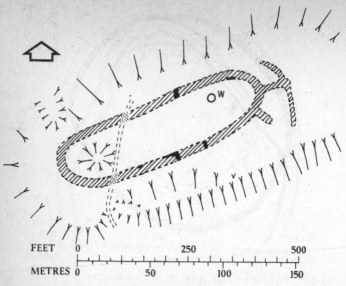

Fig. 70   Finavon. After V. G. Childe.

about 0·7 metres, and wherever tested remains of burned timbers
were found against the inside of the rampart. It seems that the
whole circuit must have been lined with timber buildings. Some
very coarse pottery was found. More recently, radiocarbon dating
of these burned remains indicated a date of probably between 400
and 600 BC for their construction.

V. G. Childe, *Proc. Soc. Ant. Scot.* LXIX (1934–5), pp. 49–80
(excavation); LXX (1935–6), pp. 347–52 (minor additional
details).
E. W. MacKie, *Antiquity* XLIII (1969), p. 17 (radiocarbon
dating).
P P, pl. 56 (air photo).

FOEL FENLLI (fig. 71; Denbigh, SJ 163 601; 510 metres).

This is one of the most impressive of the group of hill-forts on
the Clwydian Hills. The area enclosed is 10 hectares, protected on
all sides by strong ramparts; these probably represent several
phases of construction, but their development cannot be worked
out without excavation.

Round the western half of the fort the defences consist of an
inner bank (thrown up from an internal quarry ditch) separated by

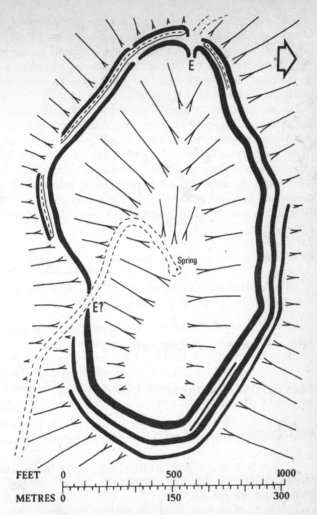

Fig. 71   Foel Fenlli. After W. Gardner and J. Forde-Johnston.

a steeply sloping berm from a ditch and counterscarp bank; the system measures about 30 metres overall. Round the remainder of the circuit the counterscarp bank becomes a second rampart, with a ditch and counterscarp bank outside it; here the overall width is 40 to 45 metres.

The only certain entrance is at the west end. It is inturned, and approached by a terraced roadway. A similar roadway leads through a gap on the south side, but there is no elaboration of the ramparts at this point to suggest an original gateway.

The interior contains numerous round platforms for timber huts, some very large, but these are often obscured by heather and no complete plan of them exists; Mr Forde-Johnston notes about two dozen. There is also a spring in the enclosure.

The occupation of the site did not end at the Roman conquest. Rough excavations, in 1849, recovered a considerable quantity of Roman material, covering the whole period from the second to the fourth century AD. This continuity of occupation is notable, for a tradition recorded before AD 800 states that the hill takes its name from Benlli, an 'iniquitous and tyrannical king' who opposed St Germanus, and who should therefore have lived about AD 450. Soon afterwards, he and his city were consumed by fire from heaven.

Willoughby Gardner, *Arch. Cambrensis* (1921), pp. 237–52 (plan).
J. Forde-Johnston, *Arch. Cambrensis* CXIV (1965), pp. 152–7 (plan).

FOEL TRIGARN, *see* **MOEL TRIGARN**.

FOLKESTONE, *see* **CAESAR'S CAMP**.

FORGANDENNY, *see* **CASTLE LAW**.

GARN BODUAN (fig. 72; Caernarvon, SH 310 393; 270 metres; pp. 43, 66, 77, 86).

This is one of the most interesting hill-forts in Caernarvonshire, and thanks to the public spirit of the owners the whole area was left free of trees when the sides of the hill were afforested; but unfortunately the unchecked natural vegetation is beginning to obscure some of the internal structures.

The top of this hill is well adapted to early settlement, as its westward slope forms a series of natural shelves, and two or three springs break out not far below the summit. The defences are of two periods. Initially, an area of some 10 hectares was enclosed by a wall about 3 metres thick, and later, by taking a part of the steeper slopes on the west, this was increased to over 11 hectares, with a stronger wall about 4 metres thick, still standing 2 metres high in places. The two entrances were simple gaps, the adjacent ends of the ramparts being slightly thickened. That to the north-east is well preserved, having been built up in antiquity. Both are approached by terraced trackways. Within the enclosure the walls of some 170 round houses can be traced, indicating a population of perhaps four to seven hundred persons, depending on the assumptions made. Excavations in four of these dwellings (during 1954) failed to produce any dating evidence, but for the most part they can be accepted as pre-Roman.

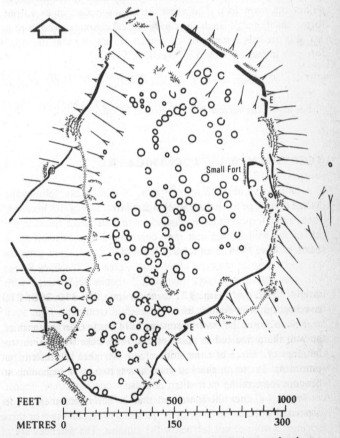

Fig. 72   Garn Boduan. After Royal Commission on Ancient Monuments (Wales).

The actual summit carries a small fort, defended by a rather more carefully built wall with steeply battered faces. Access to the top of the rampart was provided by stairs of projecting stones set in the back of the wall. There were two entrances, one (almost destroyed) from the south and another facing west. The latter is very well preserved, having been blocked during the period of use of the small fort; the rear face of the blocking contained two projecting steps. Immediately within this entrance was a round house, contemporary with the rampart and probably a guard house. The excavations mentioned above yielded some rather sparse evidence that this small fort was not earlier than the late Roman period, despite the similarity of the guard house to the dwellings within the main fort. The name Boduan signifies, in its earlier forms, the 'home of Buan', a semi-historical character who lived *c.* AD 600, so it is a tempting conjecture to suppose that the small fort may in fact have been his dwelling.

A. H. A. Hogg, *Arch. J.* CXVII (1960), pp. 1–39 (excavation report, plan).
See also *Caernarvon Inv.* III, No. 1524 (plan).

GARRYWHIN (fig. 73; Caithness, ND 313 413; 120 metres; p. 46).

A single wall about 2 metres thick, of laid blocks, follows the outline of a ridge to enclose an elongated oval fort of 0·8 hectares. There are entrances at the north and south ends, and a recess in the line of the wall on the east may correspond to a third; if so, it seems to have been intentionally blocked. The southern gateway was apparently of the type usual in this area (*cf.* Duchary Rock) with the entrance passage (about 2·5 metres wide) lined with upright slabs; one remains. The north gate, however, seems to have been given a deliberately monumental treatment. Four very large slabs, some 1·5 metres square, have been set in the faces of the wall (here doubled in thickness) to form impressive jambs to the gateway. Three of these still remain upright. The interior is featureless. The south gateway gives access to a small loch, and on the slope descending to it there is at least one hut circle, almost concealed by thick heather; but this is not necessarily to be associated with the fort.

Caithness Inv. (1911), No. 528.
Preh. Scot. p. 114.

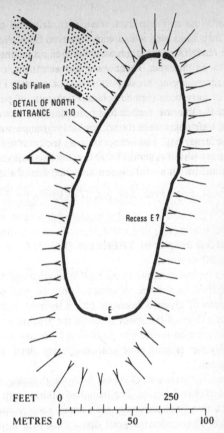

Slab Fallen

DETAIL OF NORTH
ENTRANCE x10

E

Recess E ?

E

FEET 0   250

METRES 0   50   100

Fig. 73 Garrywhin. Scale approximate.

GLENCORSE, see CASTLE LAW.

GRIMTHORPE (Yorks., SE 816 535; 150 metres; pp. 61, 62).

Although nothing remains visible, this fort deserves to be recorded here, for it has been recently and scientifically excavated.

The enclosure was almost circular, covering 3·1 hectares. It was defended by a ditch about 5 metres wide and 2 deep, of irregular profile, separated by a berm 4 to 5 metres wide from the rampart. This was represented by two rows of post holes, with traces of posts 30 centimetres in diameter. These were set 2 metres apart front to back and at 2 to 3 metres spacing along the line of the rampart, and to judge from the closeness of building behind their line they supported a wall with a vertical timber face on both sides. The chalk from the ditch would give this a height of about 3 metres, plus any parapet. A causeway across the ditch was found, with no accompanying break in the rows of posts; but a gateway could easily have been formed between two pairs of posts.

Most of the interior surface had been ploughed away, but eight settings of four posts were found, probably granaries on this site, though the larger could be houses or even look-out towers.

The pottery was of A style, H 400 say; but two radiocarbon dates were obtained which would suggest an actual age of about 800 BC.

I. M. Stead, *Proc. Preh. Soc.* XXXIV (1968), pp. 148–90.

GURNARD'S HEAD or TREREEN DINAS (Cornwall, SW 433 387; 30 metres).

This is a typical example of the way in which a coastal promontory lends itself to defence. A rampart only 60 metres long converts an area of about 3 hectares into a fortress, though indeed only about a third of the space is useful for grazing or habitation. Nevertheless, on an inland site, to defend 1 hectare would require a bank 350 metres long. The nearest landing place is some 300 metres distant.

The main rampart was of rubble with rough facing; it survived to a height of over 2 metres. The front had a fairly steep batter, and at the back two steps survived, each about a metre wide and 0·7 metres high. The section suggests that a third similar step formed the top of the main rampart, only a breastwork less than a metre thick and of uncertain height having been lost. This wall was supplemented by two shallow ditches in front of it with a dump bank between them, the whole system measuring 21 metres overall. Separated from these by a gap of 9 metres a steep-sided V-shaped ditch 3·5 metres wide runs halfway across the neck of the promontory, suggesting an unfinished addition to the defences. Slight though these appear in this description, they are commanded by a boss of rock just within the western half of the line. At the entrance, the two halves of the inner bank seem to overlap, but the actual gateway could not be excavated.

Two-thirds of the enclosed area is steep and rocky, but the eastern side forms a grassy slope, where the platforms of thirteen huts remain visible; some have been lost by erosion. They are round, the upper side cut into the slope, with a low stone wall round the lower half. Three were excavated. They produced pottery of B style, H 50–100, and rather surprisingly a scrap of Roman ware of the fourth century AD. The fort resembles some of the cliff castles found in Brittany.

A. S. R. Gordon (Mrs Gell), *Arch. J.* XCVII (1940), pp. 96–111.

HAMBLEDON HILL (fig. 74; Dorset, ST 845 126; 180 metres; pp. 35, 77, pl. 27).

This is one of the finest hill-forts in Britain, and has escaped disturbance. It stands on a narrow sinuous ridge fairly easily accessible from east and west at its southern end, but otherwise

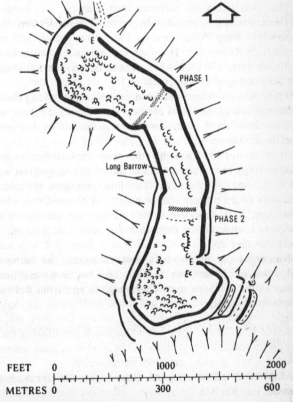

Fig. 74   Hambledon Hill. After Royal Commission on Historical Monuments (England).

steep-sided. On the ridge to the south-east the earthworks of a large neolithic 'camp' have recently been almost destroyed by ploughing; a long barrow of this period survives on the ridge within the Iron Age defences. These now consist of two banks with associated ditches, and a counterscarp bank, measuring about 45 metres horizontally overall, and still rising to a total vertical height of 15 metres. A large quarry ditch follows the inner bank for most of its length. Where the defences cross the ridge on the south-east, the easiest means of access, the outer is replaced by double banks and ditches, separated by a space 40 metres wide from the continuation of the main rampart. This is here very large, standing 10 metres high above the ditch bottom, and measuring some 30 metres wide from the rear toe of the main bank to the outer side of the counterscarp bank.

The elaboration of defences also protects the south-east entrance, which is approached by a track 150 metres long on the crest of the steep hillside, overlooked for the greater part of its length from the rampart. The south-west entrance is protected by a hornwork some 100 metres long. The third entrance, to the north, has been damaged by quarrying.

These massive defences are evidently the result of long development, and two of the stages can be traced, in part, on the ground. The northern third of the enclosure is cut off by the eroded remains of a single bank and ditch, indicating an original fort of 3 hectares at this end. Roughly the same distance further south another single cross-rampart can be traced; this second fort would have enclosed 5·2 hectares. The final extension brought the enclosure to its present size of nearly 10 hectares, but without excavation it is imposible to say whether or not the multiple ramparts correspond to more than one period of building; it is likely that they do.

Numerous hut platforms, almost all round, can be seen — eighty-two in the northern section, forty-five in the middle and eighty in the southern part. They range in size from 4·5 to 14 metres in diameter.

Dorset Inv. III (1970), pt I, pp. 82–3 (plan, profiles, photographs).

HARDING'S DOWN (fig. 75; Glamorgan, SS 437 906; 150 metres; pp. 35, 54).

This carries an interesting group of three enclosures, probably all roughly contemporary.

On the summit ('Harding's Down East') is an unfinished example of the south-western type of wide-spaced multivallate enclosure. It was planned for an internal area of 0·9 hectares, and the organization (or lack of it) applied to the work contrasts strikingly with that at Ladle Hill. Here the work seems to have been marked out with stakes (no setting out trench exists), and sections allocated to volunteers. Some of these completed the work, even to building an inner revetment of large blocks; others

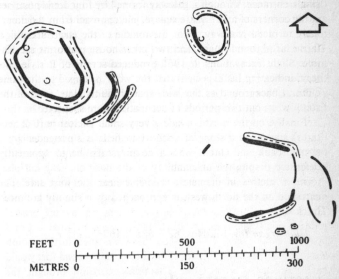

FEET 0   500   1000

METRES 0   150   300

Fig. 75   Harding's Down. After Royal Commission on Ancient Monuments (Wales).

(of a kind not unknown today) did nothing. As a result most of the eastern half of the circuit is complete, now appearing as a turf-covered bank and ditch about 2·5 metres high by 11 or 12 metres wide overall; the inner revetment, mostly removed, can be traced by a robber trench. Where the west end was to be, also, a short length of completed rampart remains. All this work, however, was rendered useless, for no attempt has been made to link up the detached sections. The outer rampart, which forms a wide enclosure on the south and east, also seems to be unfinished; but it is relatively slight.

About 250 metres away is a smaller, complete enclosure ('Harding's Down West'), of 0·6 hectare. The position was skil-fully chosen so that although the ground as a whole slopes steeply, the upper (eastern) end crosses a small local summit, giving a commanding view over the approaches. For reasons which remain incomprehensible by any modern ideas about defence, this eastern approach was (later?) crossed by two banks and ditches, widely spaced, which obstruct the view from the main rampart and can easily be passed at each end. The main (original?) enclosure was protected by a single bank, probably revetted with stone, standing some 5 metres above the bottom of a V-shaped ditch. There was a single entrance, through a gateway formed by four large posts set at the corners of a 2·7-metre square, and approached by a deliberately terraced roadway. Near the middle of the enclosure was a fairly large round house, and two other house platforms are visible. Slight excavations in 1962 produced scraps of B style pottery, indicating (as expected) that the work belonged to the same cultural background as the 'wide-spaced multivallate' forts of the south-west; but two periods of occupation were suspected.

Finally, on the northern side a very small enclosure (0·2 hectares) stands on a slope of about 1 in 6. It is surrounded by a strong bank and ditch, with a counterscarp bank, apparently defensive despite the unsuitability of the position. One hut platform, 6 metres in diameter, is visible near the west side. The entrance, to the north-west, is approached by a slightly hollowed trackway.

Glamorgan Inv. I ii, Nos. 687, 688, 646 (plans).

HASTINGS, *see* **EAST HILL.**

HEMBURY CASTLE (fig. 76; Devon, ST 112 031; 270 metres; pp. 18, 67).

This fort was the scene of an important excavation campaign by Miss D. M. Liddell from 1930 to 1935, so although the name (see p. 18) is not uncommon, 'Hembury', in an archaeological context, almost always refers to this site. The work was of high quality, and it is no criticism to say that it has suffered the usual fate of pioneer research, in that subsequent investigations elsewhere have raised questions which cannot be answered from the published report.

The structure now appears as an elongated pear-shaped enclosure, 350 by 100 metres (3 hectares), defended on all sides by close-set double ramparts with ditches. The outer ditch is accompanied by a counterscarp bank on the north and west, and is

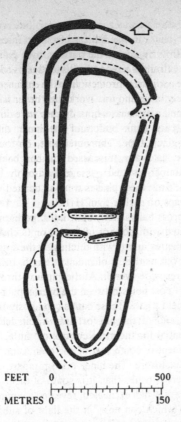

FEET   0   500

METRES 0   150

Fig. 76   Hembury Castle. After D. M. Liddell.

obscured on the east. The interior is divided near the middle by two relatively slight cross-banks. There are gateways opening to east and west.

The history of the site proved complex. Archaeologically, one of the most important discoveries was that the hill (as at The Trundle) had been occupied by a neolithic causewayed camp. These are enclosures apparently similar to hill-forts but with the ditches interrupted by very frequent causeways, often with corresponding gaps in the bank. Their function is uncertain, but they are generally accepted at present as places for seasonal assemblies. The association with the later hill-fort is almost certainly fortuitous.

Tentatively, the following evolution may be suggested for the hill-fort itself.

The initial defence was a single rampart following the line of the present inner bank. It was built up from an internal quarry ditch and faced with turf and, on the outside, by a palisade of close-set posts. At the entrances a second palisade seems to have looped outwards to give additional protection to the entrances; but the details are not entirely clear and this work may never have been finished.

In the second main phase, both ditches were dug, the outer bank and counterscarp bank built and the inner enlarged; all were probably of glacis type. The outermost, on the north, was not finished. The gateways, discussed further below, were reconstructed as timber-revetted passages, probably bridged, between short inturns. Both these phases were associated with pottery of B culture, perhaps no earlier than H 150.

The two cross-banks were built later, perhaps H 50, for they were associated with pottery of Belgic or C character. They run parallel, 13 metres apart, with ditches on the south. The northern is the larger, but neither is of much strength, being no more than some 10 metres wide overall. At the gateway through the southern bank a pair of post holes between the overlapping ends of the ditch presumably held a gate. These banks can hardly be said to convert the northern end of the hill-fort into a 'citadel', but they seem rather substantial for the mere control of cattle. They may imply the establishment of some sort of social division between the two parts of the enclosure. The inner main rampart is stronger to the north of the cross-banks than it is south of them.

The gateways, when excavated, revealed a complex arrangement of post holes which can now, in the light of subsequent work on other sites, be recognized as representing at least four periods of construction, probably considerably more. They both consisted of a passage some 10 to 20 metres long and 6 or 8 metres wide, the sides revetted with timber laid horizontally behind spaced upright posts, and probably spanned by a bridge. The gateway itself seems to have been rather narrower, at the inner end of the passage, and there are indications which can be interpreted as implying guard rooms, though the evidence is not conclusive. One of the post holes in the east gateway yielded the iron ring of the gate pivot.

Not much of the interior was examined. The only building identified seems to have been rectangular; but only one corner was found.

D. M. Liddell, *Proc. Devon Arch. Exploration Soc.* I (1929–32), pp. 40–63, 90–120, 162–90; II (1933–36), pp. 135–75 (including summary of results).

HENGISTBURY HEAD (Hants., SZ 170 908; 30 metres; p. 36).

Christchurch Harbour is to the north of the Head. The southern cliff has been greatly eroded, and saltings have formed on the harbour side where a long shingle bank running north-east from the end of the headland makes a natural breakwater. Its form when the prehistoric defences were built can only be guessed at. Probably neither the saltings nor the shingle bank was present, but even without these the estuary of the Stour must have offered an attractive natural harbour.

The main body of the head is a low hillock some 1,200 metres long rising to about 30 metres above ordnance datum; this is joined to the mainland by an almost level stretch rising only 4 or 5 metres above O.D. The defences have been built almost straight across this lower ground, protecting an area which is now (excluding the saltings) about 450 metres wide by 1,500 long; but before erosion the protected area must have been much more than the present 70 hectares.

The ramparts consisted of two close-set banks and ditches, measuring 42 metres wide overall, the inner bank still rising 7 metres above the original ditch bottom. They seem to have been of glacis type, and may have included work of more than one period. There was probably an entrance between slightly incurved banks near the north end, but this is much worn down.

The enclosed area was extensively trenched in 1911–12. The technique of hill-fort excavation at that date was barely embryonic, and very little detailed structural information was obtained (though buildings seem when identified to have been round or oval). Nevertheless, much pottery was recovered, ranging throughout the whole of the Iron Age and extending into the Roman period. What was particularly interesting was the discovery of several types of ware for which close parallels could be found on the continent, showing that the potentialities of the position as a port had not been neglected. In addition, some three thousand coins were found; the presence of a mint may be suspected, possibly *the* mint of the Durotriges.

The name Hengistbury seems to be a relatively modern invention; the place was called Hynesbury in the seventeenth century, and Hednesburia in the twelfth.

J. P. Bushe-Fox, *Excavations at Hengistbury Head* . . . , Society of Antiquaries of London Research Report III (1915).
Recently (1971) work on the site has been recommenced, by Dr D. P. S. Peacock.

HOD HILL (fig. 77; Dorset, ST 857 106; 140 metres; pp. 44, 49, 55, 77, 80, 82, 83, 84, pl. 28).

This hill-fort is the only example known in this country where an auxiliary Roman fort can be seen superimposed on earlier works. Also, the pre-Roman defences are very impressive, and almost 3 hectares of the interior have escaped modern disturbance,

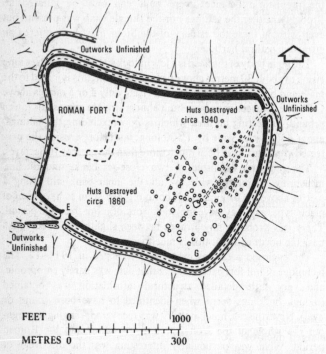

Fig. 77   Hod Hill. After Royal Commission on Historical Monuments (England).

preserving the plan of this part of the settlement as it was when the Romans took over. The clarity with which the arrangement can be followed seems to be unique in lowland Britain. As much again was destroyed in the early 1940s, without even a preliminary survey.

The site was excavated during 1951–8 on behalf of the British Museum, under the direction of Sir Ian Richmond, whose untimely death occurred while the report was in proof. The work was seen through to completion by J. W. Brailsford, who also contributed several important sections of it.

Hod Hill is a spur of the Dorset chalk uplands, with very steep scarps on the west and north, and gentler slopes on the other two sides. The defences now consist, for most of the circuit, of two close-set banks and ditches, with a counterscarp bank in places; the outer defence is omitted along the steep west side. The area enclosed is 22 hectares. There are entrances near each corner and at the middle of the east side. This last and that to the north-west are Roman, and that to the south-east is medieval or later, but the other two, to north-east and south-west, are prehistoric.

The present massive defences comprise work of three or four periods, a fifth being represented by outworks.

In phase one (of Iron Age A culture, H 400–300), there was a single rampart, accompanied by a ditch. The latter was mostly cut away by later work, but must have been some 6 metres wide and 3 deep to provide the material needed for the rampart. That was revetted on both sides with timber. In front, the uprights were set in a continuous slot near the edge of the ditch. Behind these, a level platform was first made up, running back 8 or 9 metres to meet the slope of the hill, and in the rubble composing it spaced uprights were set, holding longitudinal timber which retained the fill of the rampart. Stratification suggested the presence of transverse lacing also, but no certain evidence survived. The resulting wall was 3 metres thick and probably of similar height in front, about a metre less at the back. It followed the same line as the later ramparts, but was not built above the very steep western slope. The positions of any entrances are uncertain.

In the next phase (II A, H 200–100) this box rampart was cut down to form a continuous slope with the ditch face, and the whole was buried by a mass of new material, derived not from an enlarged ditch but from quarry pits opened behind the rampart. This new work, rising some 8 or 9 metres above the bottom of the ditch, had a parapet of flint blocks protecting a wall walk 3 metres wide. As a further protection, a palisade was set up 15 metres outside the lip of the ditch. Scattered human bones found at its foot suggest that it may also have been used to display the impaled bodies of enemies. The larger rampart, though not necessarily the palisade, was carried round the whole circuit. At the north-east gate (the only one excavated) this outer palisade curved in to join the similar revetment of the gate passage. The passage, 7 metres wide, was crossed by a bridge, supported at each end (and probably in the middle also) by pairs of posts; one of the resulting sets of three uprights presumably supported the gates. This phase and that which followed, were both of B culture.

The next step (II B, H 100–50) was to enlarge the ditch, all the material being dumped to form a large counterscarp bank 13 metres wide and at least 2 metres high, burying the remains of the palisade. The overall width of the defences was now nearly 35 metres, the ditch being 10 metres wide and nearly 5 deep. Apart from the replacement of the outer palisade by a bank, the gate plan remained essentially unaltered. Some spiritual protection seems to have been added, for immediately before the construction of the counterscarp bank a young woman was interred beneath its line, in a pit just outside the gateway.

The arrival of Iron Age C influences seems to correspond to phase three of the defences, though as will be seen this work may have been a response to the Roman invasion. The rampart was increased in width by about 3 metres, and in height by 1 metre, being provided with a flint-paved rampart walk and a parapet wall of the same material. This addition was not carried along the west side. Work on the main rampart seems to have been finished, but other improvements seem to have been left uncompleted, suggesting that these changes were a response to the Roman invasion, rather than earlier.

No skeletons of battle casualties were discovered, but the Roman attack left other dramatic evidence. One house stands out from the rest of those which survive, by its situation in a separate compound. Examination of it and its neighbour revealed eleven iron ballista bolts, still embedded as they had landed after firing from a machine just outside the south-east angle of the fort. The excavator marshals a number of arguments to suggest that this demonstration of firepower was aimed at the chieftain's dwelling, and that its success led to the capitulation of the tribe; there is no other evidence of battle.

After the conquest, the flint breastwork cresting the rampart was cast down, the dwellings destroyed, and a Roman fort built in the north-west corner. Its regularly laid out defences, a broad bank with two widely spaced ditches, contrast strongly with the gentle curves of the earlier works. The internal buildings, of timber, are no longer visible, but their plan was recovered by excavation and follows the systematic rectilinear arrangement normal to such a fort. Occupation ended after an accidental fire, probably in AD 51.

I. A. Richmond, *Hod Hill* II (British Museum, 1968).
O. G. S. Crawford and A. Keiller, *Wessex from the Air* (Oxford, 1928), p. 36, pl. I (aerial view before 1940 destruction).

HOLLINGBURY (Sussex, TQ 322 078; 180 metres).

One of the line of forts on the South Downs, very roughly 150 metres square with rounded corners, enclosing 2·5 hectares with a strong single bank and ditch, now measuring 14 metres wide overall. The crest of the bank still stands 2·5 metres above the bottom of the ditch, which was originally 2 metres deeper. The rampart was reinforced by two rows of posts about 2 metres apart in both directions, the outer line about 3 metres from the original lip of the ditch, but these did not support a revetment, at least so far as the rampart survived. They may have carried a fighting platform. The east gateway was simple, with two large posts to support the gate. The west gateway, unexcavated, had inturned ramparts. The site was initially occupied (perhaps weakly fortified) about H 450 by people of A culture, and the present rampart was built by B invaders, H 250–300.

E. C. Curwen, *Ant. J.* XII (1932), pp. 1–17 (plan).

HOLWOOD, *see* CAESAR'S CAMP, KESTON.

HONINGTON (fig. 78; Lincoln, SK 954 423; 110 metres; p. 36).

Hill-forts are rare in Lincolnshire, and this is the only one which seems characteristic, though it is rather to be described as a

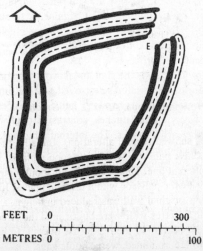

Fig. 78 Honington. Scale approximate.

'related structure', for it stands on ground which is almost flat. It is protected by close-set double banks and ditches, with a counterscarp bank, the system measuring 18 metres wide overall. There is an entrance, apparently a simple gap, in the east side. The enclosed area is 0·5 hectares.

C. W. Phillips, *Arch. J.* XCI (1934), pp. 101–2; and facing p. 103, pl. XIX (air photo).

HOWNAM RINGS (fig. 79; Roxburgh, NT 790 194; 320 metres).

This was the first site where the complex development of the small forts of the Scottish borders was demonstrated. The enclosed area remained about the same throughout, at 0·65 hectares, but

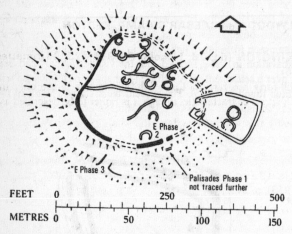

Fig. 79   Hownam Rings. After C. M. Guido.

the defences showed several alterations. Initially, the only protection was a single palisade, which was soon replaced by another on a slightly different line. Then a single wall about 3 metres wide was built just inside the palisade with a ditch in places. In its last phase as a 'fort' this original wall was reduced in height, and three more banks about 5 metres wide were built round the circuit so that the defences were nearly 40 metres across overall. In each phase the entrances, where examined, were simple gaps.

Finally, after the Roman conquest, the defences were allowed to decay, and an open settlement of round stone huts extended over the site.

The native pottery showed little change during the use of the site, but the dates are probably: palisades, H 300; first fort H 250; additional ramparts H 70; settlement, AD 100 and later.

C. M. Piggott (C. M. Guido) *Proc. Soc. Ant. Scot.* LXXXII (1947), pp. 193–225.

HUNSBURY (Northants., SP 738 583; 110 metres).

This fort now appears as a round enclosure of 1·7 hectares (axes 170 and 130 metres), defended by a single bank and ditch about 20 metres wide and 6 high overall. Part of another ditch 80 metres further north was discovered in 1903, but is no longer visible, and its date and function are unknown. The interior has been dug over for ironstone, and the main interest of the fort derives from the large collection of decorated metalwork, pottery and other objects discovered there. These are mostly in the Northampton Museum. They range in date from H 350 to H 50.

Excavation in 1952 showed that the visible rampart had been built over a settlement of A culture (perhaps to be associated with the ditch found in 1903). The present bank showed work of two phases. Initially, it had a vertical timber revetment, but subsequently this was removed and the whole rampart covered with clay to give a glacis-type of defence.

C. I. Fell, *Arch. J.* XCIII (1936), pp. 57–100 (description of objects). For note of 1952 excavation results, see *ibid.* CX (1953), p. 213.

INGLEBOROUGH (Yorks., SD 741 747; 715 metres; p. 17).

A single stone wall, curiously constructed with transverse lines of upright slabs incorporated in it, forms a pear-shaped enclosure 330 metres from north-west to south-east by 230 metres (6 hectares). There are traces of hut circles within, but although the position is magnificent it hardly seems suitable for permanent occupation.

This may be the original site known as Rigodunum.

VCH Yorks. II (1912), p. 24 (small plan).
A. King, *Early Pennine Settlement* (1970), pp. 74–6 (air photo and wall reconstruction); full account forthcoming, *Arch. J.*

IVINGHOE BEACON (Bucks., SP 960 169; 230 metres; pp. 30, 47, 62).

The fort occupied a prominent spur of the Chilterns, separated from the main range by a shallow valley on the south-west. Erosion has almost obliterated the defences, which can now be traced as a terrace below which the hillside steepens. They form an enclosure of 2·2 hectares, roughly pear-shaped in plan, 220 metres long from east to west, and 160 metres wide at the broader (western) end. Excavations during 1963–5, by Dr M. A. Cotton and Professor S. S. Frere, yielded important results.

For the greater part of the circuit the defences consisted of a mass of chalk rubble with timber revetments to front and rear, accompanied by a ditch about 3 metres wide and deep, of blunt V-section. On the south and west a small additional ditch was dug, about 4 metres outside the main ditch. The arrangement of the rampart timbering was unusual. It consisted of two lines of upright posts. The outer line ran close to the edge of the ditch, but the distance back to the inner ranged from 1 to 4 metres. The longitudinal spacing also ranged from 2 to 5 metres, though the inner and outer posts were roughly paired. The gateway was about 3 metres wide, with an entrance passage of similar length lined with large posts, showing evidence for at least one replacement. The adjacent ends of the ditch turned in slightly towards the rampart, leaving a causeway some 8·5 metres wide. A puzzling feature, not easy to explain, was the presence of a hole for a large post set in the rampart close to each ditch end. The excavators considered that the gateway was not bridged.

The area cleared inside the fort revealed numerous post holes including those for one round house of 7·5 metres diameter, and another of similar size but D-shaped, set against the rampart; also for two granaries, with four posts set in a 4·5-metre square with a central post, and for a roughly rectangular house 4·2 by 6 metres.

The finds were surprising, for although there was a considerable amount of pottery which could be regarded as of Iron Age A type (H 400–500), the metal finds were almost all typologically of the Late Bronze Age (H 700). Ivinghoe Beacon must therefore be considered one of the earliest hill-forts yet known in Britain.

M. A. Cotton and S. S. Frere, *Records of Buckinghamshire* XVIII.3 (1968), pp. 187–260.

KEMP'S WALK (fig. 80; Wigtown, NW 975 598; 35 metres).

A promontory with a fairly level top lies between the sea and a deep ravine, and is joined to the mainland at the north end, where the principal defences lie. There is an entrance, now a simple gap, at the middle of this end, and west of it three strong banks and

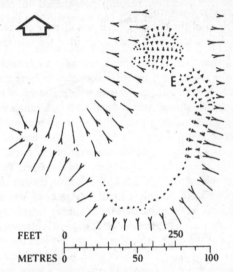

FEET   0   250

METRES 0   50   100

Fig. 80   Kemp's Walk. After Royal Commission on Historical Monuments (Scotland).

ditches, measuring about 30 metres wide overall, cut across the easiest approach. East of the entrance the outer bank and ditch are omitted. The middle bank dies away at the edge of the ravine but the inner bank, with its ditch reduced to a terrace, continues round the east and south sides, and probably on the west also though it has been destroyed by erosion. The enclosed area is oval, of 0·35 hectares, which is unusually large for the coastal forts in this district. At the tip of the promontory a narrow neck of land leads to a small hillock, on the top of which the Royal Commission's investigators considered that there had been a hut circle. More recent investigation (*ex inf.* Dr K. Steer) indicates that the hillock lay outside the enclosure and that the supposed hut circle is very doubtful; the defences seem to be unfinished.

Wigtown Inv. (1912) No. 174 (plan).
Preh. Scot., p. 161.

KESTON, *see* **CAESAR'S CAMP.**

LADLE HILL (fig. 81; Hants., SU 479 568; 220 metres; pp. 54, 56, pl. 29).

The earthwork on this hill is an excellent example of a hill-fort left incomplete, and is particularly noteworthy as one of the first in Britain where this was recognized.

About a third of the chosen circuit was already marked by an earlier boundary ditch with a bank away from the interior of the

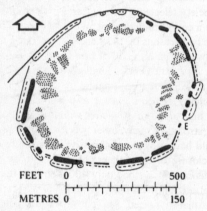

Fig. 81   Ladle Hill. After S. Piggott.

projected enclosure. The first step in constructing the defences was to cut a small ditch round the rest of the circuit, throwing the excavated material inwards. The whole perimeter was thus marked out by a ditch about 3 metres wide and perhaps 0·5 metre deep, accompanied by a bank of similar size; the area enclosed was 3·3 hectares. There were to be entrances to south-west and east. Separate gangs – probably about a dozen – then began to deepen and widen the ditch. The topsoil and loose chalk were heaped up in dumps some distance behind the line of the rampart. As larger blocks of hard chalk were reached, these were used to build the rampart.

At that stage the work stopped. The reason, of course, remains unknown; the archaeologist can only be grateful. The small setting-out ditch remains visible at many points, where work of the separate gangs has not joined up. The dumps of topsoil, which do not seem to have been recorded elsewhere, would presumably have been used as the final capping of the rampart.

S. Piggott, *Antiquity* V (1931), pp. 474–85.

LITTLE WOODBURY (Wilts., SU 150 279; 80 metres; pp. 35, 74, 75, 78).

This enclosure, previously unknown, was discovered by aerial photography in the 1920s; the name is not traditional, but was given for convenience after the discovery. Subsequently the Prehistoric Society selected it for a research excavation to uncover systematically a complete settlement. Work was halted by the war, but during the two seasons of 1938 and 1939 about a third of the area was uncovered, and a flood of new light was thrown on the nature of Iron Age settlement in southern Britain.

Had the earthwork escaped levelling by the plough, in its final state it would have formed a grass-grown bank and ditch some 2 or 2·5 metres high and 8 or 10 metres wide overall. It would thus have been as strong as many other works classed as hill-forts, though it would have looked unimpressive against a roughly contemporary enclosure of three times the area, with a much more substantial defence, which stood only 400 metres to the west.

The excavations showed that for most of its existence the settlement was merely fenced. The construction of the 'hill-fort' defence was a brief episode; the work was never finished, and the ditch was soon used as a dump for rubbish, which filled something like two-thirds of its depth before the place was deserted. Nevertheless, the results of the work provide a most valuable clue to the sort of settlement which may have stood within one of the smaller forts in southern Britain. It is for that reason that Little Woodbury needs to be described in any study of hill-forts.

The settlement stood in an almost level plain; the actual position chosen rose very slightly above the surroundings, and provided extensive views, but gave no other advantage for defence. For most of its life, the only protection was a substantial palisade, which would have been of little value for defence. It was entered by a gateway 2·5 metres wide between two pairs of posts a metre apart, the actual double gate being at the inner end of the short passage thus formed. These four posts were deeply set, and probably supported some sort of tower, which may have been merely for display, though (*pace* the excavator) a watch tower in this type of country would considerably extend the range of view. The space enclosed by the palisade was an oval, about 130 metres north-west to south-east by 100 metres wide (area 1 hectare).

At some stage in the life of the settlement, the inhabitants decided that a more substantial defence was needed. Only the ditch of this work survived, completely buried. It was V-shaped, with a narrow flat bottom, and seems to have been intended to be 3 metres deep and nearly 4 metres wide at the top; steps and irregularities show that it was never finished, and in places the excavated chalk was thrown back almost at once. An interesting feature of the fort, as designed, was a pair of ditches diverging, like antennae, one on each side of the proposed entrance, and thus providing a funnel-like approach which would simplify driving cattle into the enclosure.

Occupation continued for a long time after the threat which had led to this unfinished fortification. There were some minor changes in the palisade arrangements, but the character of the settlement remained essentially unaltered.

Within the enclosure was a maze of post holes and hollows. Two round houses were identified. The earlier, which had been rebuilt at least once on essentially the same plan, was 14 metres in diameter, comprising two rings 1·5 metres apart concentric with a framework formed by four large uprights set in at the corners of a 3-metre square, the entrance being through an elaborate porch. The detailed reconstruction still remains a matter for discussion.

This house was nearly central, and was probably the only substantial dwelling in the enclosure. After a life of some two centuries, it was replaced (or perhaps supplemented) by a smaller and less elaborate building; the general character of the settlement did not change. This can best be conveyed by describing what a visitor might have seen in, say, H 200.

Entering from the east through the gateway in the palisade, he would find a fairly open space, obstructed only by one or two drying racks. Immediately facing him would be the porch of the large house. One or two pigs would probably be rooting in the mud, but few of these animals were kept; the cattle would normally be in the fields.

To left and right of the house, drying racks would be numerous, and scattered among them, in no sort of order, would be the pits for grain storage – some still unopened, some empty, some disused except as rubbish dumps. West of the house was a large irregular hollow, some 20 or 25 metres across each way and about 0·5 metres deep. This, by modern analogies abroad, can be recognized as the area where most of the sedentary part of the farm work was carried on, the edges providing convenient seats, no doubt protected by rough temporary shelters. As one hollow became unusable, it would be filled with ashes and rubbish and another dug.

Finally, in a relatively clear space averaging 20 metres wide between the hollow and the western side of the enclosure, there would be a scatter of small buildings about 3 metres square fairly widely spaced. These would be the above-ground granaries for the seed corn; presumably the relative tidiness and cleanliness of this area were dictated by the need to diminish fire risk, for this corn, more than any other single item, was the essential on which the life of the settlement depended.

The pottery is all of late A or B culture, and indicates occupation lasting from rather before H 300 to some time after H 100, the episode leading to the incomplete fortification occurring rather before the middle of this period.

It is interesting to note that despite the impressive dwelling there is nothing to indicate that the owner was anything more than a prosperous farmer. The reports do not indicate in detail what metalwork was found, but there seem to have been no weapons and no ornate bronzes, such as would be expected if the occupant had been some sort of local 'lord'.

G. Bersu, *Proc. Preh. Soc.* VI (1940), pp. 30–111 (excavation report).
J. Brailsford and J. W. Jackson, *ibid.* XIV (1948), pp. 1–23 (pottery and animal remains).

LLANBEDR-Y-CENNIN, *see* **PEN-Y-GAER.**

LLANMELIN (fig. 82; Monmouth, ST 460 925; 100 metres; p. 41).

This hill-fort, in national guardianship, was partly excavated in 1930–32. It now appears as an oval enclosure of 1·2 hectares, protected round most of its circuit by two banks and ditches with a counterscarp bank, with a curious roughly rectangular annexe of just under 1 hectare.

The excavations suggest (but do not prove) a more complex history than that proposed by the excavator. It seems likely that the earliest work was a very elongated oval, protected by a single bank, probably revetted, with ditch and counterscarp, measuring about 30 metres wide and 4 high overall. This survives as the projecting arc of extra defences on the north-east.

It was replaced by the existing double defences, mostly following the line of the earlier work. The inner rampart was a massive dry-stone wall some 5 metres thick, with revetted faces, the inner vertical and the outer battered, separated by a berm from the ditch. Beyond this were further defences, perhaps contemporary with the wall but perhaps later. These comprised a bank of dump construction, another ditch and a counterscarp bank. This system, at its

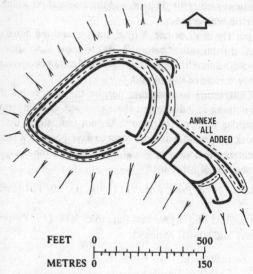

ANNEXE
ALL
ADDED

FEET   0   500
METRES 0   150

Fig. 82   Llanmelin. After V. E. Nash-Williams.

widest, measured about 30 metres across, but for much of the circuit the outer works were reduced to a wide sloping berm and a single ditch, though still measuring about 25 metres overall. In this phase the entrance was asymmetrical, one side of the passage being formed by the butt end of the rampart, the other by an inturn about 15 metres long. The gate was supported between two posts at the inner end of this passage.

Later still, the annexe was added. Its function is obscure. Interpretation of the site was rendered difficult by thick undergrowth.

All the relics found (apart from some Roman and medieval material) were of B culture. The excavator considered that the fortress was built in the second century BC, the annexe added soon after, and the gateway reconstructed *c*. AD 50. Earlier dates would now be more acceptable.

V. E. Nash-Williams, *Arch. Cambrensis* LXXXVIII (1933), pp. 237–311 (excavation report, plan, sections, etc.).

LLANYMYNECH HILL (Montgomery, SJ 265 220; 220 metres; p. 36).

Llanymynech Hill is an impressive plateau on the extreme border of Wales; indeed, the actual boundary follows part of the rampart. The circuit of the hill has been fortified, converting it into one of the largest hill-forts in Britain, an oval with axes of about 950 and 650 metres enclosing 57 hectares. It is in fact the only fort known in the region which is large enough to have been Caratacus's headquarters before his defeat by the Romans; but to make its position fit the other requirements seems impossible.

For much of the circuit, the sides of the plateau are so steep that little defence is needed, and a single rampart of no great strength was considered sufficient. This can still be seen on the west side, where it was later treated as part of the line of Offa's Dyke. On the north and east, the ramparts seem to have been double, and perhaps triple in places. They survive in fairly good condition for about 300 metres on the north, but have otherwise been damaged by gardens and quarrying. Near the middle of the northern section is an entrance with the ramparts inturned, and the damaged remains of another, similar, exist in the north-east side. There are two other gaps, which may be original, on the south and west, but they show no inturns. The interior shows many traces of mining, some of it apparently of great age, perhaps Roman; but no hut platforms have been recorded.

Immediately to the north of the main work, Blodwell Rock has been fortified by a rampart on its east side to form a long narrow enclosure 330 by 60 metres. Whether this is contemporary with the larger fort, to provide an extra defence on its more vulnerable side, must remain uncertain.

C. Fox and W. J. Hemp, *Arch. Cambrensis* (1926), pp. 395–400 (plan).

LORDENSHAWS (fig. 83; Northumberland, NZ 054 993; 60 metres; pp. 45, 73).

This is a well preserved and accessible little fort which is of particular interest as it preserves what appears to be a contemporary system of approach roads and boundary banks.

The fort itself consists of an inner oval enclosure of about 0·3 hectares, protected by a substantial bank, the toe of which is

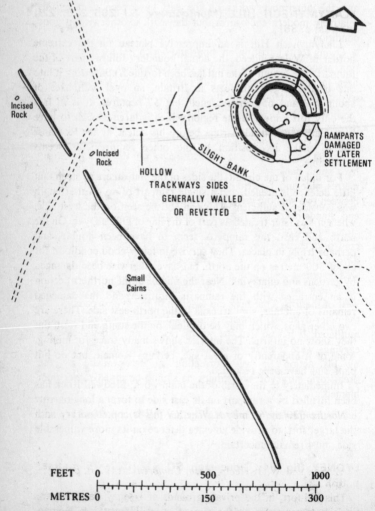

Fig. 83   Lordenshaws.

separated by a berm from its accompanying ditch; round the south-east quadrant this has a slight counterscarp bank. Roughly concentric with these defences is a further bank, with ditch and counterscarp bank. The system measures about 40 metres overall. There are entrances from east and west, leading straight through all the ramparts by simple gaps. The south-east quadrant has been largely destroyed by a settlement of stone-built huts, almost certainly of Roman date, as are the huts within the enclosure, and the outermost works on the east have been damaged by relatively modern enclosures, but the work is otherwise in good condition.

Owing to its situation on moorland which has escaped cultivation, associated features survive, of a type which must once have been far more common in this region. Hollow trackways lead towards the entrances from the south and south-east, and these are not merely the accidental results of traffic, since for much of their lengths the sides of the hollows are lined by a rough revetment of large stones. The south-eastern track leads to a former spring.

Except for the trackway the approach from the south is barred by a small bank with a ditch to the south, measuring about 3·5 metres wide and 1 metre high overall, and running nearly straight between two shallow valleys. A similar dyke, bifurcated at its west end, stands nearer the fort. These are hardly strong enough to be effective defences, and presumably had something to do with control of cattle. Half a dozen small low mounds have been noted near the fort, and may be contemporary burial places; there may well be others concealed in the deep heather. There are two carved rocks (similar to those near the Ringses on Doddington Moor) west of the fort. That near the junction of the south roadway and the outer dyke was formerly a fine example but has recently been mutilated. It is said that the person responsible believed that the carvings were intended as a map of the local hill-forts, and that by his action he was correcting an error made by the prehistoric surveyor; so perhaps he should be pitied rather than blamed.

Northumberland County History XV (1940), pp. 30–31 (plan).

LYDNEY (fig. 84; Gloucester, SO 616 027; 75 metres; p. 85).

This hill-fort, in the private grounds of Lydney Park, is particularly noteworthy as the site of a magnificent late Roman temple to the healing god Nodens. The history of the remains was elucidated by Sir Mortimer Wheeler's excavations of 1928–9. The remains of the temple and of part of the bath house have been consolidated for preservation.

The visible earthworks are almost certainly all late or post-Roman, but excavation showed that they incorporate the original bank. This was of no great size, rising only 1·5 metres above ground level and 6 metres wide; under the added material the

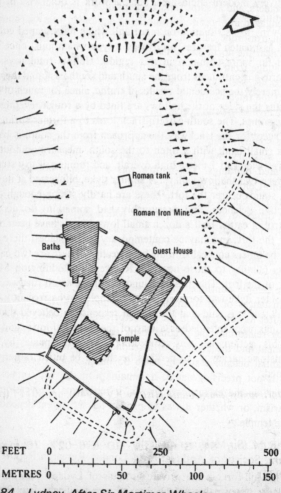

Fig. 84 Lydney. After Sir Mortimer Wheeler.

rampart walk survived, 1·5 metres wide and 0·7 metres below the crest. This first rampart crossed the neck of a steep-sided promontory, the area enclosed being 1·8 hectares, almost level.

This defence, built about H 100, protected what seems to have been an ordinary pre-Roman settlement; though, since the primary objective of the excavation was to investigate the remarkable Roman structures, relatively little is known about the earlier remains. The population seems to have been left undisturbed by the invaders, and at some time, perhaps under Roman influence, to have engaged in organized iron-mining and other metalworking; a Roman iron mine can still be seen, and there are many blocked shafts near the north end of the fort.

To judge from the frequency of coins and pottery, the inhabitants do not seem to have been very prosperous until the latter part of the third century, when finds increase remarkably, but the real change in the style of life on this hill top took place soon after AD 364.

The southern half of the hill-fort enclosure was then enclosed by a masonry wall to form a precinct for a temple and associated buildings. The temple was a basilica, not the usual Romano-Celtic double square, and it was accompanied by a large guest house, a suite of baths and a long building divided into a dozen or more small rooms, which may have been where the visitors received treatment — for the evidence of the relics suggests that the temple was the centre of a cult of healing. The name of the god is known from inscriptions, but is not recorded elsewhere.

The temple continued in use well into the fifth century; the circumstances of its abandonment are not known. But at some time after its construction the prehistoric ramparts were repaired, first by reinforcing the original bank and later by a further reinforcement and the addition of a second bank and ditch, giving a substantial defensive system some 35 metres wide overall. This work is not precisely dated. It remains a matter for conjecture whether, as the excavator suggests, it represents a reversion to barbarism, or whether it was to protect the settlement dependent on the temple.

R. E. M. (Sir Mortimer) Wheeler, ... *Excavation ... in Lydney Park*, Society of Antiquaries of London Research Report IX (1932).

MAEN CASTLE (Cornwall, SW 347 257; 45 metres).

A coastal promontory some 90 metres across the base and 130 metres long is fortified by a single stone wall 60 metres long and 3·5 metres thick, separated from the accompanying ditch by a berm not of uniform width; the average overall measurement of the defences is about 15 metres, and the enclosed area roughly 0·9 hectare. The entrance was through a walled passage some 2 metres wide (still well preserved), with a pair of post holes at the inner end; a short length of wall on the lip of the ditch gave additional protection here. The associated pot was of A style, H 300.

C. B. Crofts, *Proc. West Cornwall Field Club* I.3 (1954–5), pp. 93–108.

MAIDEN CASTLE, ARBROATH (Kincardine, NO 669 420; 30 metres; p. 18).

There are a few small promontory forts along the Kincardine coast. Maiden Castle is typical. An irregular headland is cut off by a strong earth rampart and ditch, making a fortress of about 0·1 hectare. The entrance was probably between the north end of the rampart and the cliff edge.

D. Christison, *Proc. Soc. Ant. Scot.* XXXIV (1899–1900), p. 59 (plan p. 48).

MAIDEN CASTLE, BICKERTON (Cheshire, SJ 498 528; 210 metres; pp. 18, 62).

In plan, the area enclosed forms a pointed oval, with apices 130 metres apart to north and south, and 55 metres wide (area 0·5 hectare). The west side is protected by a cliff, artificially improved; on the east two parallel banks form a system of defences nearly 30 metres wide overall.

The inner rampart was 6·5 metres thick, faced on both sides with stone revetments. These supported an earth fill, laced transversely with horizontal beams (found burned) which butted up against a central core of rubble. The same structure seems to have been used throughout the fort's life in this wall, but the outer defence showed two structural periods. In the earlier it consisted simply of a bank of sand 9 metres wide at base, with an outer stone facing, 20 metres in front of the inner wall face; there was no intervening ditch. Subsequently, a further rubble-built outer revetment about 2 metres thick was added, the bank was raised by the addition of material dug out from between the defences, and a palisade of spaced uprights was set in the top. The resulting ditch may have been lined to form a reservoir.

The entrance through the outer rampart was a simple gap. Through the inner, the ends of the ramparts were inturned to form a passage about 12 metres long, with a pair of posts 5 metres apart to support the gate about halfway along it. There were no guard chambers, but behind one of the inturns was a hut which yielded late A-style pottery (H 150?).

W. J. Varley, *Liverpool Annals of Archaeology and Anthropology* XXII (1935), pp. 97 ff.; XXIII (1936), pp. 101 ff.; summarized in *Prehistoric Cheshire* (Chester, 1940) pp. 69 ff.

MAIDEN CASTLE (fig. 11; Dorset, SY 669 885; pls. 2, 3, 4).

References to 'Maiden Castle' alone refer to this fortress, by far the most important of those which carry that name.

For description see pp. 88–92; also pp. 18, 32, 35, 46, 48, 50, 51, 55, 56, 59, 61, 71, 73, 76, 77, 78, 82, 83.

R. E. M. (Sir Mortimer) Wheeler, *Maiden Castle, Dorset*, Society of Antiquaries of London Research Report XII (1943). This has been summarized and to some extent amplified in *Dorset Inv.* II.3, pp. 493–500. The reconstruction of the gateway in period two given here (pl. 3) follows the Inventory in treating the revetments of both the main rampart and the barbican as having existed at the same time. Both reconstructions (pls. 3, 4) are from the same aspect as pl. XCIV A of the research report.

On temples: S. Piggott, *The Druids* (Thames and Hudson, 1968), pp. 61, 65, fig. 14.

There are fine reconstruction drawings by A. Sorrell in B. Green and A. Sorrell, *Prehistoric Britain* (Lutterworth, 1968), fig. 28 (general view from west); A. Fox and A. Sorrell, *Roman Britain* (Lutterworth, 1961), fig. 4 (Roman attack on east entrance); and R. F. Jessup and A. Sorrell, *Age by Age* (M. Joseph, 1967), p. 29 (east entrance). The reader may find it interesting to compare the last two with pl. 4 here, to see where independent reconstructions agree and differ.

MAIDEN CASTLE, DURHAM (Durham, NZ 283 417; 60 metres; p. 18).

A strong bank, now reduced to a scarp, with a ditch separated from it by about 20 metres, runs in a slight curve across the western end of a steep-sided spur, protecting some 2·3 hectares.

VCH Durham I (1905), p. 348 (plan).

MAM TOR (fig. 85; Derby, SK 128 838; 500 metres; pl. 30).

Despite its unusually high position, this fort contains traces of a number of huts, and on excavation these have yielded plentiful

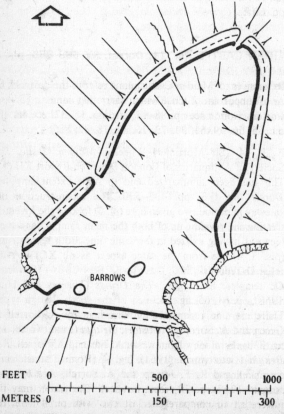

BARROWS

FEET   0   500   1000
METRES 0   150   300

Fig. 85   Mam Tor. After D. Coombs.

pottery, as well as charcoal giving a surprisingly early radio-carbon date.

The defence is a single dump rampart revetted by a stone wall in front (at least in places), and accompanied by a ditch and probably a counterscarp bank. It follows roughly the form of the hill enclosing 6·4 hectares, and there is an entrance at the north and south; the rampart is slightly inturned.

The dwellings were of timber, probably round, on levelled platforms terraced into the hillside; the lower, built-up half has been eroded away. The pottery is rough and almost all undecorated. Its character is consistent with the two radiocarbon dates obtained, which indicate occupation in about the tenth to twelfth centuries BC, corresponding to the Late Bronze Age or even earlier.

D. Coombs, *Current Archaeology* No. 27 (July 1971), pp. 100–2 (plans etc.). Preliminary note.

MEMBURY (Devon, ST 282 028; 200 metres; p. 18).

The name (p. 18) indicates a 'stone fort', but the defences now appear as a bank and ditch. The enclosure is a long narrow oval, 220 metres from north to south, enclosing 1·1 hectares. One entrance, at the southern end, is a simple gap with the ends of the banks slightly staggered, but the main gateway, on the north-east, has a curious loop of rampart curving inwards, as though to provide a false entrance to tempt attackers into a cul-de-sac. Whether this is a correct interpretation of the plan could only be decided by excavation.

VCH Devon I (1906), pp. 583–4 (plan).

MILBER DOWN (fig. 86; Devon, SX 884 698; 110 metres; p. 44).

This is a very typical specimen of the south-western type of multivallate fort. It is protected by three ramparts, widely spaced. The innermost enclosed 1·3 hectares, the outermost 7·4 hectares. A fourth bank, much slighter, would have taken in about 24 hectares, but was apparently never completed. The enclosures stand on sloping ground, with the single entranceway, through all the ramparts, approaching from downhill. The inner three ramparts were all simple unrevetted dumps of material from their ditches. All were big enough to be considered defensive, though not strong. Their overall dimensions were 15 metres wide by 5·7 high, 12 by 3·7 metres and 10 by 2·3 metres, the innermost being the largest. The heights are given from the original bottom of the ditch to the present crest of the bank, but the second and third

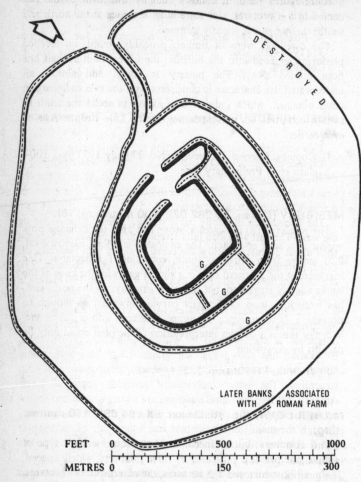

Fig. 86   Milber Down. After Lady Fox.

ditches were probably deeper elsewhere; at the section line there was a particularly hard bed of gravel. The bank and ditch of the largest enclosure only measured 7 metres wide overall; its original height is uncertain. The associated pottery was all of B style, date

H 80. No dwellings were identified. The settlement was abandoned peacefully at about the time of the Roman conquest.

Soon after, a small farming homestead was built just east of the outer bank, and at about the same time an attractive group of bronze figures – a bird, a stag, a duck carrying a cake in its beak and a ball – were buried in the silting of the second ditch.

A. Fox *et al*, *Proc. Devon Arch. Exploration Soc.* IV, 2 and 3 (1949–50), pp. 27–66 (describing excavations by F. Cottrill).

MOEL HIRADDUG (Flint, SJ 063 785; 250 metres; p. 49).

This very important and interesting hill-fort is being excavated in advance of destruction by quarrying, so will not be described in detail. Nevertheless, it must be mentioned, for it is one of the few sites which have produced positive indications of an assault on the defences by non-Roman attackers.

The site chosen is a long narrow ridge, almost precipitous on the west. The east side also falls steeply, but is broken by a broad shelf about 30 metres below the crest. A single wall encircles the ridge, forming an irregularly oval enclosure of 8 hectares, 750 metres from north to south, and varying from 55 to 190 metres in width. On the east side two further ramparts curve out from this inner line and protect the shelf, enclosing a further 2 hectares. All the ramparts are of rubble with stone facing to front and rear; the outermost is accompanied by a ditch and counterscarp bank. Excavation has shown that the interior contained both round houses, with walls probably of cob, and rectangular post-built structures. The latter individually resemble those at Croft Ambrey, but like the round buildings are widely spaced and follow no regular layout; their relative age is not yet certain. The gateway through the main (inner) rampart had a fine pair of rectangular guard chambers; buried in the rampart close by was an earlier simple gate passage.

In 1872, while making an access road, labourers discovered fragments of decorated bronze from a shield, together with other bronzes and a broken iron sword blade. These were apparently buried in the fallen debris of the middle rampart, near its north end, and the evidence suggests that they were lost during an attack on the defences. The date currently accepted for the deposit is early in the first century AD. The main rampart in its final form seems to be later than the destruction of the middle rampart, but the chronology of the site is not yet finally settled.

C. H. Houlder, *Flints. Hist. Soc.* XIX (1961), pp. 1–20 (rescue excavations, 1954–5, and discussion of shield find).

Current work (1972), *ex inf.* the excavator, J. L. Davies.

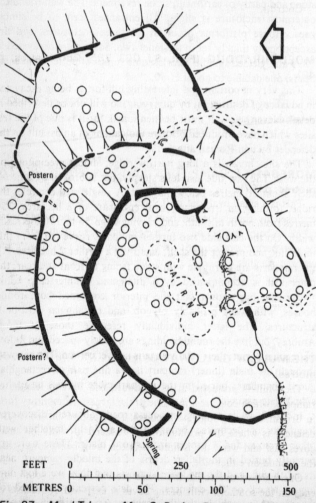

Fig. 87 Moel Trigarn. After S. Baring-Gould.

MOEL TRIGARN (fig. 87; Pembroke, SN 158 336; 360 metres; p. 77).

This fort is finely situated on the Preseli mountains, and is recognizable for long distances by the three great cairns from which it takes its name. It comprises a main inner enclosure of about 1·2 hectares, a second of about 0·8 hectare lobed out from this on the north and east, and a third of similar size on the east. Each is defended by a single rampart with no ditch, partly of dry-stone and partly of earth with stone revetment. The wall round the outermost enclosure is slight. All entrances seem to be simple gaps. House platforms occur in all three enclosures, and are exceptionally thickly set in the inner two. Some were excavated in 1899 and yielded spindle-whorls, some scraps of pottery and some beads, one datable to about H 50.

S. Baring-Gould *et al*, *Arch. Cambrensis* (1900), pp. 189—221 (plan, excavation report).

MOREBATTLE, CAMP TOPS (Roxburgh, NT 860 180; 370 metres; p. 57).

This is a small oval fort, of 0·2 hectare, axes 60 and 48 metres, enclosed by three close-set banks and ditches. The whole work seems to be of one period, so the eight hut foundations which can be seen permit a rough estimate of the number of inhabitants, and an even rougher one of how long the construction of such a work might take (p. 57).

Roxburgh Inv. II (1956), No. 653 (plan).

THE MULL OF GALLOWAY (Wigtown, NX 143 307; c. 60 metres).

The Mull is protected at its landward end by two lengths of rampart, which convert it into one of the largest promontory forts in Britain, covering some 40 hectares. The position chosen for the defences is where the promontory is reduced in width by small coves east and west, the isthmus between them being lower than the ground on either side.

One rampart overlooks the lower ground from the south, and ends on the southern cliffs of the coves at each end. It consists of an inner bank, a ditch and an outer bank, sometimes with faint traces of an outer ditch and a counterscarp bank. The whole measures about 12 metres overall. The remains of the inner bank are often very slight, and the ditch has in places been cleaned to improve drainage. There is a gap about 100 metres from the west end, which may be the original entrance. There are no obvious hut sites on the headland south of this line of defence.

The second rampart lies at the north end of the isthmus, and is a single massive bank; the higher scarp, facing north, seems to have been revetted. This line seems to have been intended to prevent approach to the two coves from the north. The only well preserved section is east of the modern road.

If these two ramparts are in fact parts of a single scheme, it seems that the headland has been converted into a very large fortress, with a protected landing place immediately outside the main defences.

About halfway between the southern tip of the promontory and these two ramparts another bank, also facing north, cuts across the promontory (*ex inf.* P. S. Gelling).

Wigtown Inv. (1912), No. 148.

MYNYDD BYCHAN (Glamorgan, SS 963 756; 80 metres; p. 73).

This is a very small enclosure, only 0·2 hectare, and for its size is elaborately fortified. It must surely have been the Iron Age equivalent of a castle, if such an anachronism may be allowed. Except for the defences, the prehistoric features were concealed by the round houses of an unfortified Romano-native village and by a medieval croft with outbuildings, so the full original plan of the interior could not be recovered.

The enclosure is roughly shield-shaped, with the entrance at its apex on the west. The enclosed area measures 50 metres from north to south by 60 metres from east to west. The position is not naturally strong, but had an extensive view.

The main protection was a rampart about 5·5 metres wide, with its outer face revetted with large blocks, probably standing about 2 metres high and fronted by a ditch 3·5 metres wide and 1·5 deep, with a small counterscarp bank. On the more accessible north-west side were a second ditch and bank, now almost all obscured by a modern lane. The defences were thus of no great strength. Nevertheless the gateway was substantial and elaborate. On one side it was overlooked by a massive bastion, revetted partly with a row of close-set tree trunks set upright, and partly with stone. The gateway itself had a framework of four posts in line, forming a triple portal, and stood at the inner end of a slightly curved barbican approach between stone walls. This was further obstructed by a curving palisade slot, but the full purpose of the design is not easy to understand.

Within the enclosure there were at least three round timber houses, as well as a cooking oven and other structures, but except for one building 6 metres in diameter most details were obscured by the later remains. The general impression is that the builder felt that his prestige depended on displaying a large and impressive gateway; the rest was of minor importance.

The relics found in this phase indicate occupation from about H 50 up to the arrival of the Romans.

H. N. Savory, *Arch. Cambrensis* CIII (1954), pp. 85–108; CIV (1955), pp. 14–51 (excavation report, two parts).

OLDBURY (fig. 88; Kent, TQ 582 566; 170 metres; p. 48).

A very large fort, enclosing about 49 hectares, mostly by a single bank and ditch round the edge of a steep-sided plateau, near the northern edge of the Kentish Weald. It is generally well preserved, but wooded. Excavation showed that the defences comprised work of two periods. Period one, of H 80, was a large but simple bank of dump construction, accompanied by a ditch. In period two, perhaps as late as AD 43, the bank was enlarged, revetted, and given a parapet walk with a wooden breastwork. An additional bank and ditch were added in places and in others the ditch was enlarged to give a wide flat-bottomed profile like that at Fécamp in Normandy. Sling stones were introduced in this period. The south gateway, damaged by a modern access road, was inturned. At the north-east gateway, which was excavated, the primary arrangement was not clear, but holes for the two posts of the second period gateway were located; they had been burned. There had been some dwellings inside the enclosure, but it was not intensively occupied.

The excavator gave reasons for regarding the second period of refortification as a reaction to the Claudian invasion, but this makes the Fécamp-type ditch a century later than its continental parallels. Dates of H 50 and before H 100 for the two periods are perhaps rather more likely than those given.

J. B. Ward-Perkins, *Archaeologia* XC (1944), pp. 128–76.

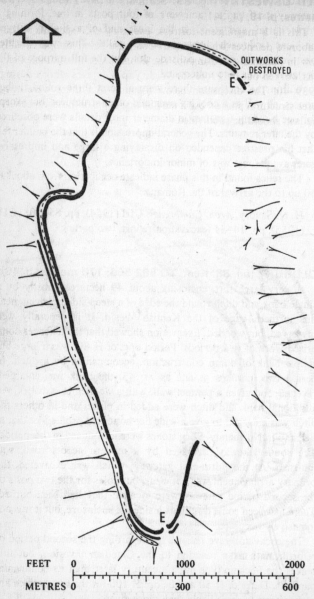

OUTWORKS
DESTROYED

E

E

FEET	0		1000		2000
METRES	0	300		600	

Fig. 88   Oldbury. After J. B. Ward-Perkins.

OLD OSWESTRY (fig. 89; Shropshire, SJ 296 310; 165 metres; p. 19, pl. 31).

This is a magnificent fortress, enclosing 5·3 hectares within elaborate defences which in part comprise seven ramparts. It is now in national guardianship. The evolution of this complex site was worked out by Professor W. J. Varley in excavations during 1939–40. The discussion below assumes that there were only three structural phases; but it may be that some of these, especially the last, should be subdivided.

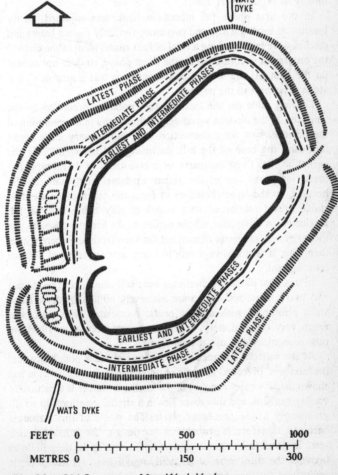

Fig. 89 Old Oswestry. After W. J. Varley.

The earliest settlement, of timber-built round houses, was unfortified. After this had been deserted for some time, and the remains had become turf-covered, the hill-top was enclosed by a rampart about 3 metres thick, with a stone revetment to front and rear. This was accompanied by a ditch and a second rampart of dump construction, also with a ditch. The ditches were separated from their associated ramparts by some 10 metres, possibly to allow for the instability of the hill slopes, which are of glacial gravel. The dwellings of this phase also were round, but of stone; beneath the hearth of one was a piece of Iron Age A pottery, of a type found mostly in Wiltshire (H 200?).

In the next phase the innermost bank was enlarged, partly burying at least one hut, and two more similarly spaced banks and ditches were built, making a total of four round most of the circuit; the outermost is concealed by the latest phase, so does not appear on the plan. At the same time the entrance was inturned, with a stone revetment to the passage.

Leaving aside for the moment the problems presented by the 'annexes' at the western entrance, the final stage in the evolution of the defences saw the construction of a pair of very large banks following the base of the hill, enclosing and partly burying the earlier works. These ramparts were essentially of dump type, but made ingenious use of the rather unstable local materials by heaping up the larger boulders to form the outer edges, the less stable gravel reinforced with layers of clay being used as fill. Logically, in this phase, all the earlier banks became obsolete, for the large new ramparts obstructed the view from anywhere within them; but it is not always safe to carry modern ideas of defence into the past.

In this final phase the dwellings were still round, but one at least had two rooms, and they were massively built with thick stone walls reinforced with upright posts. Associated with them was much very crude pottery, regarded as post-Roman in 1948 but now recognizable as of the Iron Age.

At the western entrance the plan suggests as a possibility that the 'annexes' preceded the pair of outer banks; but excavation has shown that the outer rampart of the northern annexe is structurally similar to them, and moreover lies in a similar relationship stratigraphically to the preceding phase. The whole of this elaborate barbican, therefore, is probably of one design. The annexes, which seem in detail to be unique, seldom hold water in the deep hollows between the transverse banks, and cannot have served as cattle enclosures for they have no entrances. It may be that they were designed solely to protect and define the very long entrance passage, and that the space within served no practical purpose but was not worth the labour involved in refilling. The sides of the entrance passage were revetted in stone, but it seems to have been narrower than its precursor, and owing to erosion its floor was at a lower level.

During the Roman period the place seems to have been deserted, though a few scraps of Roman pot were found in the ditch silting. Finally, several centuries later, the earthworks formed a landmark on the boundary between Wales and Mercia; Wat's Dyke was carried up to the Iron Age ramparts.

The traditional name of the place was Caer Ogyrfan, the 'fort of Gogyrfan', who was the father of Guinevere; but in view of the revised dating of the coarse pottery associated with the latest occupation one must now regretfully abandon the romantic vision of King Arthur riding through the ruins of the great west entrance to visit his future in-laws.

W. J. Varley, 'The Hill-Forts of the Welsh Marches', *Arch. J.* CV (1948), pp. 41–66 *passim*. Full report forthcoming (1974). For name and associated tradition see I. Watkin, *Oswestry* (Oswestry, 1920), pp. 348–9.

OLD SARUM (Wilts., SU 137 327; 110 metres; p. 17).

Most of what can now be seen here is medieval, but the great outer rampart follows that of an Iron Age hill-fort, area about 20 hectares. Occupation continued into the Roman period, the place is mentioned in 552, and is known to have been inhabited from the time of Alfred at least until the middle of the fourteenth century, though its importance declined after the establishment of New Sarum (Salisbury) about 1220. Whether occupation was in fact continuous throughout remains uncertain, but the survival without much change of its original name of Sorviodunon is notable.

D. H. Montgomerie, *Arch. J.* CIV (1947), pp. 130 ff. (plan).

OLD WINCHESTER HILL (fig. 90; Hants., SU 641 206; 190 metres; p. 18).

The fort forms an almost regular oval, on the end of a steep-sided ridge. The defence is a single bank and ditch, originally fairly uniform in profile and about 30 metres wide overall, still mostly 6 metres high. The enclosed area is 5 hectares. There is an entrance

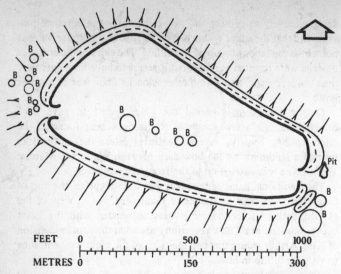

Fig. 90   Old Winchester Hill. After J. P. Williams-Freeman.

to east and west, with inturned ends to the ramparts. At the eastern entrance, which has the easier approach, there is an additional hollow outside each end of the main ditch; these are now rather eroded, and their nature is not clear.

The enclosure contains a few vague depressions which may be hut emplacements, and there are several Bronze Age burial mounds in and near the fort.

The legend implied by the name is lost.

J. P. Williams-Freeman, *Field Archaeology* [in] ... *Hampshire* (London, 1915), p. 391 (plan).

OVERTON DOWN (Wilts., SU 129 707, p. 56).

This is the location of a section of bank and ditch thrown up, under the auspices of the British Association for the Advancement of Science (BAAS), in order to study the processes of construction and weathering in earthworks.

P. A. Jewell (ed.), *The Experimental Earthwork on O.D., Wilts., 1960* (BAAS, 1963), and P. A. Jewell and G. W. Dimbleby, *Proc. Preh. Soc.* XXXIII (1966), pp. 313–42 (report on first four years).

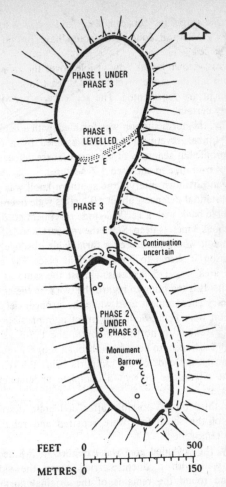

PHASE 1 UNDER
PHASE 3

PHASE 1
LEVELLED

E

PHASE 3

E

Continuation
uncertain

E

PHASE 2
UNDER
PHASE 3

Monument
Barrow

E

E

FEET 0 500

METRES 0 150

*Fig. 91 Pen Dinas, Aberystwyth. After Royal Commission
on Ancient Monuments (Wales).*

PEN DINAS, ABERYSTWYTH (fig. 91; Cardigan SN 584 804; 125 metres; p. 35, pl. 32).

Excavations by Professor C. Daryll Forde in 1933–7 have given some clues to the history of the site, though much still remains to be discovered. The fort occupies the top of a ridge which rises into knolls at the north and south ends, connected by a saddle. The ridge lies between the Rheidol and Ystwyth rivers, which under natural conditions would have provided excellent landing places.

The grass-grown banks now visible cover the remains of ramparts with tall dry-stone revetments; at least four main stages of development are represented. The sequence is probable, but not absolutely certain.

Initially, the north summit was fortified, with a bank faced by a battered timber revetment and accompanied by a ditch, of irregular profile but generally of V section. These defences measured 13 metres overall, and enclosed 1·6 hectares.

After an unknown interval the southern knoll was given much more substantial defences, about 10 metres wide overall, comprising a rubble bank with a vertical stone revetment accompanied by a ditch about 3 metres deep. Since the rampart stood at the top of a steep slope it would have been a formidable obstacle, but for the same reason it seems to have failed in places by sliding. The enclosed area was 1·5 hectares, almost the same as that of the earlier fort. It is tempting to regard the work on the north knoll as a temporary encampment used while the stronger defences on the south knoll were being built, but proof is impossible. The south fort had gateways to north and south, and these, as in all subsequent phases, seem to have been through roughly square settings of four posts, the ends of the ramparts being thickened; but the successive alterations prevent a complete understanding of the arrangements.

In the third phase, possibly after deliberate destruction, the defences of the south fort were repaired and rebuilt, and the gateways remodelled.

Finally, the defended area was extended to 3·8 hectares by a revetted wall with a ditch, carried along the sides of the saddle and round the remains of the original north fort. The entrance to the isthmus was originally 12 metres wide, but was narrowed in four stages to a normal type of gateway with four posts. Remains of a pot indicate that the full extent of the enclosure must date from about H 100. Finds generally were very sparse.

In the south fort, the only area which has not been cultivated, about eight platforms for dwellings can be traced. The buildings were probably round, though one (excavated) seems to have been D-shaped in plan. A setting of four posts in a rectangle 1·7 by 2·1 metres was found on the isthmus; it was not a granary, as a hearth was associated with it.

C. D. Forde, W. E. Griffiths, A. H. A. Hogg, and C. H. Houlder, *Arch. Cambrensis* CXII (1963), pp. 125–53 (excavation report).

PEN-Y-GAER, LLANBEDR-Y-CENNIN (fig. 92; Caernarvon, SH 750 693; 380 metres; pp. 19, 48).

This fort is noteworthy as one of the rare examples of the use of *chevaux-de-frise* for defence. The ramparts are also interesting, but puzzling; although they are certainly of more than one period their evolution cannot be worked out from surface evidence alone.

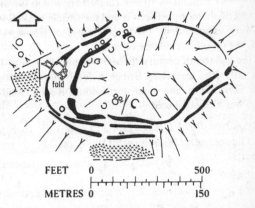

| FEET | 0 | | 500 |
| METRES | 0 | | 150 |

Fig. 92   Pen-y-gaer, Llanbedr-y-Cennin. After Royal Commission on Ancient Monuments (Wales).

The area enclosed is about 2 hectares. It is protected by three ramparts except on the west, where the two outer banks converge, and on the north-east, where the ground is very steep and they have been omitted. All are faced with large blocks roughly coursed, and are about 4·5 metres thick. For the innermost the fill is clean rubble, as also for the middle rampart except for about 100 metres along the south side of the fort. That section is filled with earthy rubble, and so is most of the outer bank. Only this last is accompanied by a ditch.

Outside the ramparts, to the west and south, there are two large patches of *chevaux-de-frise*; the southern patch is bounded by a slight bank and ditch, a feature also found in central Spain (see

p. 48). This patch also extends into the space between the outer and middle ramparts, suggesting that the outer bank at least is later than the *chevaux-de-frise*.

A modern break has been made through all the ramparts on the south, but the only original entrance was at the west end. The gateway through the innermost rampart is well preserved, 4 metres wide, the sides of the passage faced with large blocks; the rampart ends are thickened to 7 metres. The entrance through the combined middle and outer ramparts seems to have been similar, but only the south side of the passage is visible, the actual opening being filled with rubble. The detailed arrangements here are obscured.

The eastern half of the interior has been cleared, but the western half contains remains of twelve round huts within the inner rampart, and of six more between it and the middle bank. Some of the huts were excavated in 1905, and traces of ironworking were found, but no other evidence of date.

In the eighteenth century the site was also known as Pen Caer Helen, after the legendary British wife of Magnus Maximus, to whom Sarn Helen, the main north–south Roman road through Wales, was also attributed.

Caernarvon Inv. I (1956), No. 315 (plan). H. H. Hughes and W. Gardner, *Arch. Cambrensis* (1906), pp. 241–67 (excavation reports).

PREIST (near Bitburg, Germany; pp. 48, 61).

This was a promontory fort beside a tributary of the Moselle, roughly 30 kilometres north of Trier, excavated in advance of quarrying by Professor Dehn, in 1938. It is taken as type site for the system of timber lacing in which the rampart is reinforced by a row of equally spaced uprights at front and back, connected by transverse horizontal members.

For an accessible description, with references to original reports, see

M. A. Cotton, *Arch. J.* CXI (1954), pp. 26–9, 64–5.

PUY D'ISSOLU (near Vayrac, Lot, France; p. 50).

Probable location of Uxellodunum, captured by Caesar.

E. Castagné, *Congrès Archéologique de France*, XLIe Session (Paris, 1875) (41e sess, Agen et Toulouse) p. 440 (plan).

A. H. A. Hogg, *Antiquity* XLIII (1969), pp. 262–3, 272 (brief note with sketch plan).

QUARLEY HILL (Hants., SU 262 423; 170 metres; p. 44, pl. 33).

The investigation of Quarley Hill was one of the important series of excavations organized by the Hampshire Field Club.

The enclosure is pear-shaped, the narrower end to the north-east, and measures 310 by 146 metres (area 3·6 hectares). There are entrances at the north-east and south-west, as well as a gap in each side. These gaps seem to have been places where the rampart was left unfinished, not intentional entrances. The ground falls away fairly steeply in all directions, particularly to north-west and south-east, but although the position is strong the defences are massive, consisting of a glacis-type bank and V-shaped ditch measuring nearly 20 metres wide overall, the crest of the bank still rising 6·5 metres above the original bottom of the ditch; in addition there was a counterscarp bank, now much eroded. No evidence of timberwork was found in the rampart.

The north-east entrance was excavated, and details indicated that it was never completed. As designed, it was to comprise a passage some 12 metres long and 6 metres wide between timber revetments, with a portal of large posts at its inner end framing a gateway 2·5 metres wide. About 5 metres in front of this the passage was similarly restricted by smaller posts, presumably for a bridge. A later series of four posts had been set up in the holes dug for the north-west side of the unfinished gateway, suggesting that after giving up the monumental design the builders had decided to finish off the work in rather a makeshift way.

The approach causeway at both entrances preserved short lengths of a slot for an earlier palisade, most of which had been destroyed by the main ditch.

Earlier still, the summit of the hill had formed a junction point for a number of Late Bronze Age banks and ditches interpreted as ranch boundaries. These had largely silted up before the hill-fort was built. Two appear as faint dark lines converging on the enclosure from the bottom corners of plate 33.

The dates tentatively assigned to the various phases, in the context of the chronology accepted at the time of excavation, were the first half of the first millennium BC for the ranch boundaries, fourth century BC for the palisade, and third century BC for the hill fort. Both palisade and hill-fort belonged to phases of Iron Age A culture.

C. F. C. Hawkes, *Proc. Hants. Field Club* XIV, pt. 2 (1939), pp. 136–94.

RAINSBOROUGH (figs. 6, 10; Northants., SP 526 348; 145 metres; pp. 46, 49, 58, 64, 68, 69, 71).

This site has been the subject of a campaign (1961–5) by members of the Oxford University Archaeological Society, as part of their programme of excavating hill-forts in the eastern Cotswolds. The account of their work is one of the most valuable of recent excavation reports.

The fort stands on the edge of a plateau, and its surroundings are almost level except on the north-west, where the ground falls away gently to give a wide view across the Cherwell valley. In plan it is roughly a trapezium with rounded corners, the east and west sides being about 220 and 160 metres, the width 150 metres, enclosing 2·5 hectares. The entrance is near the middle of the west side. The defences appear as a large bank with ditch and counterscarp bank, but there was an outer ditch, now entirely filled.

The excavations were primarily to examine the defences, but enough work was done in the interior to show that it was intensively occupied. The only structures of identifiable plan consisted of holes for four posts set sloping inwards as if to meet in a point; these may have carried a roof protecting a shallow hollow. Two such arrangements were found; the larger was 3 metres square at base, the smaller 2·5 metres.

The defences were not the result of long evolution, but were initially built to an elaborate and sophisticated design on a site already occupied. These impressive works have been described above (p. 63–4 and figs. 6, 10). The excavator suggests a date in the fifth century BC.

This phase lasted for a century or so. The defences and gateway arrangements were maintained, with occasional repairs, but not in a state of great cleanliness or efficiency. Then some threat inspired a fairly thorough overhaul; the gateways were fully rebuilt and the ditches cleaned. Nevertheless, these precautions were not enough. The timberwork of the gateways was set on fire, including the guard houses, and even the timber lacing of the inner rampart was burned. The skeleton of one of the defenders was found among the ruins of a guard house.

The victors left after their raid, and a few inhabitants lingered among the charred ruins; but they did not remain long, and the enclosure remained almost deserted until the arrival of new occupants during the second century BC.

These re-established the defences in the simplest way possible, by cleaning out the ditches and using the spoil to heighten the banks as glacis-type ramparts. The gateway consisted of three large posts forming a double portal. Within the camp, behind the line of the rampart, was a pair of posts set 4 metres apart, perhaps for some formal 'arch'. There was no road surface associated with this gateway, which may have been destroyed before completion.

After this, the site was again abandoned, but there was some re-occupation in the Roman period, the most notable feature being a stone building 3 metres square just outside the main entrance, dated to the late fourth century by coins. This suggests as a possibility that a temple awaits discovery in the interior.

M. Avery, J. E. Sutton and J. W. Banks, *Proc. Preh. Soc.* XXXIII (1967), pp. 207–306.

RANSCOMBE (Sussex, TQ 438 092; 120 metres).

For the possible relation to The Caburn, see that entry.

Some time about H 500 the inhabitants of the eastern downs decided to build a fairly large fort on a spur above the Ouse. To judge from the shape of the ground, it would have been about 350 by 200 metres, enclosing some 6 hectares. About a quarter of the rampart was finished, on the south, and work then stopped. The place is of interest both as an example of an unfinished fortification and because its excavation is one of the few which has yielded evidence for horizontal timberwork in ramparts in the south.

The defences were placed on a slope, and as designed seem to have comprised an almost flat-bottomed ditch about 5 metres wide by 1 metre deep, behind which a berm also 5 metres wide sloped up fairly steeply to the foot of the rampart. This was reinforced by vertical posts front and rear, each about 0·3 metre in diameter. These presumably held up a revetment of timbers laid horizontally. The space between was filled with chalk from the ditch; this must have given a massive wall at least 2 metres high, probably with a breastwork in addition. A particularly interesting discovery was evidence for horizontal beams linking the front and back uprights; they were 0·13 metre in diameter, set at 0·2 metre and 0·6 metre above the chalk surface.

G. P. Burstow and G. A. Holleyman, *Sussex Arch. Coll.* CII (1964), pp. 55–67.

RAVENSBURGH CASTLE (fig. 93; Herts., TL 099 295; 150 metres).

This oblong contour fort, of 6·6 hectares, stands on chalk, about a kilometre north of the Icknield Way, and belongs to a

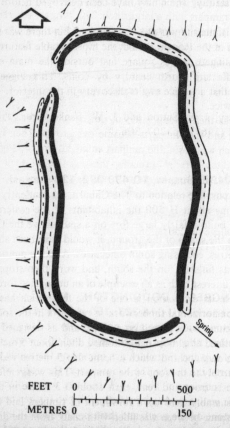

FEET   0   500

METRES 0   150

Fig. 93   Ravensburgh. After J. Dyer and Royal Commission on Historical Monuments (England).

series each of which, as J. Dyer has shown, was probably the centre of a defined territory; these were separated by dykes which controlled traffic along the Way. Steep natural scarps protect the position round the greater part of three sides, but the massive rampart continues round the whole circuit. On the east, where the approach is gentle, it still stands 5·5 metres high above the silted ditch. On the north and west there is an outer bank with an accompanying ditch, both slight. There are two entrances, that on the north-west having the end of the northern rampart clubbed.

Excavations in 1964 and 1970, by J. Dyer and (in 1964) J. Moss-Eccardt, showed that the earliest occupation was as an unfortified farming settlement. This was followed in H 400–300 by a single rampart with a large ditch. The rampart was reinforced by vertical timbers following the front and back of the rampart and linked by horizontal beams set transversely and longitudinally. There was probably a continuous front revetment of vertical timbers. This structure, associated with Iron Age A pottery, remained in use long enough for the timbers to require replacing twice.

There was then a long interval, during which the ditch silted completely and the ramparts became overgrown. Then (H 100–50), the ditch was recut, the rampart enlarged, and the slight outer bank and ditch formed, bringing the defences to their present form. Finally, the western rampart was slighted.

These excavations are continuing.

J. Dyer, Second Interim Report (1970), duplicated (Putteridge Bury College of Education, Luton).
Herts. Inv. (1910), pp. 114–15 (plan).

THE RINGSES, DODDINGTON MOOR (fig. 94; Northumberland, NU 014 327; 150 metres; p. 45).

Doddington Moor is notable not only for the five small forts close together and easily accessible, but for some excellent examples of cup and ring markings incised on the native rock.

Of the forts, the best is The Ringses, near the north edge of the moor. The interior, of about 0·1 hectare, was protected by a broad stone wall, now much robbed, with two further ramparts of earth and stone on the north and three on the south. The entrance passage is zigzag, between banks linking the ramparts. On the south a separate entrance through the outer banks leads to the

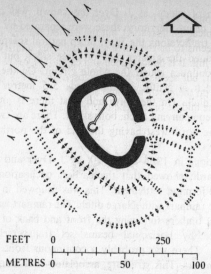

FEET   0   250

METRES 0   50   100

Fig. 94   The Ringses, Doddington Moor.

space between the ramparts, which is partitioned by smaller banks, probably to protect livestock. Two huts which can be traced in the interior are almost certainly later and of Roman date, but whether the defences represent work of one period or of several must remain uncertain without excavation.

About 1·5 kilometres to the south-west, on Dod Law, three forts close together show an interesting transition, from one barely visible, on the east, to the western specimen which is well preserved. This probably corresponds to the sequence of construction. The best carved rocks are in this area, but the association is probably accidental. The fifth fort, just over 1 kilometre due south of The Ringses, is a simple enclosure protected by a single bank and ditch, probably unfinished.

A. H. A. and N. Hogg, *Arch. Aeliana* 45. XXXIV (1956), pp. 142–9.

RUBERSLAW (fig. 95; Roxburgh, NT 580 155; 425 metres; pp. 45, 84).

This structure, though badly ruined, is of particular interest in that part of it incorporates re-used stones which show Roman workmanship.

It occupies a very irregular rocky hill, and most of the ramparts form a typical 'nuclear fort', but the earliest feature, probably pre-Roman, seems to be the outer wall, following a fairly level course round the hill. It is badly ruined and can no longer be traced for its full circuit, but seems to have enclosed about 2·8 hectares, with entrances on the north-west and south.

Near the middle of this enclosure the summit is protected on all

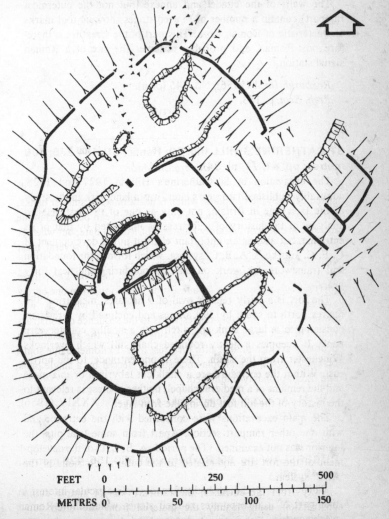

FEET 0 250 500

METRES 0 50 100 150

Fig. 95 Ruberslaw. After Royal Commission on Historical Monuments (Scotland).

sides except the north-east by cliffs 12 to 15 metres high, but the top of this has been enclosed by a wall to form a 'citadel', with the main entrance on the north-east. On the south-west side a track from another entrance leads down to an annexe enclosing a plateau and part of a gully south of the summit. Another gully lies north of the summit, and on the ridge between the two an additional wall protects the approach to the 'citadel'.

The walls of the citadel and annexe (but not the outermost rampart) contain a number of re-used stones showing tool marks characteristic of Roman work. This part of the structure is therefore post-Roman, and probably occupies the site of a Roman signal station.

Roxburgh Inv. I (1956), No. 145 (plan).
Preh. Scot. p. 153.

ST CATHERINE'S HILL (fig. 10; Hants., SU 484 276; 100 metres; pp. 41, 71, pl. 34).

The excavation of St Catherine's Hill in 1927 and 1928, admirably published two years later, was a landmark in the study of the Iron Age in Britain, not only as one of the first detailed analyses of the history of a fortress as illustrated by that of its entrance, but also as an important element in the development of C. F. C. Hawkes's 'A, B, C' system, which formed the foundation and framework for work on that period during the next forty years.

The fort is a fairly regular oval of 9 hectares, measuring 390 metres north to south by 290 metres and enclosed by a rampart consisting of a large bank and ditch with a smaller counterscarp bank. It occupies a gently rounded chalk hill which overlooks Winchester from the south. There is one entrance, to the north-east. Within the enclosure are a chalk-cut labyrinth or miz-maze and the remains of a medieval chapel; neither of these is relevant to the history of the hill fort during the Iron Age.

The main excavations were concerned with the entrance and with one other rampart section. Apart from some trial pits, the interior was not examined. (The periods A, B, C, D of the development of the fort are not related to the cultural divisions of the 'ABC' system.)

Away from the entrance, the rampart was of simple dump construction using mainly the material from the ditch supplemented by a little scraped up from behind it. It was originally some 8 metres wide, and still stands 3 metres high. In front was a berm 2 metres wide, and then the ditch, also 8 metres wide and originally 3·5 metres deep, of blunt V profile. The counterscarp bank was very slight. No evidence was found of any revetment, nor of a breastwork; it seems inherently likely that one must have existed, but if so it can have been little more than hurdling.

The entrance was more informative. In its first stage (period A of the excavator) it was an elaborate structure with guard chambers, but these were not symmetrical, that on the left when entering being an elongated building with a door, that on the right apparently an open-fronted shed. There seem to have been two gates hinged on a central support and opening inwards against a stop.

In period B the guard houses were dismantled, and the plan was not otherwise altered, but in period C elaborate changes were made. The sides of the approach passage outside the gate were faced with walls of chalk blocks, and a similar wall was extended halfway across the entrance to the old gate post socket. The inner part of the passage was given a new revetment of clay, partly covering the smaller guard chamber. The ditch also was deepened and the material added to increase the height of the rampart.

Finally, in period D, the gate and blocking wall were removed. While the entrance was thus unprotected, all the timberwork of the gate was burned, presumably as a result of a raid, for the place was not re-occupied.

The history of the site thus shows a period of emergency (A), when the settlement on the site was first fortified; a period of relative peace (B) when the gates were maintained; a second emergency (C), with refortification; and a further period of peace (D), rudely terminated by the final destruction of the fortress before the defences could again be put into order.

The earlier pottery on the site is of Iron Age A character, and the first defences were presumably built by the people who used it, perhaps about H 400. The final destruction may be assigned to H 50. The general history of this region in relation to the phases of peace and emergency is discussed in dealing with the South Downs group of forts.

C. F. C. Hawkes, J. N. L. Myres and C. G. Stevens, *Proc. Hants. Field Club* XI (1929), pp. 1–188.

ST DAVID'S HEAD (fig. 96; Pembroke, SM 722 279; 50 metres).

This headland is well suited to defence, being partly separated from the mainland by natural clefts. These are joined by a dry-built wall about 100 metres long, and originally perhaps 3 metres wide and 4 high, accompanied by two slighter walls or banks of rubble perhaps with shallow ditches between. The entrance seems

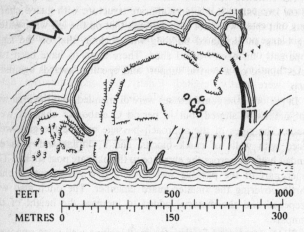

| FEET | 0 | | 500 | | 1000 |
| METRES | 0 | | 150 | | 300 |

Fig. 96   St David's Head. After S. Baring-Gould.

to have been a simple gap 2·3 metres wide. The area enclosed is some 3 hectares, but most of it is bare rock. On a shelf not far from the entrance is a group of seven round stone-built house foundations, mostly about 6 metres in diameter, but the largest over 10 metres. These were examined in 1898 and yielded spindle-whorls, beads and a few indeterminate scraps of pottery. There are extensive enclosures outside the fort to the east, which may well be contemporary.

S. Baring Gould *et al.*, *Arch. Cambrensis* (1899), pp. 105–31 (plan).

SALMONSBURY (Gloucester, SP 173 208; 130 metres; p. 18).

A large fort, almost square, enclosing 22 hectares, within two banks and ditches, close-set. Four seasons of excavations, from

1931–4, remain unpublished save in brief notes. The inner rampart, probably originally revetted with stone, was 18 metres wide and is still 0·8 metre high, the outer was 12 metres wide but is almost levelled; the corresponding ditches were 10 metres wide by 3·7 metres deep originally and 6 by 2·7 metres, both V-shaped. Some A-style pot was found under the banks, and round timber huts with B ware in the enclosure. The sides of the entrance passage were revetted with dry-stone walling, and the timberwork was of two periods. In the earlier, two pairs of double gates were hung on posts set against the walling; in the later, a transverse row of six large posts blocked almost the whole passage, leaving only a small gate on each side.

Occupation continued into the Roman period, when the ramparts were partly levelled. Finally, at some unknown date, probably late Roman, a stone blocking wall was built across the partly filled entrance gap.

G. C. Dunning, *Antiquity* V (1931), pp. 489–91.

Reports of Congress of Archaeological Societies: No. 39 (1931), p. 16; Nos. 40 and 41 (1932, 33), p. 25; No. 42 (1934), p. 26.

SANDY, *see* **CAESAR'S CAMP.**

SCHOLES COPPICE, *see* **CAESAR'S CAMP.**

SKELMORE HEADS (Lancs., SD 274 751; 90 metres).

Although the remains on the site are not impressive, it is important as the only hill-fort in the Furness peninsula. It was excavated by Professor T. G. E. Powell in 1957–9, unfortunately without yielding evidence of date, though some of the structural history was elucidated.

In plan the enclosure is roughly trapezoidal with rounded angles, about 135 by 95 metres average, of 1·3 hectares. Natural rocky scarps seem to have been accepted as defences on all sides except the north, which is protected by a bank and ditch, now much worn down and appearing irregular. Where sectioned, the ditch proved to be 2·5 to 3 metres wide and about 1 metre deep, separated by a berm 1·5 to 2 metres wide from a bank of rubble now 4 or 5 metres wide; this may have been revetted in front by upright timbers. The entrance was examined, and showed a complicated system of shallow post holes, but was too ruined for its arrangement to be worked out.

A palisade trench was identified in the south-east angle of the enclosure, and may have continued round the whole circuit, but owing to the irregularity of the rock this could not be confirmed.

T. G. E. Powell, *Trans. Cumberland and Westmorland Ant. and Arch. Soc.* LXIII (N.S. 1963), pp. 1–30.

SOUTH CADBURY (Somerset, ST 628 252; 150 metres; pp. 20, 61, 62, 79, 81, 82, 83, 86).

Huge banks and ditches, four round most of the circuit, enclose the top of a steep-sided hill to form a fortress of some 8 hectares, roughly trapezoidal in plan. The excavations directed by Professor L. Alcock on behalf of the Camelot Research Committee have been one of the most important recent archaeological investigations. The definitive report is in preparation, but the publication of a general preliminary account justifies some discussion here. Dates are given as suggested by the excavator.

The hill top was first inhabited during the third millennium BC, but the main occupation started during the eighth century and continued with few or no breaks until the Roman period. The earliest defence dates from the mid-fifth century. It was slight and simple, comprising a small ditch behind which was an earthen bank with an outer revetment of horizontal timbers, supported by spaced vertical posts probably tied to inclined posts set 1·5 metres further back.

Each subsequent stage in the elaboration of the ramparts seems to have been preceded by a period of neglect, and to be associated with the appearance of new influences of continental origin. Nevertheless, with one exception, there seem to have been no breaks in the occupation; and it remains uncertain whether the continental influences should be attributed to the arrival of additional settlers, perhaps as rulers, or to trade.

The next rampart, built somewhere about 400 BC, was more massive and was accompanied by a larger rock-cut ditch, all following the line of the earlier works, which were destroyed or buried. The rampart was mostly of rubble from the ditch, with spaced upright posts to front and rear; the front revetment between these was built of lias slabs brought from some distance away.

By about 200 BC the defences had attained essentially their present form, generally consisting of four ramparts, all except the outermost with accompanying rock-cut ditches, some 35 to 50 metres high from the outer toe to the crest of the inner bank and twice that in width overall. These works almost certainly incorporate remains of earlier reconstructions, but details of these have been obscured. At this stage also, if not earlier, the gateway was provided with paired semicircular guard chambers, and the settlement had evolved from a large fortified village into something which can justifiably be called a town, though it remains uncertain whether there was any approach to regular planning. Some buildings were round and some rectangular, all of timber. Both types tended to be rather large in comparison to most of those known in other hill-forts. Several had been rebuilt more than once on the same site, implying continuity of tenure, and there were indications that the round buildings may have been the later. There were also many storage pits of the kind familiar at Little Woodbury and elsewhere in southern Britain.

At about the beginning of the first century AD the defences and gateway were repaired and rebuilt, apparently after a period of abandonment, for the earlier gateway was turf-covered and ruinous. At the same time the use of storage pits was given up, and wheel-made pottery was introduced. No dwellings could be assigned to this phase with certainty, but on the summit of the hill there was a small square building with a deep verandah which could be identified as a shrine. Twenty burials of sacrificial animals were found in front of it. Some tradition of sanctity for this part of the enclosure may have survived through the period of abandonment, for there were other square buildings nearby which were probably shrines during earlier phases, though the evidence is not quite so compelling.

This ultimate Iron Age occupation came to a violent end. On the floor of the gate passage lay the remains of some thirty persons, men, women and children, whose bodies had been left where they fell to be dismembered by wild animals. Some time later the gateway was systematically demolished under the supervision of Roman troops, who set up regular rows of temporary huts within the fort. Surprisingly, this destruction was not an incident in Vespasian's campaign in the mid-40s, but must have taken place about AD 70 or 80, as part of some police action the context of which is not known. During the rest of the Roman period there was no large settlement on the hill, but numerous coins, especially of the third and fourth centuries AD, strongly suggest the presence of a temple; no building has been found, but tiles and worked stones were re-used in the later rampart.

Subsequently South Cadbury was refortified on two occasions, and work was begun on a third. The first of these, the 'Arthurian' occupation, lasted for a generation or two from about AD 470. The great enclosure contrasts strongly with the little fortlets in Wales and Scotland, such as Dinas Emrys or Dunadd. The new rampart followed the old inner bank. It was faced on both sides with dry walling between wooden uprights linked both transversely and longitudinally. Although superficially very similar to many Iron Age structures, the uprights were not set deeply in the ground, and the arrangement owed much of its stability to the rubble fill. The gateway was formed by a roughly square setting of four posts. In the enclosure, the only building certainly of this period was a post-built aisled hall measuring about 19 by 10 metres, but a fairly plentiful scatter of pottery indicated occupation widely distributed in parts of the site which remain unexcavated.

Next, in the time of Ethelred the Unready, the defences were rebuilt to provide a stronghold against Danish invaders. The rampart was 6 metres thick, mainly a bank of earth and rubble but faced with a well built revetment of mortared masonry 1·3 metres thick. This was intended to protect a town, and coins exist which were minted here; but they imply a life of only a decade, from 1009 to 1019. Only one excavated feature, apart from the rampart, could be assigned to this phase. This was the foundation trench for a large masonry building, in plan an equal-armed cross, 25 metres across with square-ended arms 9 metres wide. Despite its eccentric orientation, 30 degrees from the cardinal points, there seems no satisfactory alternative to the excavator's identification of it as a church. No masonry was ever laid in the trench, which is consistent with the short life indicated by the coinage.

Finally, in the reign of King John, a small amount of money was spent for unspecified work at Cadbury, probably this site. Some pottery of the right date has been found, associated with a foundation trench for a wide masonry wall; but no fortification was ever built. Apart from this, the only medieval work on the hill was a dry-stone wall following the *inner* face of the rampart, probably to make it a safe enclosure for cattle.

L. Alcock, *By South Cadbury is that Camelot* (London, 1972). This gives a good preliminary account of the results of the excavation, and in addition provides the reader with an excellent description of the genesis, progress and analysis of a major piece of archaeological research.

Interim excavation reports: *Ant. J.* XLVII (1967), pp. 70–6; XLVIII (1968), pp. 6–17; XLIX (1969), pp. 30–40; L (1970), pp. 14–25; LI (1971), pp. 1–7. For a convenient summary, *Antiquity* XLVI (1972), pp. 29–38.

For comments on the identification as Camelot, see C. Thomas, *Antiquity* XLIII (1969), pp. 27–30, and especially L. Alcock, *Arthur's Britain* (London, 1971), p. 163.

SOUTH DOWNS.

The line of forts following the chalk downs was studied systematically by E. C. Curwen and several co-workers, mostly during the 1930s, usually by means of selective excavations on a relatively small scale. Some of the most important forts in this series are St Catherine's Hill (excavator C. F. C. Hawkes), Old Winchester Hill (unexcavated), The Trundle, Cissbury, west of the River Adur; and Thundersbarrow, Hollingbury, Ranscombe and The Caburn to the east. West of the Adur, the sites seem to have been occupied in Iron Age A (H 450), but not fortified until the arrival of B influences (H 250–300). The defences comprised a strong rampart and ditch with a counterscarp bank, of uniform profile all round the circuit. East of the river the defences seem mostly to have been put up at the initial (A) occupation, though repaired or enlarged when the B influences arrived. Their profile is not necessarily uniform, and counterscarp banks are absent. In this region, the large enclosure envisaged at Ranscombe Hill was never finished, and The Caburn close by stands out as an exception, not having been built until after H 300.

An important group of papers, summing up the results of work on these forts, was published by A. E. Wilson, E. C. Curwen, C. F. C. Hawkes and L. F. Field in *Sussex Arch. Coll.* LXXX (1939), pp. 193–292.

The recent discussion in a paper on 'Stock Raising and the Origins of the Hill-Fort on the South Downs', by R. Bradley, *Ant. J.* LI (1971), pp. 8–29, is stimulating and valuable.

STANWICK (fig. 97; Yorks., NZ 180 115; 100 metres; p. 41).

These earthworks are the most notable in the north of England, not merely for their great size and for the huge area enclosed, but because the excavations by Sir Mortimer Wheeler in 1951–2 enabled him to work out a convincing account of the whole complex, linked with recorded history. His analysis is followed here, but for brevity the necessary scientific reservations in his own account are omitted.

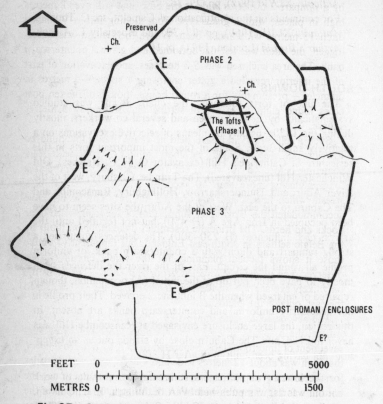

Fig. 97 Stanwick. After Sir Mortimer Wheeler.

The fortress stands in the northern part of what was then the territory of the Brigantes, corresponding roughly to Yorkshire, Lancashire, Durham, Westmorland and much of Cumberland. For a quarter of a century after the Roman invasion, the tribe was split into two factions, one led by the king Venutius and hostile to the invaders, the other friendly and supported by his queen Cartimandua. Apart from a brief interlude in AD 48, the pre-Roman party kept the tribe at peace until soon after AD 50, when open war broke out, the queen being supported by the Romans.

The Stanwick earthworks can be regarded as the 'capital' established then by Venutius.

The first phase, probably soon after AD 50, was the fortification of the hill now called The Tofts. This is the only part of the complex which can properly be called a hill-fort. It was protected by a rampart 7·5 metres wide at the base, and still over 2 metres high in places, with a glacis-type front sloping into a V-shaped ditch 13 metres wide and 5 deep. Where the ground was waterlogged, the ditch was left flat-bottomed and given a counterscarp bank. The area enclosed was 5·3 hectares, and excavation of part of the interior revealed a gutter enclosing a space 8·5 metres in diameter – presumably for a round house, though of the ten post holes found eight form a neat setting almost exactly 5 metres square.

Such a hill-fort would have held no more than a few hundred warriors, if accompanied by their families. The next step, sometime before AD 60, was to build a great rampart 3 kilometres long, enclosing more than 50 hectares, and taking in part of a stream which flowed past the original hill-fort. This would have accommodated the Brigantian supporters of the king, with their flocks and herds. The principle resembles dyked 'oppida' built by the Belgic settlers in south-east England, but (apparently) unlike those it shows tactical planning, for the whole circuit can be observed, and its defence directed, from The Tofts. This seems the only likely explanation for leaving Henah Hill, some 500 metres to the east, outside the enclosure.

The new defences were impressive. The rampart was 12 metres wide at the base and at least 3 metres high, faced with a vertical revetment of limestone slabs. Separated from it by a narrow berm, the ditch was about 12 metres wide and 4 deep, with vertical sides for the lowest 1·5 metres where it was cut into limestone; the bottom was flat, 5 metres wide. Part of this structure, north of the modern road from Forcett to Stanwick, has been preserved by the Department of the Environment. Near the entrance the waterlogged bottom of the ditch had preserved a sword still in its wooden scabbard, with bronze fittings. Nearby was a human skull showing three sword cuts, presumably that of an enemy which had been exhibited on a stake at the gateway. Relics of occupation were fairly plentiful, the pottery including imported Roman wares.

This second structural phase corresponds to a period of civil war among the Brigantes; the Romans gave some support to Cartimandua, but in AD 69 they were in danger of civil war themselves, with four rivals competing for the post of emperor. At the same time, the queen alienated the sympathies of many Brigantes by taking a new consort. Venutius therefore planned a major offensive, and called in aid from other tribes.

The third phase of the defences corresponds to this event. A rampart similar to that of phase two was set out to enclose a further 240 hectares, bringing the fortified area up to nearly 300 hectares in all. But before this huge work was quite finished, the Romans attacked.

This last stage was strikingly illustrated by excavation at the new south gateway. This was planned as a monumental structure, with the ends of the ramparts overlapping, and commanded by a high bastion on its south side, but the holes for the necessary timber framework were not dug, the approach causeway was cut away, and large stones still remained on the bottom of the ditch. Relics of occupation were almost absent. The vast size of the enclosure made central direction from The Tofts impossible, but whether this contributed to the defeat cannot, of course, be known. Finally, much of the great enclosing rampart was slighted.

This was not quite the last phase in the history of the earthworks, for a further enclosure was at some time added to the south, but these banks are of different character and are almost certainly post-Roman, unconnected except by location with the Iron Age defences.

The ancient name of the place is not known. Stanwick comes from *steinvegges* ('stone walls'), and the adjacent village of Aldborough St John takes its name from the 'old fort'.

Sir Mortimer Wheeler, *The Stanwick Fortifications*, Society of Antiquaries of London Research Report XVII (1954).

STAPLE HOWE (Yorks., SE 898 749; 110 metres; pp. 35, 61).

Staple Howe is a steep-sided chalk knoll on the northern edge of the Yorkshire Wolds, overlooking the Vale of Pickering. Its recognition as an archaeological site dates from 1950, when a schoolboy noticed a fragment of ancient pottery, and brought it to the attention of Mr Brewster, who organized the excavation. The work was almost entirely voluntary, and the resulting report is a model of its kind, a classic of British archaeology and of major importance.

In its earliest phase the hill-top was protected by a simple rather slight palisade, enclosing an oval of about 60 by 25 metres (0·1 hectare), with four gaps for access. Before very long, this was replaced by a line of posts lower down the hill, more deeply set and tied to a row of short posts about 2 metres further back. At this stage the posts formed a revetment to a platform of earth and rubbish, so the hill was in fact enclosed by a fairly substantial rampart. This can have been of no great height, perhaps only 2 metres, but the steep slope of the hillside would have rendered attack difficult. This enclosure was rather larger, about 70 by 30 metres (about 0·15 hectare). Later, this revetment was rebuilt, mostly on the same line. There was a single entrance, on the south. Nothing remained to show how it was closed, perhaps by a movable hurdle.

In its first phase, the enclosure protected a single oval house, about 10 by 6 metres. Later, this was replaced by a round building (10 metres in diameter) at the western end and an irregular oval of similar area at the eastern end. Almost exactly central to the enclosure was a strongly built square structure. The position suggests a watch tower, but the excavator rejects this interpretation in favour of a granary; carbonized grain was found in other parts of the site.

The settlement was rich in pottery, in A style, as well as objects of bone and jet, but perhaps the most noteworthy discovery was a bronze razor, of a type well known in Europe and assigned to about 500 BC. A radiocarbon indication confirmed a date within the fifth or sixth century BC for the foundation of the settlement.

T. C. M. Brewster, *The Excavation of Staple Howe* (E. Riding Archaeological Research Committee, 1963) with numerous illustrations.

SUTTON WALLS (fig. 98; Hereford, SO 525 464; 90 metres; pp. 49, 84).

This fort, north of the Lugg valley in western Herefordshire, is an impressive local landmark, and is important because of the salvage excavations of 1948–51. It is all on private ground, though footpaths run near. The ramparts, overgrown with woodland, have been preserved, but the whole of the western half of the interior has been gutted for the sake of the gravel of which the hill is composed, and is now (1972) used as a dump for toxic waste.

The enclosure covers 11·5 hectares, and was protected by a single bank and ditch, now eroded to a scarp with a terrace at the foot. It is a long irregular oval in plan, with an entrance, originally inturned but now damaged, at each end. The excavations produced

numerous 'finds', but structurally the most important information
related to the defences. These showed an initial occupation under
the existing bank, probably protected by a palisade. The first
rampart was built up with material from a deep V-shaped ditch,
giving an overall width of about 32 metres and a height from the
bottom of at least 15 metres; there was a revetment of timber and
dry walling at the front of the bank. This was associated with B

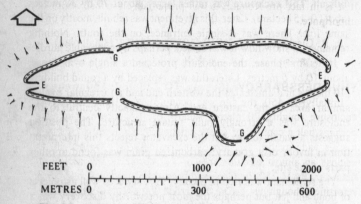

*Fig. 98   Sutton Walls. After K. M. Kenyon and Royal
Commission on Historical Monuments (England).*

style pottery, of H 100. A burial, perhaps sacrificial, was found in
the make-up. After an interval long enough for a thick turf layer to
develop, the bank was raised with material from a quarry ditch
behind it. This was after the arrival of Belgic influence, probably
early in the first century AD. Finally, perhaps after some hurried
and incomplete refortification, the fort was captured, many of the
defenders being killed and their bodies thrown casually into the
ditch. Some had injuries which suggested wounds suffered during
battle, while others had been decapitated, but none had been cut to
pieces, as at Bredon Hill. The excavator suggested that this battle
had been fought against the Romans, about AD 75. The rampart had
been thrown down to cover the bodies, but occupation of the site
continued during most of the Roman period.

K. M. Kenyon, *Arch. J.* CX (1953), pp. 1–87.

TASBURGH (Norfolk, TM 200 960; 35 metres; p. 41).

Although in its present mutilated condition Tasburgh is no
longer very impressive it deserves mention on account of its

position and size. It stands isolated from other hill-forts in the middle of East Anglia, some 40 kilometres from its nearest neighbour; it encloses 7·6 hectares. Its plan approximates closely to a quadrant of a circle of radius 300 metres, the north and east sides being nearly straight, and the included angle 98 degrees. The defence seems to have been by a single rampart, probably with a ditch now filled; the whole site is damaged by roads and buildings. If it is in fact pre-Roman, it was presumably a tribal centre of importance.

R. R. Clarke, *Arch. J.* XCVI (1939), pp. 48–9 (small plan).

THUNDERSBARROW (Sussex, TQ 229 084; 150 metres).

Initially, H 450, the site was occupied by a lightly protected enclosure roughly 70 metres square, or 0·5 hectare, but after perhaps half a century or so the existing bank and ditch, about 9 metres wide overall and now 3 metres high, was thrown up to enclose an almost circular area of 1·3 hectares, 130 metres in diameter. By H 250 the place had been abandoned, and was never refortified, though just before the arrival of the Romans an agricultural village grew up outside the fort. The rampart seems to have contained no timber reinforcement; the gateways are damaged, but may have been strengthened by inturning the rampart ends.

E. C. Curwen and K. P. Oakley, *Ant. J.* XIII, pp. 1p9–51.

TRAPRAIN LAW (fig. 12; East Lothian, NT 581 746; 210 metres; pl. 6).

For description see pp. 95–9; also p. 18.

General Account: R. W. Feachem, *Proc. Soc. Ant. Scot.* LXXXIX (1955–6), pp. 284 ff., *q.v.* for other refs.

See also A. H. A. Hogg in *Aspects of Archaeology in Britain and Beyond* (ed. W. F. Grimes, 1951), pp. 204–13 (with some notes on pottery and additional references).

On metalwork: E. Burley (Mrs Fowler), *Proc. Soc. Ant. Scot.* LXXXIX (1955–6), pp. 118–226.

On treasure: A. O. Curle, *The Treasure of Traprain* (Glasgow, 1923).

On Pictish chain: A. J. H. Edwards, *Proc. Soc. Ant. Scot.* LXXIII (1938–9), p. 326.

On the name: *Watson, Celtic Place Names of Scotland* (Royal Celtic Society, Edinburgh, 1926), p. 345.

TREGEARE ROUNDS (fig. 99; Cornwall, SX 033 800; 150 metres; pl. 35).

The fort is a good example of the type with wide-spaced ramparts which is characteristic of south-western Britain. It stands on ground which falls gently from 155 metres above ordnance datum on the north-west to 140 metres above on the south-east.

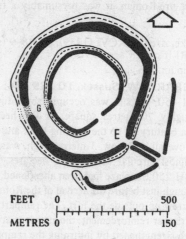

Fig. 99   Tregeare Rounds. After S. Baring-Gould.

In plan, it consists of two roughly concentric enclosures, with a crescentic outwork. The inner enclosure, of 0·7 hectare, is protected by a bank and ditch 10 metres wide by 5 high overall; the outer, of 1·9 hectares in all, has a similar rampart 16 by 7 metres. The main entrance, on the south-east, is approached through the crescentic 'barbican' by a hollow way, and on the south-west there are gaps which may be original leading through both ramparts. The outer rampart is thickened at both gaps.

Some excavations just within the outer bank, in 1904, recovered decorated pottery of B culture, about H 100. There is no evidence to show whether the ramparts are contemporary or of several periods. The plan of the larger enclosure and 'barbican' is similar to that of Castle Dore, but at that site the bank which protects the barbican continues as a close-set outer defence round the remainder of the circuit.

S. Baring-Gould, *Journal Royal Inst. Cornwall* XVI (1904), pp. 73 ff. (plan by I. K. Anderson).

TRELISSEY (Pembroke, SN 175 078; 90 metres; p. 41).

This was a defended farm rather than a hill-fort. It is now almost ploughed out, and can never have been of great strength. Two close-set banks formed an almost circular enclosure, 103 metres in diameter overall, within which stood a simple rectangular Roman farmhouse.

W. G. Thomas and R. F. Walker, *Bulletin of Board of Celtic Studies* XVIII (1958–60), pp. 295–303 (excavation report).

TRE'R CEIRI (fig. 4; Caernarvon, SH 373 446; pls. 1, 5).

For description see pp. 92–5, also pp. 46, 59, 77.

A. H. A. Hogg, *Arch. J.* CXVII (1960), pp. 10–39, *q.v.* for other refs.

Also, in summary, *Caernarvon Inv.* II, No. 1056.

THE TRUNDLE (ST ROCHE'S HILL) (fig. 100; Sussex, SU 877 110; 200 metres).

This is one of the South Downs group, and is archaeologically of particular interest as the Iron Age fort is superimposed on a

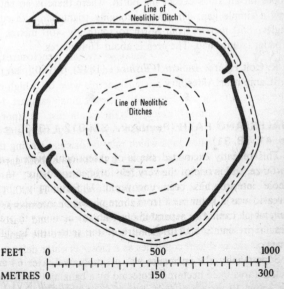

FEET 0 — 500 — 1000
METRES 0 — 150 — 300

Fig. 100   The Trundle. After E. C. Curwen.

much earlier neolithic causewayed camp. The excavations of 1929 were directed primarily towards investigating that, but pottery yielding information on the history of the hill-fort was also recovered.

The Iron Age defences enclose about 5 hectares. They are set out as an irregular polygon with rounded corners, and are of uniform profile, comprising a bank, ditch and counterscarp bank. There are two inturned entrances. The pottery suggests an open settlement of A culture, starting about H 500, fortified at the time of the arrival of B influences (H 250) and abandoned when the Belgae entered the area (H 50).

E. C. Curwen, *Sussex Arch. Coll.* LXX (1929), pp. 33–85 (plan).

VESPASIAN'S CAMP (Wilts., SU 146 417; 90 metres; p. 21).

This hill-fort is much obscured by tree-planting and landscaping. It is of interest as an early example of antiquarian identification; the name goes back well into the eighteenth century, and is associated with Chlorus's Camp (now Figsbury Rings).

The defences, a single bank and ditch, utilize a spur with steep slopes on all sides except the north, where there is an entrance, now a simple gap. The fort is roughly triangular with rounded angles, 850 metres from north to south, by 400 metres at the broader (south) end. The area is about 16 hectares.

R. Colt Hoare, *Ancient Wiltshire* I (1812), p. 160; plan p. 128 ('Camp near Amesbury').

WALESLAND RATH (Pembroke, SM 912 170; 30 metres; pp. 41, 78, 81).

This recently excavated site is of exceptional interest and importance, and is one of the very few fortified enclosures where the whole interior has been uncovered. Unfortunately, the plan revealed was a palimpsest from three phases of intensive occupation, which cannot be separated out with any certainty to present a clear representation of the nature of the settlement at different times.

Superficially, the enclosure was a simple oval, axes 64 and 48 metres (area 0·25 hectare), protected by a bank and ditch measuring about 12 metres overall. Excavation showed that there were two pre-Roman structural phases. In the first, H 100, there were entrances to the south-west and south-east. They were of different character, the south-west having a rectangular framework of four small posts at the inner edge of the rampart, approached by a stone-revetted passage. That on the south-east seems to have been under a wooden tower set on the line of the rampart and supported on six massive posts. In this phase, six round dwellings (several times rebuilt) stood near the middle of the enclosure.

In the second phase, early in the first century AD but still pre-Roman, the bank was enlarged, burying the south-west entrance, and the round houses were replaced by a line of smaller rectangular buildings standing close to the inner face of the rampart.

Finally, after a century or more of disuse, a small one-roomed (?) Roman farmhouse was built partly over the south-east gateway.

G. J. Wainwright, *Britannia* II (1971), pp. 48–108 (excavation report).

WANDLEBURY (fig. 5; Cambridge, TL 493 534; 70 metres; pp. 61, 64).

This fort stands on the chalk ridge of the Gog-Magog Hills, south-east of Cambridge. When complete, it was protected by two large banks and ditches forming an almost circular enclosure of 6 hectares. It is still impressive, though the inner bank was levelled into its ditch when the grounds of the house were laid out in the eighteenth century. The history of the defences has been worked out by careful excavation; the entrance and most of the interior were not available for investigation.

The ramparts have been illustrated earlier (fig. 5). Both periods were associated with A-style pottery, dating from H 450 and H 350, the occupation ending perhaps H 250.

In the small part of the interior which could be excavated, and under the inner bank, were found pits for storage and post holes of buildings which may have been rectangular, as well as of 'four-poster' granaries.

B. R. Hartley, *Proc. Cambs. Ant. Soc.* L (1957), pp. 1–27.

WARHAM (Norfolk, TF 944 409; 15 metres; pl. 36).

Two massive ramparts accompanied by ditches, measuring nearly 50 metres wide overall, enclose 1·4 hectares.

The inner bank still was 5·25 metres above the ditch, which was originally 1 metre deeper. The plan is almost exactly circular, 130 metres in diameter, suggesting intentional setting out. Slight excavations failed to locate the entrance and produced few relics, mostly Roman.

H. St G. Gray, *Ant. J.* XIII (1933), pp. 399–413.

WHITE CATERTHUN (fig. 101; Angus, NO 548 660; 299 metres p. 45, pl. 37).

This strong and impressive fortress stands less than a mile from its neighbour the Brown Caterthun. They are clearly intervisible,

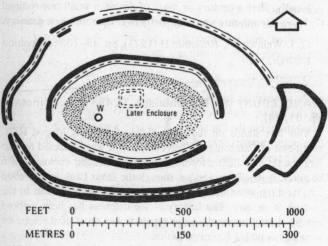

| FEET | 0 | | 500 | | 1000 |
| METRES | 0 | 150 | | 300 | |

Fig. 101   The White Caterthun. After D. Christison.

but their difference in character suggests different dates and functions.

The White Caterthun has features in common with timber-laced forts such as Castle Law (Forgandenny) or Barry Hill – a central stone-walled fort with earthen outworks (see p. 45) – but is far larger and stronger. The area enclosed is some 0·7 hectare. The plan is essentially three concentric ellipses. The outer rampart consists of a ditch between two banks, the outer bank being generally rather stronger than the inner. Outside this at the east end is an annexe enclosed by a substantial bank with no ditch. There is no direct access from the annexe to the enclosure, but their entrances are adjacent. The second ellipse is formed by a ditch with a fairly slight outer bank. This is separated from the outer ellipse by a space ranging from 25 to 80 metres.

The final defence is represented by a huge bank of rubble, the toe of which lies 5 to 10 metres from the edge of the ditch. This bank is almost certainly the remains of a very large timber-laced wall, the complete collapse being the result of the wood decaying. It differs from most such in having two crests with a hollow between. This may indicate that there were two walls, but a more probable explanation is that either there was a particularly high proportion of timber in the middle of the wall, or even that to economize on material – for the wall is exceptionally large – the centre was left hollow. This hypothesis can only be tested by excavation.

There are entrances through the outer defences at each end of the ellipse, and corresponding gaps in the second line, but no gateway can be traced with any certainty in the ruins of the stone wall.

Within the enclosure is a deep hollow, no doubt a well, and a slight rectangular enclosure which is probably quite recent.

The history of this fortress can only be determined, if at all, by excavation; but the impression given is of a single coherent design. The outer rampart follows the edge of what, from the main wall, would have been dead ground.

D. Christison, *Proc. Soc. Ant. Scot.* XXXIV (1899–1900), p. 103 (plan).
Preh. Scot., pp. 106–7.
Now see also J. K. St Joseph, *Antiquity* XLVIII (1974), p. 53 and pl. VIII (air photo); from this, Dr St Joseph has identified a fourth line of defence, probably the earliest, set rather unsymmetrically within the outer line. This is very difficult to trace on the ground and has not previously been recorded; it is not shown on the plan.

WIMBLEDON, *see* **CAESAR'S CAMP.**

WINKLEBURY (fig. 102; Wilts., ST 952 217; 260 metres; p. 18, pl. 38).

A recent re-survey and reconsideration of the surface evidence by R. Feachem has enabled him to work out the evolution of this site. It displays three structural phases, all unfinished.

The earliest comprised two straight lengths of bank and ditch

21 metres overall cutting off the end of a steep-sided promontory. The area enclosed was 5·7 hectares, with an oblique entrance between the two sections of rampart. Next, work was begun on a rampart round the steep edge of the promontory. Then, finally, a much slighter bank and ditch, only 10 metres wide overall, was

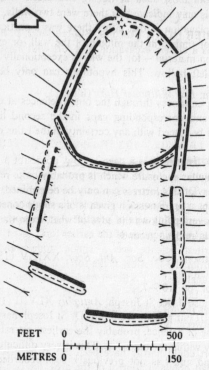

Fig. 102   Winklebury. After R. W. Feachem.

constructed to form an oval enclosure of 1·8 hectares at the tip of the spur. All these structures show the irregularities in height, and the breaks corresponding to the work of separate gangs which are characteristic of unfinished earthworks.

Excavations by Pitt-Rivers in 1881–2 produced pottery from the site. The evidence of this is not discussed by Feachem, but it now seems probable that the large fort should be of Iron Age A culture (H 250), and that the smaller enclosure is the work of Belgic (C) arrivals in about H 50.

R. Feachem in *I A H F* pp. 32–3 (plan).

A. H. L. F. Pitt-Rivers, *Excavations in Cranborne Chase* II (1888), pp. 233 ff.

C. F. C. Hawkes, *Arch. J.* CIV (1947), pp. 30–2 and n. 22 (but requiring reconsideration in the light of Feachem's survey).

WITTNAUER HORN (Aargau, Switzerland; p. 63).

Noted as a classic excavation of a fort with massive timbered rampart.

G. Bersu, *Das Wittnauer Horn* (Basel, 1945).

WODEN LAW (fig. 103; Roxburgh, NT 768 125; 420 metres; p. 84, pl. 39).

The notable complex of earthworks on this hill has been analysed by Dr St Joseph and the late Sir Ian Richmond. In brief, it comprises a pre-Roman fort showing two periods of construction, two overlapping sets of practice Roman siege-works, and a post-Roman refortification of the earlier fort.

The earliest defence was a single stone wall (the second counting from the interior of the fort). It had no accompanying ditch. By analogy with other forts in the region, it is attributed to H 100. Later, perhaps about the time of the Roman invasions, it was reinforced by the addition of two outer ramparts with a ditch between, and one or perhaps two annexes on the southwest.

This fort could hardly have been left in occupation after the Romans had obtained control of the area, for one of their main military roads, now known as Dere Street, runs close by. So the Roman siege-works, the next structures on the hill, must have been training works set up round an empty fort. There were at least two practice campaigns, but the banks cannot be completely sorted out into different periods.

The main feature is a double bank and three ditches, set round the accessible side of the fort just outside the theoretical range of hand-thrown missiles. Outside these are three further lines of rampart, double in places; two cross, and are thus of different periods. There is also a mound similar to the supposed ballista platforms at Burnswark.

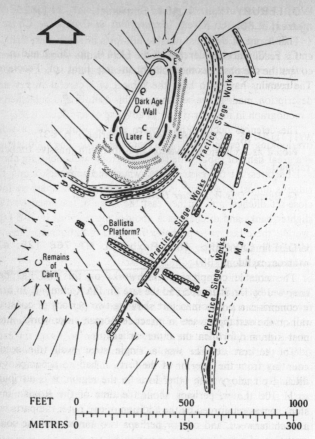

Fig. 103   Woden Law.   After Royal Commission on Historical Monuments (Scotland).

Finally, after the Romans had left the area, the top of the hill was refortified by what is now the innermost wall, about 2·7 metres thick, faced with large boulders or orthostats as in other late Roman and Dark Age structures in this district.

There are traces of four round stone hut foundations in the enclosure; these may belong to any of the occupation periods.

Roxburgh Inv. I (1956), No. 308 (plan).

WOODBURY, *see* LITTLE WOODBURY.

WORLEBURY (figs. 4, 104; Somerset, ST 314 625; 75 metres; p. 60).

This is one of the most notable hill-forts of south-west Britain, and is readily accessible, though the picturesque woodland which covers the site obscures the archaeological features to some extent. The remains have also been the subject of a careful survey and description, made at the beginning of this century and published as a monograph in many ways far in advance of its time.

The defences occupy the western end of Worle Hill, a ridge overlooking Weston-super-Mare from the north. The main feature is a great bank of rubble, the ruin of a strong wall enclosing about 4·1 hectares. At the eastern end, where the approach along the ridge is almost level, there is a second wall accompanied by four close-set ditches, and further east the ridge is traversed by two slighter banks and ditches, each about 9 metres wide by 1·5 high overall; these last were probably no more than boundary banks, perhaps limiting grazing grounds.

The excavations showed that the stone walls were originally 10 or 11 metres thick and they are still more than 3 metres high. They were of very elaborate construction, with multiple concealed revetments carried up through the full height (fig. 4). In the outer wall on the east there were in places three such revetments on the inner side and two on the outer, in addition to those on each side of the 'core'. Unlike simpler examples of *murus duplex*, the outer layers were very thick and not of uniform width but tapering off and ending in places. Except along the very steep north side the walls were almost always accompanied by a ditch, some 4 metres wide and a metre deep. The inner face of the southern wall was provided with curious additions, each consisting of a wall nearly a metre thick, from 13 to 16 metres long in typical cases, parallel to the main wall and separated from it by about 1·4 metres. Presumably these either provided means of access to the wall top or formed the base of some sort of tower, but pending further research the original author's purely descriptive term of 'internal rectangular appendages' seems best.

The main gateway opened towards the south-east, and the rampart here was thickened and inturned, giving a passage over 20 metres long and about 4 metres wide. The other two were apparently merely simple passages through the rampart.

The narrower end of the interior, east of the main entrance, was cut off by a ditch running north and south. This can no longer be traced for its full length, but the description of its southern end, as

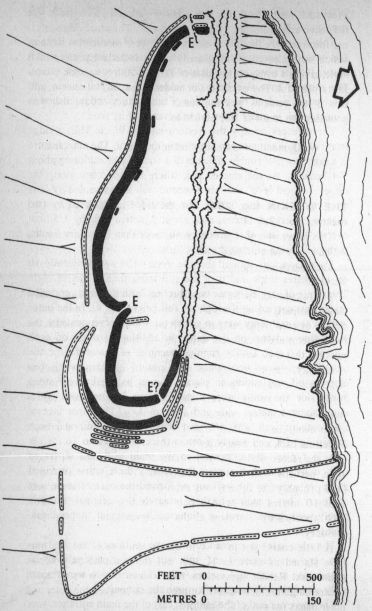

Fig. 104 Worlebury. After C. W. Dymond.

excavated, seems to justify the original author's view that it was defensive and protected a 'keep' or 'citadel'. The chief other internal features were the pits – ninety-three were recorded – some of which were cleared yielding many relics, including pottery of B style, giving a conventional date of H 100–200. Sling stones were fairly plentiful. The excavator considered that the ruinous condition of the remains was the result of slighting. If so, that was probably the result of Roman action.

C. W. Dymond, *Worlebury* (2nd edn. Bristol, 1902) (plan).

THE WREKIN (fig. 105; Shropshire, SJ 629 082; 400 metres; pp. 17, 71).

This impressive fort is noteworthy also as one of the very few which retain their original names little altered. Excavations begun in 1939 were interrupted by the war, so many problems remain unsolved.

The remains comprise an inner enclosure of 2·6 hectares, with a single rampart, set within a larger one of nearly 8 hectares, with a double or even triple rampart in places. The plan suggests that the two systems are of different dates, but the excavator considered it possible that they were contemporary.

Initially, the inner rampart was a flat-topped bank 6 metres wide, with a sloping back, a fairly well built stone revetment in front and no accompanying ditch; the entrance was slightly inturned. The outer rampart now appears as two terraces, the upper being the remains of a similar bank and the lower the result of cutting back and steepening the natural hill slope.

In the second period the inner rampart was enlarged, in 'dump' style, perhaps with a stone breastwork. The southern entrance (and probably the others) was extended inwards to form a passage 10 metres long with a pair of rectangular guard rooms each about 8 by 3 metres at the inner ends, all in very poor masonry.

A little coarse pot in A style was found. Use of the site may have started as early as H 300, but the evidence only allows guesswork. Recent excavations have shown that rows of small square buildings (as at Croft Ambrey) stood between the outer and inner banks (*ex inf.* S. C. Stanford).

K. M. Kenyon, *Arch. J.* XCIX (1942), pp. 99–109.

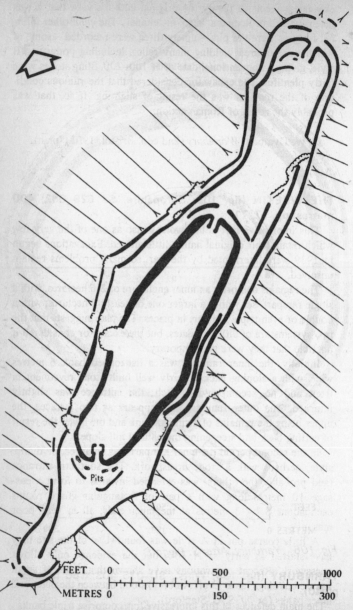

Pits

FEET   0   500   1000
METRES 0   150   300

Fig. 105   The Wrekin. After K. M. Kenyon.

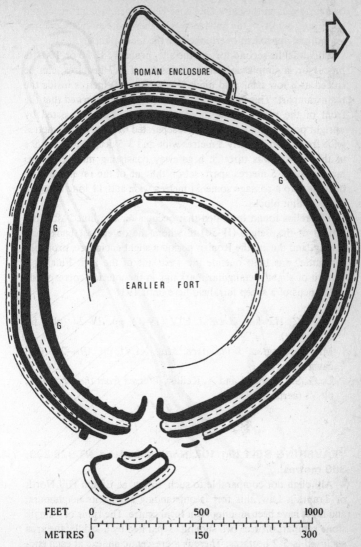

ROMAN ENCLOSURE

G

G

EARLIER FORT

G

| FEET | 0 | | 500 | | 1000 |
| METRES | 0 | 150 | | 300 | |

Fig. 106 Yarnbury. After S. Piggott.

YARNBURY (fig. 106; Wilts., SU 035 403; 160 metres; pl. 40).

The main defences of this impressive fort comprise triple banks with accompanying ditches, the outermost being relatively slight, the others substantial. The area enclosed is 10·5 hectares. There is one entrance, on the east. The inner banks there are inturned, and additional banks on the outside give further protection and enforce an indirect approach, overlooked by the inner rampart.

This was the second fort on the site, probably H 50 or 100. Its precursor, a simple univallate enclosure of 3·7 hectares, can be traced as a low bank and ditch about 50 to 80 metres inside the main rampart. This was of A culture. Excavation showed that the front of the rampart was faced with a revetment supported by upright posts about a metre apart, separated by a berm 4·5 metres wide from a ditch nearly 5 metres wide and 3·5 deep. The entrance at this period was through a gateway consisting merely of two large posts 3·5 metres apart, set on the line of the revetment and opening into a passage some 5½ metres wide and 11 long between kerbs of flint blocks.

The relics found indicated that occupation continued after the arrival of the Belgae (H 50) to whom the outermost bank may belong, and during the Roman period a slight enclosure, probably for cattle, was built outside the west side of the fort. Finally, a pattern of slight rectangular markings in the interior corresponds to the pens of a sheep fair, held here until 1916.

C. F. C. Hawkes, *Arch. J.* CIV (1947), pp. 29–31 (plan by S. Piggott).

Mrs Cunnington, *Wilts. Arch. Mag.* XLVI, pp. 198–217 (excavations).

O. G. S. Crawford and A. Keiller, *Wessex from the Air*, p. 68, pl. VI (aerial view).

YEAVERING BELL (fig. 107; Northumberland, NT 928 293; 360 metres).

Although not comparable to such 'towns' as Eildon Hill North or Traprain Law, this fort is outstanding among its neighbours, and must have been an important local centre. The ruins of a single stone rampart protect two summits separated by a saddle; the area enclosed is 5·2 hectares. There is a crescentic annexe at each end, protected by a rather slighter wall, the relation of which to the main rampart is not clear. The entrances, on north, east and south, are simple gaps. Within the enclosure the sites of some 130 huts can be traced mostly as levelled platforms in the hill slopes. All (save perhaps one) were round and of timber; there are none of the stone-built houses typical of the later Roman settlements in this

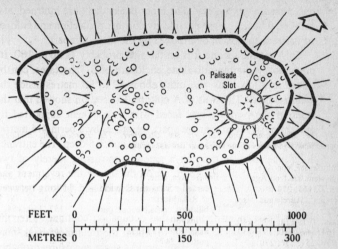

Fig. 107 Yeavering Bell. After G. Jobey.

region. Round the higher, eastern summit is a palisade slot, earlier than some of the house platforms.

The occupation of the site probably started in the pre-Roman period, but despite the absence of stone buildings a few relics found by the slight excavations which have been made indicate occupation continuing into the second century AD or perhaps even later.

G. Jobey, *Arch. Aeliana* 45, XLIII (1965), pp. 31–5 (plan).

For all the place-names and hill-forts see Gazetteer. The Introduction, Bibliography and Bibliographical References in the Gazetteer are not indexed.

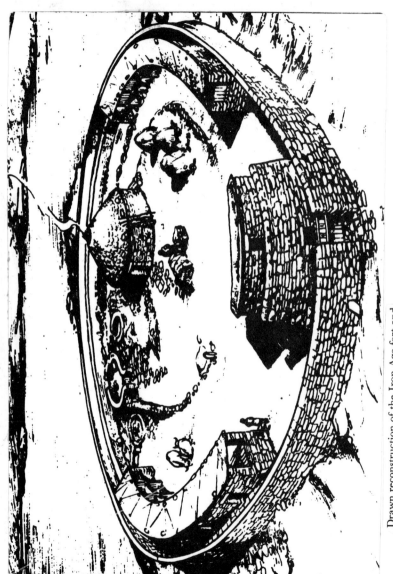

Drawn reconstruction of the Iron Age fort and blockhouse at Clickhimin, Shetlands.